Manifestation through
GARBHA SANSKAR

Dr Sonal Jain Jayaswal, armed with formal degrees in engineering as well as management, embarked on an extraordinary journey to master Garbha Sanskar. As an accomplished mother of two and with a doctorate in prenatal education, she has positively impacted and empowered the lives of countless aspiring mothers with her transformative approach. Her groundbreaking book and online app on Garbha Sanskar, DreamStar Baby App, holistically blend ancient wisdom with modern science, igniting a revolution in nurturing divinity in the womb—a vital step for Manifesting the Superpowers of Tomorrow right from the Womb.

Scan the QR code below for Dr Jayaswal's Linktree:

'I understand that the book blends ancient wisdom with modern science to offer a comprehensive guide for expectant mothers. I congratulate the author Dr Sonal Jain Jayaswal for her book and wish the publication success.'

—**Ramesh Bais**
Governor of Maharashtra

'Having known Sonal for the past 20 years, what I admire the most is her dedication, commitment and perseverance. Under the mentorship of my late wife, Jyotsna Darda, she conducted numerous motivational sessions with the Lokmat Media Group, showcasing her passion and expertise. I wholeheartedly endorse her current work on Garbha Sanskar as a testament to her desire to nurture values in the womb which is an important step towards achievement of an empowered future.'

—**Dr Vijay Darda**, Chairman, Lokmat Media Group
Sr Member of Parliament Rajya Sabha (1998–2016)

'This book goes beyond pregnancy and childbirth; it serves as a blueprint for creating an empowered nation and catalysing India's journey towards a 30-trillion-dollar economy by 2047. As a mother myself, I wholeheartedly recommend this book as a must-read for all expectant mothers, contributing significantly to the vision of "Viksit Bharat".'

—**Amruta Devendra Fadnavis**
Banker, Singer, Social Activist

'*Garbha Sanskar*, with its focus on the holistic development of the fetus and the nurturing of the mother's mind, body, and spirit, aligns perfectly with India's comprehensive growth objectives. [This is a] much-needed book towards creating a healthy and empowered youth population, which is the cornerstone of a thriving economy.'

—**Rekha Sharma**
Chairperson, National Commission of Women

'I commend Dr Sonal Jain Jayaswal for her dedication to promoting Garbha Sanskar and empowering expectant mothers with holistic guidance. By promoting relaxation, positive thinking and emotional balance, Garbha Sanskar contributes to reducing stress and anxiety, which are common concerns during pregnancy. This book is a testament to the potential synergy between ancient practices and modern medicine in supporting optimal pregnancy outcomes.'

—**Dr Sadhana Desai**
MD, FRCOG, (ENG) FICOG
Consulting Obstetrician and Gynaecologist
Infertility and ART Specialist

'A much-needed book to remind ourselves of what we have forgotten. Bringing a blessed soul into this world is a science and this book most beautifully encapsulates that ancient science. A must-read for everyone to usher in a new era of sanity.'

—**Nityanand Charan Das**
Spiritual Counsellor, Author

'Sonal's research on Garbha Sanskar is truly remarkable, as she has structured this ancient science into a step-by-step model known as "Sonal's Intelligence Model for Holistic Development". This is a perfect self-help book for all aspiring mothers, regardless of caste, creed or religion, who aspire to give birth to a divine and genius child.'

—**Dr Manju Jain**
PhD Guide, Spiritual Healer and Bhaktamar Global Mother

Manifestation through GARBHA SANSKAR
UNLOCK THE SECRETS TO YOUR DREAM BABY

SONAL JAIN JAYASWAL

Important:
Please use this book in consultation with your doctor.

Published by
Rupa Publications India Pvt. Ltd 2024
7/16, Ansari Road, Daryaganj
New Delhi 110002

Sales centres:
Bengaluru Chennai
Hyderabad Jaipur Kathmandu
Kolkata Mumbai Prayagraj

Copyright © Dr Sonal Jain Jayaswal 2024

The information contained in this book is **not** intended as a substitute for medical consultation with a physician and may not be construed as medical advice or instruction. Instead, readers should consult appropriate health professionals on any matter relating to their health and well-being. Before starting any diet/exercise, you should speak to your physician. All information contained in this book but not limited to text, graphics, images, information, third party information and/or advice, food, recipes, exercise, diets and psychology are for informational and educational purposes only. No action or inaction should be taken based solely on the contents of this information. This book is not meant to be used, nor should it be used, to diagnose or treat any medical condition. The publisher and the author are in no way liable or responsible with respect to any loss or incidental or consequential damages caused to any person or entity, or alleged to have been caused, directly or indirectly, by use of the information contained in this book.

The views and opinions expressed in this book are the author's own and the facts are as reported by her which have been verified to the extent possible, and the publishers are not in any way liable for the same.

All rights reserved.
No part of this publication may be reproduced, transmitted, or stored in a retrieval system, in any form or by any means, electronic, mechanical, photocopying, recording or otherwise, without the prior permission of the publisher.

P-ISBN: 978-93-6156-137-5
E-ISBN: 978-93-6156-677-6

Fourth impression 2025

10 9 8 7 6 5 4

The moral right of the author has been asserted.

Printed in India

This book is sold subject to the condition that it shall not,
by way of trade or otherwise, be lent, resold, hired out, or otherwise circulated, without the publisher's prior consent, in any form of binding or cover other than that in which it is published.

To all the mothers who nurture the miracle of life within and illuminate the universe with boundless love and light.

Contents

Foreword		*xi*
Author's Note		*xv*
1.	The Beginnings	1
2.	Creating Intelligence in the Womb	32
3.	Maintaining Physical Well-Being	68
4.	Developing Mental Well-Being	118
5.	Ensuring Emotional Well-Being	137
6.	Imbibing Spiritual Well-Being	161
7.	A Miracle Is Born	190
8.	Care of New Moms and Newborns	217
Annexure 1		262
Annexure 2		281
Annexure 3		284
Endnotes		292
DreamStar Baby—Manifest your Divine Genius		299
Acknowledgements		301

Foreword[*]

Each of us is born with the sole purpose of experiencing a journey of blessings and challenges woven intricately into our karmic plan. Our experiences, whether joyful or painful, are mere chapters in the script written by our souls for growth and learning. Like a butterfly emerging from its cocoon, we must embrace resilience and perseverance to break free from our own limitations and soar high with open wings. Sadly, many in the mortal realm forget this fundamental truth and engage in a cycle of blame and desperation. Yet, true *Shivyogi*s view challenges as opportunities and every 'suffering' as a stepping stone towards divine realization.

I vividly recall Sonal's first visit to our *shivir* in Shimla way back in May 2008. Married for four years, her deepest desire was to conceive. A dedicated *sadhak*, she diligently followed the protocols and teachings of *Shivyog* with unwavering faith. Despite facing multiple miscarriages, Sonal remained steadfast, drawing strength from each setback to continue her pursuit. Her surrender to her Guru and the Divine was absolute and her determination unshakeable. Little did she realize that the journey that she was going on was deeply rooted in ancient wisdom, guided by the Vedas and Upanishads. Unknowingly,

---

[*]As narrated to Ishan Shivanand, mental health researcher and professor. He is also the founder of Yoga of Immortals.

Sonal embodied the essence of Garbha Sanskar, the sacred practice of nurturing and holistically developing the foetus through ancient Indian wisdom and practices.

With her surrender and dedication, Sonal gave her all to the sacred practice and was blessed with two vibrant and divine children: Ishaan and Shambhavi. Yet, her journey didn't end there. Driven by empathy and love, she decided to pay back to the Divine by selflessly serving others, which prompted her to earn her doctorate in this sacred subject. During her journey, she developed simple and easily understandable models that can assist any woman on her path in a highly organized manner. She skilfully integrated ancient wisdom with a modern scientific approach, making it accessible to everyone. Her journey from personal achievement to becoming a beacon of hope for thousands of women is a testament to her resilience and devotion. She demonstrates the true spirit of Shivyog by becoming instrumental in '*Jyot se jyot jagaoo*' (Ignite one flame with another).

This book on Garbha Sanskar is a treasure trove of Shivyog teachings that Sonal practised with dedication, yielding extraordinary results. It is not merely a theoretical discourse but a practical guide rooted in self-help and result-oriented approaches. Furthermore, Sonal has developed an app to provide daily guidance to mothers to nurture the womb's holistic development. Her belief is simple: if she could achieve these results by walking the path shown to her by her Guru, so can others. However, it requires the same level of trust, surrender, dedication and resilience that Sonal demonstrated.

In the realm of Shivyog, it's not just about giving birth. It is also about birthing a divine child and becoming a divine mother. Sonal's journey embodies this ethos, inspiring countless others to embark on their paths of divine motherhood.

I extend my heartfelt blessings to Sonal, a true Shivyogi, for becoming an inspiration and spreading the transformative power of Shivyog to future generations. This book has the potential to usher in a world of divine mothers and divine children, shaping a powerful and enlightened society.

Bless You.

—Dr Avdhoot Baba Shivanand
Father of Indian healing and founder of Shivyog

Author's Note

My journey of motherhood has been a profound and transformative experience, filled with challenges, victories and divine blessings. In sharing my story, I hope to inspire and empower women who may be facing similar struggles on their path to becoming mothers.

Married in 2004, I embarked on a challenging path to conceive my first child, which led me through three failed IVF attempts and two miscarriages before the successful birth of my son in 2012, with the committed and sincere efforts of Dr Sadhana Desai. I was extremely blessed to be guided and supported by my Guru, Dr Avdhoot Baba Shivanand, through this difficult time. His teachings and divine guidance were instrumental in my journey.

The experience of my first pregnancy, though filled with anxiety and challenges, taught me valuable lessons about surrendering to divine powers and trusting in the guidance of my Guru. Despite being on bed rest for most of my pregnancy, I devoted my time to spiritual practices, such as mantra chanting, meditation, affirmations and visualization, which ultimately helped me overcome obstacles and ensure the safety and well-being of my baby. Though I was victorious, my entire experience right from conception to delivery had been very traumatic. I then resolved to rewrite it with divine grace.

Staying steadfast to the Guru's guidance, my second pregnancy was a transformative experience, wherein all steps, from conception to delivery, were extremely blissful. Through intense mantra chanting along with other sacred practices, I could invoke the energies of the Divine Mother and was blessed with a divine girl child, defying astrological predictions and reaffirming the power of divine intervention.

Driven by an ardent desire to serve others, I then pursued a doctorate in Garbha Sanskar under the mentorship of Dr Manju Jain. For my research, I drew inspiration from the works of Dr Howard Gardner, which led to the development of Sonal's Intelligence Model for Holistic Development©, which is a structured approach that harmonizes ancient wisdom with modern scientific insights. This model is presented in the book as a systematic, step-by-step process that focusses on enhancing physical, mental, emotional and spiritual well-being to assist in creating the child of one's dreams.

Additionally, I have launched an app called 'DreamStar Baby' based on my model, which will provide expectant mothers with daily activities focussed on developing the desired neural pathways for their holistic brain development in a scientific manner. Together, the book and the app will offer a comprehensive solution for mothers during their pregnancy. Furthermore, the proceeds from both will be contributed to women and child welfare activities.

During my counselling sessions for conception and pregnancy, I realized the power of empathy and shared experiences in empowering others on their journey to motherhood. Success stories, including my own, became sources of strength and inspiration for women seeking to fulfil their dreams of motherhood.

This book on Garbha Sanskar is a culmination of my personal journey, experiences of those I have counselled, years of study, practise and observation and, most importantly, the divine teachings of my Guru. The stories and examples shared in this book are based on real-life experiences, though names and settings have been changed to respect the privacy of the individuals. Honestly, this book is the result of divine grace, and I am full of gratitude towards the Almighty for choosing me to share something meaningful with the world.

The purpose and scope of this book is to support expectant mothers in creating a nurturing and positive environment in the womb. However, it is essential to recognize that every pregnancy is unique, and it is strongly recommended that one seeks medical guidance from one's general physician and/or gynaecologist in conjunction with the practices outlined in this book. Furthermore, this book does not endorse any motive or bias and there is no intention to hurt any professional, cultural, religious or regional sentiments.

Today, I am grateful to be a mother of two divine children and I am confident that the reservoir of knowledge shared in the book will bring immense confidence, direction and inspiration to all women starting the wonderful journey of motherhood. I extend my heartfelt wishes for a happy and fulfilling experience to every seeker.

1

The Beginnings

'The first seeds of good values are planted in the womb and create the blueprint for life.'

Shakuntala waited with bated breath as she looked towards the horizon. She delicately placed her hands over her stomach, which was now home to the embodiment of her love—a love that was so pure that no darkness could dim its light. She felt the evening breeze prick at her eyes, which were moist with the knowledge that her beloved must have forgotten her.

'You need to chant and be peaceful within,' said the father-like sage, Rishi Kanva. 'You are home to this soul that has chosen you as its mother—a soul whose character, nature and virtues will be defined by you.'

She followed his advice, and she would do so for the months that were to follow. She would give birth to a king that no other could rival. It was her will, her only endeavour and her promise to her beloved.

Shakuntala was aware that the curse that had been bestowed upon her by Rishi Durvasa could not be undone. The king of

Hastinapur was her beloved husband, and this was a fact that none were aware of—none except her and the king himself. This was the era of Gandharva Vivah, and King Dushyant had married her for love.

The love they shared was so true that she had been lost in his thoughts. However, one fateful day, while she had been lost in thoughts of the king, she had forgotten the presence of the godly sage, Rishi Durvasa, and had failed to welcome him properly. The sage, who was known for his wrath and proclivity for dishing out curses, had been quick to take offence and curse her. He had said that the person whose thoughts she was lost in would forget her entirely.

The possibility of such a curse had shaken Shakuntala's entire being. She had immediately begged the sage for forgiveness. Rishi Kanva, the man who had raised her, had beseeched Rishi Durvasa, 'Please forgive her. She is oblivious of the world and lost in the thoughts of the king who she has married recently. She carries his child in her womb. I request you to please bless her with your kindness.'

The sincere apologies that followed had made him ease the strictness of the curse. He had limited her banishment from the king's heart and mind and told her that King Dushyant would remember her if she showed the king something of his own, a ring in this case.

While she was pregnant, she stayed at Rishi Kanva's ashram and began her endeavour of raising a son who would be the heir to the throne of Hastinapur and then lend his name to a kingdom that would be the embodiment of his glory. She willed herself to raise the greatest warrior and king of all time. She would chant the mantras that she was told to chant and talk to the child in her womb, letting it know 'who' she wanted him to become. She would eat foods that would nurture her child and would sing him sacred hymns. She would never indulge her tears, and she let go of her every fear. Her penance was diligent and, as a result, the boy who was born was divinity personified. He was courageous, kind and had the virtues of someone who would rule the kingdom with dignity and honesty.

Seven years later, Shakuntala left the ashram to remind King Dushyant of their marriage. But, on her way, she lost the ring in a river while trying to cross it. The king was ignorant of the truth and angry at such an allegation. He turned her away, and she returned to the ashram, heartbroken all over again.

As fate would have it, the king's chef found the ring as he was cutting open a fish. He thought it wise to bring it to the king. The mere sight of the ring rekindled his memory: it instantly brought to mind the wearer he had fallen in love with. King Dushyant inhaled sharply as a pang of regret—stronger than any physical pain—pricked his heart. Not wasting another minute, he stormed to Shakuntala's village.

King Dushyant was filled with regret. He fumbled to find the right words to apologize and justify his actions. He could not fathom how he could have forgotten a love that had defined him.

As he neared the ashram of Rishi Kanva, he saw an unreal sight. A boy was sitting in front of a lion, holding its jaws wide open and counting its teeth! The bravery of the young child took him by surprise. Before he could stop himself, he asked, 'Who are you, little one? Are you some supreme being? Where have you come from?' The boy responded with a smile. He said, 'I am Bharata, son of King Dushyant.'

Later, King Bharata went on to rule the kingdom of Hastinapur and lent his name to our country; a name that spells wisdom, truth, virtue, kindness, supremacy and modesty.

We believe that every stage and aspect of human life is sacred. Accordingly, the journey that the soul makes from the time of its conception to its cremation should be celebrated. These practices and beliefs are compiled in ancient scriptures that were created by Vedic seers. They prescribe a set of observances known as the *Sanskar*s. Every step of the journey is celebrated and marked by rituals and customs, as they remind us that our existence in the lap of this planet's abundance is a valuable gift from the Almighty; that each step has its significance, whether our mortal self is aware of this or not; and that each moment must be duly respected and regarded.

In ancient times, there were over 40 such rituals and rites that marked the human journey, as mentioned in the Gautam Smriti. Later, Maharishi Angira differentiated between them and contained them within 25 rites. Further down the timeline, the Vyas Smriti ultimately codified them in 16 rituals, or the Shodasha Sanskars that begin with conception and end with the funeral rites.[1]

The essence of these stages lies in the fact that they begin from the prenatal period—choosing to have a child, its conception and the nine-month-long wait—and how it is dealt with. This essence is grounded in the eternal belief of Hindu practices that the moment a foetus comes into existence, the development of its brain and personality depend on the communication between the parents and their unborn child, the physical and emotional environment and what they want their child to be. This ancient art and science of educating the foetus is known to us as Garbha Sanskar. Its powers, applications and results remain unmatched, as the practice emphasizes the overall well-being of the child, the parents and their lives ahead.

Table 1.1
The Sixteen Sanskars

The Sixteen Sanskars of Mankind Mentioned in the Vyas Smriti	
Before Birth (Prenatal Stage)	
Garbhadhan	Conception
Pumsavana	Achieve Progeny of Desired Health and Gender
Simantonayana or *Godh Bharayi*	Hair-parting/Baby shower
Within the First Year of Birth	
Jatakarma	Birth rituals
Namakarana	Name-giving
Nishkrama	First outing
Annaprashana	First solid food
Chudakarma or *Chaul*	Shaving the head
Karnavedh	Ear piercing
From the Age of Five	
Vidyarambha	Learning the alphabet
Upanayana, *Janeyu* or *Yagnopavit*	Sacred thread initiation
Vedarambha	Beginning Vedic study
Keshant or *Godaan*	Shaving the beard
Samavartan	End of studentship
Vivaha	Marriage ceremony
Antyeshti	Death rites

Charkacharya, a renowned Ayurvedic teacher, shared in the following verse:

शुक्रशोणितजीवसंयोगे तु खलु कुक्षिगते गर्भसंज्ञा भवति ॥5॥

The union of the sperm (*shukra*) and the eggs (*shonit*) is merely a physical act. It is only when the soul (*jeev*) enters the womb (garbha) of the mother that it becomes the embryo. Once the soul enters the garbha, the process of instilling the right wisdom, virtues, empowerment and enlightenment in the child within is called Garbha Sanskar.

> Garbha Sanskar is the holistic development of the foetus in the womb and is aimed at nurturing the physical, mental, emotional and spiritual well-being of the life within, with the belief that these influences will create an everlasting impact upon the child's overall growth and well-being.

When a farmer does not focus on the land that he is cultivating, weeds start to grow. However, when he is completely aware, provides the right care and takes proper precautions, he is blessed with the best produce! Growth happens according to the laws of nature, but whether it is desirable or not will depend upon our consistent and focussed efforts. A similar scenario plays out with the baby in the womb. The growth and development of the baby is bound to happen, but whether it is holistic and desirable or not depends on the focus and desire of the mother. So, instilling the desired values, intelligence and skills through consistent focus and efforts is what Garbha Sanskar is all about.

Pujya Pramukh Swamiji Maharaj, the fifth spiritual successor in Bhagwan Swaminarayan's succession of Gunatit

Gurus, says that one can rectify the seed but never a tree. The quality of the seed decides the quality of fruit the tree will bear. Similarly, if a mother has envisioned particular qualities, traits or skills for her unborn child and wishes for them to be manifested, she has to work on instilling the qualities during the prenatal stage to make her wish a reality.

There once was a woman who asked Socrates about a daily ritual that could ensure the virtuous and holistic upbringing of her five-year-old son. Socrates replied that she had been late to initiate the procedure by five years and nine months. This throws light on the fact that the right time to impart value education to a child is when the child is still in the womb.

The Three Prenatal Sanskars

Garbhadhan (Conception)

Garbhadhan Sanskar, also called Garbhalambhanam, in the literal sense, refers to attaining the wealth of the womb. This is the first sanskar (rite) that begins when a couple plans to conceive. This step is the most important one as the strength of the tree is determined by the quality and strength of the seed.

Conception should happen not by chance but by choice!

The couple should start working towards the holistic development of their physical, mental, emotional and spiritual well-being, as this will help them attract a blessed soul. This positive lifestyle should be inculcated at least a year before the couple plans to conceive. However, if that is not possible, then spending a minimum of three months in good health and mind-space will help immensely. During this period, the couple should inculcate the best value-system in their lifestyle and be in a blissful state of mind and immerse themselves in divinity.

Pumsavana (Achieve Progeny of Desired Health and Gender)

Pumsavana is a ritual conducted when the pregnancy becomes visible, ideally in or after the second month and usually before the foetus starts to move within the mother's womb. The ceremony celebrates the early signs that the foetus' head, limbs and reproductive organs have started developing. Many believe that this ritual is performed to bring about the birth of a male child, but in reality, it is more broad-based and aimed at the child's holistic and healthy development as desired by the expecting mother. The master gland—the pituitary gland—which controls the secretions of the other glands in other parts of the body, takes shape during the second month and protects the child from diseases caused by hormonal imbalances.

During this sanskar, the couple is guided by various aspects of Garbha Sanskar. All efforts must be made by the couple towards achieving Garbha Sanskar throughout the pregnancy. The mother should know that every thought, emotion and action that she exhibits is going to have a profound impact on the growth of her child. She must be very careful about what attributes, emotions and thoughts she wishes to impart to her baby.

Simantonayana (Hair-Parting)

This ritual is performed to pray for the healthy development of the baby and ensure a safe delivery by the mother.

Generally, in the third trimester, the pregnant woman is pampered by her husband and blessed by other married women. It begins with the husband gently parting the hair of his wife, signifying the care, love and affection that he wishes to bestow upon her in the coming months. When the other family members and married women pamper the mother-to-be as a part of the ritual, the love, happiness and affection she feels is divine. This love is absorbed by the child within and this helps the baby's growth. The objective of this sanskar is to protect the pregnant mother, while aiding the holistic growth of the child and giving the mother the strength to have a successful delivery.

We have described the basic sanskars that must be practised before the birth of the child. History is filled with examples of how mothers and fathers have invoked divine characteristics in their children through these methods. However, the need and requirement of these practices are much higher and more relevant in today's time than they have ever been before.

Need for Practising Garbha Sanskar in Modern Times

In today's world, the importance of Garbha Sanskar has reached an unprecedented peak. With fertility rates plunging globally, Garbha Sanskar is no longer a luxury but a necessity. According to a recent *Lancet* report published in March 2024, the total fertility rate (TFR), which measures the average number of children a woman is expected to give birth to, has shown a worrying decline. In 1950, India's TFR stood at 6.18, which fell to 4.6 by 1980, and by 2021, it dropped further to 1.91, which is below the replacement rate of 2.1.[2] This signifies a shift where more people are passing away than are being born, leading to a significant slowdown in population growth. Over the past 50 years, fertility in the Indian subcontinent has been cut in half, leaving our generation half as fertile as our grandparents.[3]

If this trend continues, by 2050, our TFR could dwindle to an alarming one child per woman, leading us towards an ageing population. Presently, the average age in India is 28, but projections show this could rise to 38 by 2050.[4] This shift threatens India's demographic advantage, as our young and dynamic population, which is our nation's backbone, may diminish. To achieve our vision of 'Viksit Bharat', it is crucial that we not only preserve a youthful population but also ensure that each new generation is healthy, powerful, intelligent, dynamic and grounded in values.

With families now often limited to one or two children, it is our responsibility to nurture each child's full potential—physically, mentally, emotionally, and spiritually. Garbha Sanskar becomes an essential pathway, encouraging couples to enhance their fertility and give birth to a 'divine genius'. Through the practices outlined in this book, which focus on holistic well-being and detoxification, we aim to empower parents to cultivate the optimal environment for nurturing future generations who can lead us towards a prosperous and enlightened future.

As we proceed, you will understand how to make simple changes in your lifestyle to accommodate this mammoth change and hold the divine child of your dreams in your arms.

Stages of Garbhayatra

The journey that the soul undertakes as it goes through life in human form can be separated into various stages. These form the various stages of the Garbhayatra or the divine journey of the foetus.

Conception: Before the Journey Begins

Garbhayatra begins with Garbhadhan and is the most important phase. But it is most often ignored. This is the phase when the seed is planted, so it is important to ensure that only the highest-quality seed be planted to give birth to the best-quality produce. While one might think that it begins when the mother is impregnated, in the realm of Garbha Sanskar, it ideally begins as early as one year or a minimum of three months before the couple actually conceives. Thus, the couple needs to invest quality time to bring about lifestyle corrections to ensure the production of healthy and powerful ovum and sperm.

It is written in the Sushruta Sharirsthan:

ध्रुवं चतुर्णां सान्निध्याद्गर्भः स्याद्विधिपूर्वकम् ।
ऋतुक्षेत्राम्बुबीजानां सामग्र्यादङ्कुरो यथा ॥33॥

The Sushruta Sharirsthan says that in order to harvest a healthy crop, it is important that the season be appropriate, the soil be fertile, the water requirement be adequately met and the seed be of high quality. So when a farmer puts in so much effort to get the desired quality of produce, how can we mothers leave our conception to chance? Garbhadhan is a planned conception—not by chance but by choice. Thus, for the ideal conception, the couple must ensure that the timing be conducive, the mother's womb be fertile and free of all illnesses, the foetus receives proper nutrition, and the sperm and ovum be healthy and potent.

Garbhadhan is the period dedicated to the purification of a couple's thought processes, behavioural patterns and lifestyle choices in order to invoke the choicest soul for their child. This includes embracing a positive lifestyle, adopting healthy food habits, engaging in meditation, performing prayers, chanting mantras, thinking positive thoughts, reading scriptures and indulging in activities that contribute towards one's holistic development. Let's read about the ways in which a couple can regulate their lifestyle and practise simple living and high thinking modules so that they attract a blessed soul for their child.

The theory of karma states that it is the child who chooses its parents in accordance with its karmas. The vibrations of the soul travel from the astral world and attract similar-frequency vibrations of a couple planning to become parents. Therefore, when one wants to conceive a divine child with specific qualities, they also need to emit similar vibrations as that of the soul. Only divine parents with high frequency of vibrations can invoke a divine child. In the spiritual realm, the higher the frequency of vibration, the higher the divinity of and the power to manifest a divine child.

When Maharaja Dashrath wanted to invoke divine souls for his sons, he went through extreme penance, walking barefoot to gather the things needed for the *yagna* (offerings to the gods) that he was asked to perform. After a lot of hardships, he completed the Putrakamyeshthi Yagna and was thus blessed with Ram, Lakshman, Bharat and Shatrughan.

According to our scriptures, even the great sage Agastya

and Maa Lopamudra had attained superior abilities by doing penance before conceiving a child. Only after purifying themselves—physically, mentally, emotionally and spiritually—and becoming free from vices did they get engrossed in the process of conception with the intention of having a divine child. Having received the true blessings of the gods, he and his wife gave birth to a divine child named Drishtasyu, who was a great poet of the Vedic period.

The great achievement by Maa Lopamudra and Rishi Agastya is within the reach of all couples planning to have a baby. In this regard, the couple should manifest their dream child by saying the following prayer: 'O Lord! While behaving as per the dignity of Grihastha Ashram, we husband and wife wish to have the best children. Please give us such wisdom that our child is strong, intelligent, brave, of a good character, service-oriented and an ideal devotee; one who brings glory to themselves, their parents and the country.'

Although the mother plays a major role, the influence of the father cannot be emphasized enough. Lankapati Ravan's father Vishrava was a pious sage, but his mother Kaikasi had a devilish personality. During her first two pregnancies, her thoughts were more dominating and, as a result, Ravana and Kumbhakarna were born. But in the third pregnancy, Sage Vishrava did not stay silent and awakened his spiritual powers through his penance, which resulted in the birth of the righteous king, Vibhishana.

In the words of Osho, 'Invocation of the higher consciousness gives birth to a superior soul. Atmosphere can be created by understanding the art of love and the knowledge of science and then being born as an individual who has been called a superhuman by Maharshi Arvind and Nietzsche.'[5]

Impregnation: Invoking the Child within the Womb

Impregnation is a divine act and should happen by choice and not by chance. The importance of the impregnation stage—when the actual conception happens—is very vividly talked about in the Mahabharata.

When King Vichitravirya of Hastinapur died, he left his wives—Ambika and Ambalika—childless, making Vichitravirya's mother Maharani Satyavati anxious about the progression of the royal lineage. She called upon one of her sons, the ascetic Vyasa (one who was born through Sage Parashara), to bestow motherhood upon the two widowed queens. This was done through Niyog Pratha. Since the sage was leading a life of severe austerity, he looked unpleasant and fearsome. Ambika shut her eyes tight with fear when she saw him, while Ambalika went pale with fear. Vyasa told his mother that because of this, they would birth sons who would be blind (Dhritarashtra) and jaundiced (Pandu). However, Vidura—half-brother to the kings of Hastinapur—was also born of Sage Vyasa, but his mother Parishrami, who had been the lady-in-waiting to the sister queens Ambika and Ambalika, was absolutely bold and blissful during the process, which resulted in her giving birth to one of the most intelligent characters in the Mahabharata.

Thus, the thoughts, feelings and emotions of the expectant mother at the time of conception play a significant role in the overall development of the child. As mentioned earlier, when the sperm meets the ovum, it might not necessarily result in an embryo. Conception only occurs when life force (*chetana*) also enters the seed and merges simultaneously with the five gross elements. This then gives rise to the live embryo. It is very important that we understand and realize that impregnation is not merely a physical act but also a divine process where parents invoke a soul. This is explained further in the following shloka from the Carak Sharirsthan:

गर्भस्तु खल्वन्तरिक्षवाय्वग्निनतोयभूमिविकारश्चेतनाधिष्ठानभूत:।
एवमनया युक्त्या पञ्चमहाभूतविकारसमुदायात्मको
गर्भश्चेतनाधिष्ठानभूत: स ह्यस्य षष्ठो धातुरुक्त: ॥6॥

Conception, thus, is nothing short of a natural miracle as the life force independently enters the embryo of its own free will.

In the year 1900, in Switzerland there were 9,000 children who were born almost at the same time, and all had low IQ levels. When a researcher named Bejola researched this, he found that all these children were conceived during the Vintage and Swiss Carnival, which was known for heavy drinking. This leads to a pertinent question: if the couple conceives their child under the influence of alcohol, then how can the child be born healthy and intelligent?

Thus, the couple should follow the guidelines given below to make the environment conducive for the divine act.

1. According to the code of the Carak Samhita, consummation is a spiritual and divine process, and it is important that the couple harbour only positive and loving thoughts to ensure the arrival of a divine soul. This has been clearly expressed by Charakacharya in the following shloka:

गर्भोपपत्तौ तु मन: स्त्रिया यं जन्तुं व्रजेत्तत्सदृशं प्रसूते ॥25॥

(The woman gives birth to the child with characteristics in accordance with her thoughts during conception.)

So, it is very important to ensure that the couple is in the best state physically, mentally, emotionally and spiritually during this crucial period.[6]

2. The fertile period, known as 'Ritukaal' in Ayurveda, typically spans from the eighth to the twenty-second day of the menstrual cycle, and varies based on individual cycle length. During this phase, a woman is most fertile and likely to conceive.

3. While everything has a bearing on the process of invoking a divine child, the ambience of the bedroom is also extremely vital. One must give due importance to ensuring that the ideal qualities that are soothing to our senses are maintained. Visually, the room must be clean and beautifully decorated. The use of white bed sheets and curtains provides a more peaceful and serene environment. Scented candles, incense sticks and jasmine flowers can be used to accentuate the positive vibrations. Soothing and melodious music can help build the serenity of the space.

4. It is also highly important for the couple to be physically and mentally relaxed at the time of fertilization.

5. Emotionally and spiritually, the couple should be very loving, blissful and positive during the entire process. Under no circumstances should they have any negative emotions like anger, jealousy, lust, greed, irritation, etc. They should have the desire to invoke a pure and divine soul by chanting the following shloka as suggested by Charakacharya, and then commence with the divine physical act.

ॐ अहिरसि आयुरसि सर्वत: प्रतिष्ठासि
धाता त्वां दधातु विधाता त्वां दधातु ब्रह्मवर्चसा भवेति
ब्रह्मा बृहस्पतिर्विष्णु: सोम सूर्यस्तथाऽश्विनौ
भगोऽथ मित्रावरुणौ वीरं ददतु मे सुतम् ।

(Dear foetus, may you shine bright like the Sun, may you be protected by the creator of the universe, may you be blessed with divine knowledge. I pray to all the Gods—Brahma, Vishnu, Mahesh, Moon, Sun, Mitra and Varun—to bless me with a brave child.)

In fact, Acharya Sushruta also explains in the following verse in Sushruta Sharirsthan that the diet, behaviour and activities of the couple at the time of impregnation manifests into similar characteristics in their offspring:

आहाराचारचेष्टाभिर्यादृशीभि: समन्वितौ ।
स्त्रीपुंसौ समुपेयातां तयो: पुत्रोऽपि तादृश: ॥४६॥

Thus, the shloka reaffirms the importance of Garbhadhan in one's life. It reiterates the Mahabharata story by stating that at the time of impregnation, the exact bearing of the couple's physical, mental and emotional conditions defines the nature of the progeny being birthed.

During Pregnancy: When the Divine Soul Has Arrived Within

With the divine soul now in the mother's womb, it is important that we nurture it in a way that it receives all the right supplements it needs to blossom into a beautiful human being, with all the qualities that the parents desire. This book is actually dedicated to all expectant mothers and unlocks all the secrets to manifest your dream baby in a structured, step-by-step process as shared below.

1. First, the parents should have complete clarity on the qualities, skills and intelligences that they want their child to possess. This includes the foresight to develop the physical quotient (PQ), intellectual quotient (IQ), emotional quotient (EQ) and spiritual quotient (SQ) of the child by using a step-by-step, structured approach as outlined in Sonal's Intelligence Model for Holistic Development©. We will take this up in greater detail in Chapter 2.
2. The parents should ensure their proper physical well-being by adopting the right lifestyle practices as enumerated in Chapter 3.
3. The expectant mother should focus her thoughts on the development of the PQ, IQ, EQ and SQ of the child in the womb by repeating affirmations on a daily basis to manifest their dream child. In fact, the couple should create a vision board with pictures of the people whose qualities they wish to see in their child. Chapter 4 gives us a step-by-step guide on how to achieve the desired mental well-being through mind programming with the help of affirmations and visualization.
4. The mother should be in a state of bliss and maintain her emotional well-being at all times as outlined in Chapter 5.
5. The mother can raise the consciousness of the child in the womb and help its release from the karmas of its past lives by engaging in spiritual acts such as selfless service, chanting mantras, performing prayers, reading powerful scriptures and meditating upon the holistic development

of the child. Chapter 6 takes a closer look at how one can go about achieving the spiritual well-being of the foetus.
6. Garbha Sanskar helps make childbirth a divine and peaceful experience. The process of a miracle taking birth through divine delivery is explained in depth in Chapter 7.
7. The care during the first 40 days post childbirth is very crucial for both the mother and the child. In fact, Garbha Sanskar continues even after the child is born, in the form of breastfeeding, which is highlighted in Chapter 8.

Ritu was well into her 30s when she finally became pregnant. She was new to the mammoth changes her body would go through as it was her first pregnancy. However, she had worked and prayed hard to conceive. She had read many books and followed the advice of many dieticians to help her regulate her body in a manner that provided a conducive environment for the pregnancy, and the good news was finally here. She envisioned a fabulous personality for her offspring. But she wasn't aware of how exactly that would come to be.

It was her second month into the pregnancy and she was still battling nausea and other symptoms that wreaked havoc on her. She lived with her in-laws and was on a sabbatical from her work as a chartered accountant for a month until she felt better.

It was during one of those days that Ritu decided to unwind and sit back. The television was on, and a detective show was playing in which she was quite engrossed.

'Ritu, what are you watching? Please don't watch such television shows. It will have a negative impact on the baby,' her mother-in-law said softly as she joined her on the sofa.

'But Ma, how is that? It is just a TV show. Besides, it has only been a month. The baby will hardly even realize what I am doing,' Ritu said, smiling back.

'I know. But then, the moment the child is within you, its brain starts developing, and it absorbs whatever you are thinking and feeling,' her mother-in-law responded.

'Oh Ma, it is just a TV serial. It will be over in half an hour and then I will sleep for some time. Both of us will get rest and I can unwind,' she said politely, unable to comprehend how the things her mother-in-law had said could even be possible. *Yes, she had tried hard to conceive and had made all the necessary dietary changes to make that possible. She had taken medicines and vitamins to strengthen her womb and practised yoga for a better and stronger body that could handle pregnancy. But this? I think I deserve a break,* she thought to herself.

'Bring the Ramayana, let us sing it together. You will enjoy it,' said Ritu's mother-in-law as she noticed Ritu's reluctance to switch off the TV. It was difficult for her to explain things to her daughter-in-law, and thus, she decided that she would actually do all the necessary things with her.

Then, mother-in-law and daughter-in-law sang in unison the birth chaupaayis—the stanzas that recited the birth of Lord Rama in the Ramayana. As they sang, Ritu began to enjoy the rhythm of the scripture. The mother-in-law clapped her hands and sang as both of them enjoyed the description of the birth of Lord Rama.

नौमी तिथि मधुमास पुनीता। सुकल पच्छ अभिजित हरिप्रीता।
मध्यदिवस अति सीत न घामा। पावन काल लोक बिश्रामा।।1।।

सीतल मंद सुरभि बह बाऊ। हरषित सुर संतन मन चाऊ ।
बन कुसुमित गिरिगन मनिआरा। स्रवहिं सकल सरिताऽमृतधारा ।।2।।

सुर समूह बिनती करि पहुँचे निज निज धाम ।
जगनिवास प्रभु प्रगटे अखिल लोक बिश्राम ।।।191।।

They sang for an hour, and it became an afternoon ritual for them. Ritu also began reading the Hari Gita, a poetic rendition of the Bhagvad Gita in Hindi, and sang it to her baby every evening, making it a pattern for the next few months. Through this everyday ritual, the baby in the womb had connected to Ritu's voice. By then, Ritu was a changed person and loved spending time listening to the stories of great scholars and yogis told by her mother-in-law, who was a very spiritual person.

Ritu had to get a sonography done in the sixth month of her pregnancy. She was with her husband, who lovingly held her hand until they reached the clinic. Ritu was all smiles and greeted the doctor and took her place on the examination bed.

The doctor smeared the gel on her belly to begin the scan. On the monitor, the baby turned the other way; the doctor wasn't too happy with it.

'Why don't you drink some more water and chew a candy? We need to wait for the baby to change its posture to resume the scan,' the doctor said.

'Oh, I really cannot have any more water. And ma'am, if I have candy, I will feel pukish,' Ritu replied, helpless. She was too full and needed to use the washroom. However, the scan wasn't possible on an empty bladder.

'But then what do we do? You will have to wait for some time,' the doctor said patiently.

'Can I just get a minute here if that's okay with you?'

'Sure,' said the doctor.

'Hi baby, it is Mumma,' Ritu said as she placed a hand fondly over her belly.

'Doctor Aunty here really needs to see you and if you keep turning the other way, we will have to stay here for a really long time. Please could you turn around for me? Please turn around, sweetheart,' she said these words while rubbing her belly softly. The doctor sat there smiling, a bit impatient, wondering what was going on.

'I don't think it works this way, dear. You will have to wait outside,' she said to Ritu, who kept stroking her hand over her belly softly.

'Ma'am, I think you should try again. I felt it move just now,' Ritu said happily.

The doctor smeared some more of the cool gel over her belly and placed the transducer over her. To her surprise, the baby had listened to its mother's request and turned.

The doctor was surprised but dismissed it as a coincidence, while Ritu knew exactly what had caused it. She knew that her baby was tuned to listening to her and this was the first time it had let her know. Her eyes brimmed with happy tears as the doctor completed the scan and dismissed any concerns.

'The baby's growth is very good. You can continue whatever you are doing and keep taking your vitamins. I will see you next month,' said the doctor.

As Ritu nodded and left with her husband, she was eager to talk to her mother-in-law and tell her about the experience. She knew that she would be over the moon.

Relevance Redefined

Though the centuries have witnessed mammoth strides in human progress, development and growth, we have fallen behind when it comes to imbibing the positive aspects of our traditional wisdom in our daily lives. For instance, from an era where no one doubted the fact that the baby begins to learn inside the womb, we have entered an era where no one believes anything without proof. While people have subjective understanding of diets, yoga and meditation and engage in selective learning, they are able to reap benefits that are limited to their actions. Today, people are willing to go overboard with medication, clinical intervention and the like to conceive, but are unaware of the potential of the mind, meditation and the mystic universe. In this book, we bring together this ancient wisdom with modern scientific research to unlock a deeper understanding of prenatal development and its impact on the holistic well-being of both the mother and the child in the womb. This ancient wisdom is definitely finding its way into scientific research and journals, which is discussed in depth below.

Scientific Orientation to Garbha Sanskar

It is amazing to note that one tiny cell grows into a fully-developed brain with 100 billion cells by the time a baby is born. To achieve this extraordinary feat, at least 250,000 brain cells are created every minute on average! It is important for the mother to have an in-depth understanding of this rapid growth that leads to the development of the child's brain.

The table below shows the gigantic growth of the foetal brain happening on a month-to-month basis.

Table 1.2
Month-to-Month Growth of the Foetal Brain

Month	Foetal Brain Development
First	In the first month, just 16 days after fertilization, an embryo forms the neural tube, which is the earliest nervous system tissue and eventually develops into the brain and the spinal cord.
Second	During the second month of development, the neural tube begins to separate into brain cells and nerve cells.
Third	In the third month, this basic brain development allows the embryo to display reflexes and react to its environment.
Fourth	During the fourth month, the foetus begins to prepare itself for the outside world by developing its senses of sound and touch.
Fifth	By the fifth month, the foetus begins learning to control its movement and its reaction to these sensations.
Sixth	The ability to consciously react to sensations becomes even stronger during the sixth month. Another major brain development occurs as the cerebral cortex splits into two separate hemispheres.
Seventh to ninth	In the third trimester, i.e., from the seventh to the ninth month, the cerebral cortex takes over from the brain stem and prepares the baby for future learning, which is marked by increased responses such as yawning, resting (arms crossed) and self-touch. These responses frequently occur when there are stimuli from the mother, like her voice or when she touches her abdomen. When the baby is full-term at nine months, the foetal brain has as many neurons as an adult brain, though smaller in size.

Furthermore, in his article 'Foetal Brain Behaviour and Cognitive Development', Prof. R. Joseph lists the spontaneous brain developments of the foetus throughout the pregnancy.

From head turning and bodily reflexes to sleeping, the entire journey of nine months is a learning experience for the child.[7]

During the foetal period, the developmental changes occurring in the brain are phenomenal. New synapses are constantly being formed in response to external cues being delivered to the foetus. The development of neural connectivity enables the foetus to recognize and analyse complex information, thus enhancing the learning-related capabilities in the womb, which is the essence of Garbha Sanskar, showing that learning can happen in the womb. It is worthwhile to note that in just nine months, the embryo, which could only be seen under a microscope and was almost weightless, gets transformed into a baby weighing a few kilos with all the functional organs in place.

Development Phases and the Impact of the Mother's Interventions

The prenatal phase is not only concerned with the development of physical organs but also with the development of sensory organs. A number of scientific studies have been conducted to observe foetal behaviour, which reiterate and reaffirm the learning happening in the womb through the development of the five senses.[8]

Hearing

A large amount of evidence proves the development of the auditory nervous system in the foetus. A research paper claims that prenatal experiences have a remarkable influence on the brain's understanding of sounds, which may support, for example, the ability of an infant to learn multiple languages faster.[9] It has been found that this also helps the child in improving genetic disorders such as dyslexia, speech-sound correlation, or the inability to learn a language.[10]

In another study by Prof. Peter Hopper of the School of Psychology at Queen's University, Belfast, the foetus was regularly made to listen to the tune of the soap opera *Neighbours* through a speaker taped to the abdomen of the mother. Then, as the music played, every movement the foetus made—its heart rate and so on—were constantly monitored by ultrasound. The study revealed that memory developed in the womb.[11]

Table 1.3
Foetal Hearing Development: A Timeline

Week of pregnancy	Development
4–5	Cells of the embryo begin to arrange themselves into a baby's face, brain, nose, ears and eyes.
9	Indents appear where the baby's ears will grow.
18	The foetus begins to hear sounds.
24	The foetus is more sensitive to internal sounds such as the mother's heartbeat, air moving through the lungs, the growling of the stomach and even the sound of the blood coursing through the umbilical cord.
25–26	The foetus responds to noise/voices while in the womb, especially the mother's. The response is marked by an increased heart rate, which suggests that it is more alert when the mother is talking.

Scientists have discovered that while in the womb, babies also begin to learn language through their mothers. This is seen when babies that are born only a few hours ago are able to differentiate between sounds from their native language and foreign ones.

Vision

The eyes, which are formed in the first trimester, are sealed shut until almost the seventh month. After they open, the foetus can see, but there's little to no light to see anything inside the mother's womb. However, it has been reported by doctors that if very bright light is focussed on the mother's belly, then the foetus turns away from it.[12] Ultrasounds have revealed that the foetus gradually opens and closes its eyes more regularly as it approaches the day of its delivery. It is as if it is blinking and is ready to look at the outside world.

Taste

The taste buds begin to develop around the seventh or sometimes the eighth week. By the fourteenth week, there is evidence that suggests that the baby in the womb can taste bitter, sweet and sour flavours in the amniotic fluid.[13] Ultrasounds prove that many foetuses often lick the placenta and uterine wall. Studies also indicate that the food that the mother eats during her pregnancy may affect her baby's taste preferences long after its birth. According to Julie Mennella, PhD, biopsychologist at the Monell Chemical Senses Center in Philadelphia, the more varied a mother's diet is during her pregnancy, the more likely it is that the infant will accept new food with ease.[14] In fact, according to researchers from Ashton University and Durham University's Foetal and Neonatal Research Lab, the evidence of foetal reactions to what their mothers are eating and smelling could have important implications regarding our understanding of the development of our taste and smell receptors and thereby translate into a better understanding of our perception and memory of food.[15]

Smell

An unborn baby can not only taste food but also smell it. It is well established by doctors that at the time of birth, the amniotic fluid sometimes carries the smell of cumin, garlic, fennel and other spices that the mother ate while she was pregnant.[16] The amniotic fluid, which babies swallow and breathe in during their time in the womb, contains the smells not just of the foods the mother has eaten but also of the mother herself. This proves that many newborns can instantly recognize their mothers in the first few hours after birth. The credit goes to the baby's sense of smell that can help it identify its mother instantly. In fact, studies have shown that if a mother washes just one breast right after birth, the baby will prefer to nurse at the unwashed breast because of the natural aroma present there.[17]

Based on research by Marshall Klaus, MD and the author of *Your Amazing Newborn*, every time a newborn baby is placed upon its mother's bare abdomen, it is guided mostly by smell and within the first hour of its life, will push its way up towards its mother's breast.[18]

Touch

Babies eagerly explore whatever they can get their hands on as early as 20 weeks. A foetus can react to everything around it. Ultrasounds have shown that some foetuses also try to grasp the amniocentesis needle when it's inserted into the uterus.

The foetus entertains itself by sucking on its own hands and fingers, especially the thumb, which it discovers around the eighteenth week. They also 'walk' around by pushing on the uterine walls with their feet. They really enjoy pulling on and swinging from the umbilical cord.

This extent of their playfulness helps them develop important reflexes that they would need once they are born. The act of thumb-sucking will not only be crucial to taking in food but will also become a source of comfort to them. Feeling things with their mouths is an important way for babies to explore things. The process of filling their lungs and moving the diaphragm up and down, with fluid instead of oxygen, is also good practice for the foetus because, when it is born, it would have learnt how to breathe on its own.

Developing Focus

Through ultrasound tests, researchers have visualized evidence that babies that are in utero can experience rapid eye movement (REM) sleep. This is associated with dreaming and occurs around the thirty-second to the thirty-sixth weeks. It is still unclear if they are actually dreaming because their brain waves cannot be monitored at that stage. However, doctors do believe that there is a possibility.

It has also been found that the sleep pattern of foetuses at this stage of development closely resembles that of newborns. They invest a lot of their time in REM sleep. However, they also indulge in quiet and deep sleep with no eye movement. Researchers have also observed babies in utero in a state of quiet alertness. This suggests that they may be concentrating—perhaps listening intently to their mother talk.

All these development processes prove that a baby is not passively waiting to be born in the womb but is already learning and working on building important skill sets to make a comfortable entry into this big world.

Right Time to Start Garbha Sanskar

The brain of the foetus in the mother's womb develops as many as 100 billion neurons at the astounding speed of 2.5 lakh per minute. This colossal task begins as early as the sixteenth day after conception.[19] Interestingly, this remarkable feat of neuron formation occurs even before the pregnancy is confirmed, and the mother remains unaware of her pregnancy. So, the best time to imbibe the practices of Garbha Sanskar is not when the mother confirms her pregnancy but rather when she plans it.

The making of a human brain from a tip of a 3-mm neural tube is indeed a marvel of biological engineering.[20] Considering the extraordinary development rate, we can say that the mother's womb is actually the 'Divine School for the Unborn', where one could achieve considerable character-building in nine months.

The thoughts, emotions and lifestyle of a mother during her pregnancy have a profound effect on the growth and development of the child residing within. Thus, the process of nurturing your child and teaching ethics actually begins right from the time the child enters the womb. So, when a mother is focussed entirely and incessantly upon applying the principles of Garbha Sanskar, she can ensure that the brain development of her child happens in a way she deems fit. It is in fact the most blissful work that any mother can engage in.

The Divine Curriculum

School: The Divine Womb
Guru: Mother
Course : Manifestation through Garbha Sanskar
Syllabus: Holistic development of the baby
Duration: The nine months in the womb
Fees: Focussed attention
Eligibility Criteria: The desire to give birth to a divine genius

Course Highlights:

1. Enhance the child's PQ, IQ, EQ and SQ by working on physical, mental, emotional and spiritual well-being
2. Create a holistic child, empowered with qualities and possessing the skills and traits as desired and worked upon by the mother
3. Protect the womb
4. Learn to exercise caution and adopt a healthy lifestyle to prevent diseases
5. Develop an eternal bond between the mother and her unborn child
6. Create an empowered generation that will be a force to reckon with

The Divine Womb is the most powerful school where the first Guru, the Mother, imparts the most significant lessons of life in just nine months through Garbha Sanskar.

Let's get started with your journey to unlock the secrets to your Dream Child.

2

Creating Intelligence in the Womb

'The Divine Womb is the most powerful school where the first seed of intelligence is sown.'

There is a popular mythological lore involving Maharshi Vashishtha—one of the most revered Vedic rishis—and his wife Arundhati, whose spirituality and levels of penance put her at par with the Saptarishis. She is held in such high regard that one of the stars linked to the constellation Saptarishi has been named after her.

Legend has it that the Saptarishis, including Rishi Vashisht, reached a lake during their travels. They plucked some lotuses and kept them on the bank before taking a dip in the lake. When they came out, the flowers were missing. The theft at such a location raised the suspicion that one of them was involved.

To uncover the mystery, the rishis cast a curse: stealing lotuses will be as big a sin as not offering evening prayers (Sandhya Aarti).

Arundhati's curse was a little different: stealing lotuses will be no less a sin than a mother conceiving a weak child from infidelity.

The tale shows how procreating a frail child was considered a sin in ancient times. It was up to the resolve of the mother to shape her child. They would chant, practise their virtues and observe penance at the heart of everyday life in order to have benevolent, brave and bright offspring. The rishis believed that the possibility of weak children could be easily ruled out if the parents followed the diktats of the shastras from conception to birth.

This is even more applicable in today's dynamic environment. The coming generations need to be equipped to face this challenge. The responsibility lies with us—the current generation—to ensure that we nurture a powerful future that is progressive, intelligent and equipped with the right values to handle this dynamism. However, ironically, despite living in such an advanced world, we tend to leave important parts of our life up to destiny. It completely depends upon the artist as to what he creates when he is bestowed with the best brushes, canvas and colours. Similarly, a mother can be considered to have the power to manifest the child of her dreams by simply regulating her lifestyle, mindset and behaviour patterns.

The child is created in the womb not by accident but as a combination of three major factors. These are:

1. The child's own karma: The life script of every soul is based on its karmas. In fact, it is the soul that chooses parents who can support it in its journey and not the other way round.

2. The genetic makeup of its parents: The inherent strengths and unique attributes of the family's genetic lineage play a vital role in the development of the child.
3. Nurture and care during pregnancy: This has the most profound influence on the development of the baby in the womb. This potential of the human mind is what is tapped into under the science of Garbha Sanskar. This is explained by Charakacharya:[1]

सत्त्ववैशेष्यकराणि पुनस्तेषां तेषां प्राणिनां मातृपितृसत्त्वान्यन्तर्वन्त्या:
श्रुतयश्चाभीक्ष्णं स्वोचितं च कर्म सत्त्वविशेषाभ्यासश्चेति ॥

It says here that a baby's mind in the womb is neither empty, nor fully mature. At the embryo stage, the mind of the foetus is strongly connected to that of its parents. It can listen, be moulded and directed by the types of stories and music the mother listens to when she is pregnant. Thus, whatever the mother listens to and focusses on with rapt attention contributes to the development of the mind of the child. This becomes clear when we examine historical incidents that supposedly back it.

In 1874, a 15-year-old boy named Jesse Pomeroy in Boston, USA, brutally murdered many boys. While the case was being investigated, it was revealed that the boy's father was a butcher. When interviewed, the mother revealed that she had watched her husband killing the animals. The shock and trauma of the sight could have seeped through her to the child in her womb. The child would also have grown up seeing what his father's profession entailed. This could also have fanned the flames that resulted in his becoming a murderer.[2]

On the other hand, Lord Buddha's mother Mayadevi was very kind. Her heart used to overflow with compassion when she saw people suffering from oppression, burdened with taxes and fighting slavery. She always had a strong desire to mitigate the suffering of others. So strong was her compassion that from her womb Lord Buddha was born. He later abandoned the family and the riches and comfort of his life to lead countless people to enlightenment.

What emotions do you feel in your heart? What thoughts attract you the most? What actions primarily hold your interest? Depending on your emotions, thoughts and actions, you can give birth to the child of your dreams and ideals. The power lies with the mother. A mother is blessed by God with the power to create, so it is of utmost importance that she use this power responsibly.

Holistic Human Intelligence

Human intelligence is the mental ability to learn from experiences. It is all about being able to adapt to new and random situations, understanding and handling abstract occurrences, and deploying this knowledge to navigate one's environment. The mother can try to guide the development of the mind of the baby in the womb by following the principles of Garbha Sanskar.

If the mother has extreme clarity regarding the attributes she wants to develop in her child and is focussed on them, then there is no doubt that her child will be an exact replica of what she envisions. However, the million-dollar question remains: what does one manifest? Every parent wants for their child to excel, to embody wisdom, possess a profound understanding of the world, and navigate life's challenges with resilience. But what are these attributes, and how does one go about imbibing them to ensure that their child is fully empowered? This is something which puzzles almost every parent. Many of them, when asked about the qualities they want in and for their child, give answers that are limited to gender, complexion and a few personality traits. However, we will fail to navigate and will not arrive at our final destination unless we know the address of where we want to go. So, the better the clarity we have on the qualities and skills we desire to see in our child, the closer we are to holding the child of our dreams.

This chapter throws light on the various types of intelligence a child can possess, their characteristics and ways to achieve them.

Holistic human intelligence can be separated into four different levels which can be measured with the help of their respective quotients. The four levels of human intelligence and its related quotients are:

1. Physical intelligence measured by PQ
2. Mental intelligence measured by IQ
3. Emotional intelligence measured by EQ
4. Spiritual intelligence measured by SQ

Physical intelligence is all about a person's ability to perform physical tasks efficiently. It is a measure of the kinaesthetic skill sets of a person and is called physical quotient. A long time ago, people were merely involved in manual labour and their PQ was the primary source of power, status and earning a livelihood.

However, with the advent of technology, the dependability on physical prowess has reduced and intellectual intelligence (measured by one's intellectual quotient) has been introduced. Intellectual intelligence is defined as an individual's thinking capacity for abstraction, logic, understanding, reasoning, planning, creativity and problem-solving by using various skill sets like the application of logic, verbal communication, spatial awareness, musical atonement, etc.

This is furthered by the ability of a person to understand and manage not only their own feelings and emotions but also of those around them. This is the emotional intelligence of a person and is measured by the EQ.

However, just handling feelings at the surface level is not enough. In order to have a holistic understanding of one's needs, one must understand the true reason behind their actions, emotions and thoughts, and what actually triggered their reaction and led to the subsequent feelings. The ability of a person to know one's true self, have clarity of purpose in life and understand the underlying motives behind his thoughts, emotions and actions is spiritual intelligence and is measured by SQ.

When it comes to the holistic growth of an individual, all of the above intelligence measures need to work in tandem. Having said that, one must note that it is wrong to assume that higher intelligence levels need to replace the lower ones. In fact, it is the lower levels of human intelligence that act as the building blocks and aid the development of the higher orders of human intelligence.

A popular saying goes, 'The hand that rocks the cradle, rules the world.' One of the most beautiful roles that a woman plays is that of a mother. The Markandaya Purana has a beautiful story of the powerful mother and Queen Madalasa. She was a pious and legendary mother who bore four children and shaped

their personalities while they were in her womb. She was an ideal wife, mother and woman who was well versed with the ancient scriptures, and imbibed their teachings in her thoughts as well as her actions.

When Madalasa bore King Ritdhwaja his first son, all through her pregnancy, she spoke of the Vedas, the spiritual journey of a soul, the purpose of life and many more teachings to her unborn child. She taught him about being pure and that worldly desires and attachments only led to great suffering and misery.

Soon, the son was born and the king named him Vikranta. As he grew up, she taught him all the Vedas, scriptures and more. She went on to have two more sons and repeated the process with them. They were named Subahu and Shatrumardan. Her ways of raising her three sons were such that eventually they renounced all worldly pleasures and embarked on the path of sanyas or renunciation.

When Madalasa became pregnant again, the king requested her for an heir to the throne. Respecting his desires, the queen handled her child in the womb differently. Unlike her previous pregnancies, she did not focus much upon renunciation and sacrifice but gave lessons on bravery, courage and righteousness. Queen Madalasa focussed on doing all the things that were required for a king—learning warfare techniques, handling court proceedings, understanding the code of conduct for a ruler, and so on. Queen Madalasa demonstrated that the thoughts and characteristics of a child are created while they are in the womb, and these are directed by the mother's thoughts, actions and words. As predicted, Alarka, the fourth son of Queen Madalasa, went on to become one of the most powerful, respected and righteous kings in the history of mankind.

Creating Intelligence in the Womb

Queen Madalasa thus rightly justified what is suggested by Acharya Sushruta in the following verses:[3]

राजसंदर्शने यस्या दौहृदं जायते स्त्रिया: ।।
अर्थवन्तं महाभागं कुमारं सा प्रसूयते ।।22।।

दुकूलपट्टकौशेयभूषणादिषु दौहृदात् ।।
अलङ्कारैषिणं पुत्रं ललितं सा प्रसूयते ।।23।।

आश्रमे संयतात्मानं धर्मशीलं प्रसूयते ।।
देवताप्रतिमायां तु प्रसूते पार्षदोपमम् ।।
दर्शने व्यालजातीनां हिंसाशीलं प्रसूयते ।।24।।

अतोऽनुक्तेषु या नारी समभिध्याति दौहृदम् ।।
शरीराचारशीलै: सा समानं जनयिष्यति ।।28।।

(A pregnant lady who desired to see a king delivered a wealthy and righteous child. The desire for headbands of fine cloth, silken garments, ornaments, etc., led to the birth of a child with materialistic desires. The desire for a hermitage leads to a self-controlled and righteous child. The desire to see the idol of a deity gives birth to a devoted child. The desire to see ferocious animals led to the birth of a violent son. Therefore, we can see that the mother's desire affected what the child grew up to be.)

Acharya Sushruta further shares:[4]

कर्मणा चोदितं जन्तोर्भवितव्यं पुनर्भवेत् ।।
यथा तथा दैवयोगाद्दौहृदं जनयेद्धृदि ।।29।।

(The desires that arise in the heart of the mother are in accordance with previous karmas and are guided by destiny.)

The Nine Intelligences by Dr Howard Gardner

We understand that when it comes to the science of Garbha Sanskar, a mother actually has the power to instil within the unborn child all the characteristics, thinking abilities, intelligence levels and other nuances based on her will and aspirations. Before we move on to those processes, let us look at the different types of intelligences that one can measure within themselves or instil in their offspring.

Dr Howard Gardner was a professor of cognition and education at the Harvard Graduate School of Education. He is known for the development of his theory of multiple intelligences way back in 1983. In that study, he stated that people deploy several types of intelligences, rather than one general kind on any given aspect. According to him, intelligence should be understood as a multifaceted and diverse set of abilities rather than a single measure of cognitive capacity.[5]

The different intelligences include:

1. Bodily-kinaesthetic intelligence: This refers to mind and body coordination. It is highly important in athletics and the performing arts. Quite mistakenly, while this is not often referred to as intelligence, kinaesthetic intelligence is the skill of using one's body effectively and expressing oneself through physical activities, such as sports, dance or fine motor tasks, thereby making one 'body smart'. How a sportsman uses his body to catch a ball, how a dancer moves his feet to a particular rhythm, or how an actor enacts a particular scene,

are all examples of where bodily-kinaesthetic intelligence comes into focus. In fact, the kings of old derived all their power and status through kinaesthetic intelligence.

You possess high bodily-kinaesthetic intelligence if:

- You can recognize your physical capabilities and limits.
- You can efficiently communicate with body language, gestures and actions.
- You can command your body as well as respond to it with great ease.
- You possess a good sense of timing when it comes to physical activities.
- You can handle objects with a high degree of deftness, assertion and ease of movement.
- You can use your hands creatively.

Great career areas for people with bodily-kinaesthetic intelligence include physical therapy, dance, athletics, as fitness coaches or instructors, as gym owners, acting, mechanics, carpentry and the like.

Do you know where the great Shivaji Maharaj was trained in warfare? The school was none other than his mother's womb! Jijabai Bhonsle, or Rajmata as they lovingly called her, was the revered mother of Shivaji Rao, the founder of the Maratha Empire, whose name was enough to make the British tremble. Shivaji was evidently blessed with superior kinaesthetic intelligence than his peers. Jijabai was the embodiment of courage and strength. Right from her birth, she was exposed to the heroism of her father who

served the Nizams. Encouraged by his valour, she also learnt sword fighting, arms training and the like.

When she was three months pregnant with Shivaji, her husband Shahaji was away fighting the Mughals. It is believed that during the time Shivaji was in her womb, Rajmata Jijabai would recite stories of valour of his father and would herself practise with weapons like swords. She was very keen on having a son who would bring light into the lives of the Marathas and put an end to their shame of working only for the Nizams.

She recited the epics and Puranas, and taught him to serve people and be a friend to all irrespective of caste, creed and religion. Justice, fair play and staying true to one's duty were her preachings to the young Shivaji that started in her womb.

She was thus bestowed with a son who ended Aurangzeb's rule. This shows that just as a potter's skills define the shape and quality of a pot, the mother can define the true essence of the child she gives birth to.

Such feats achieved by mothers were not only limited to the Indian subcontinent. French mother Letizia Bonaparte also imparted the knowledge of war strategy to the great emperor Napoleon Bonaparte in her womb.

The display of kinaesthetic intelligence can be seen in the performing arts as well. Charlie Chaplin's mother Hannah Chaplin was a famous actress, singer, dancer and performing artist who had done stage shows in England since the age of 16. She seemingly imparted all these skills to the child in her womb when she was pregnant. Later, her first son Charlie Chaplin became the world's most famous comedian and her second son Sidney Chaplin was also a good actor in his time.

The mother is an artist creating her masterpiece, giving it shape, size, colour in accordance with her desires. If you want your child to have thick, curly eyelashes or a dimpled cheek, then from the day you know that you are pregnant, start visualizing your child with those physical attributes.

Shefali was very focussed on having a baby with thick, curvy eyelashes and dimpled cheeks. As a follower of Jainism, Shefali was well acquainted with the divine power of the Bhaktamar Stotra, especially the ninth shloka that emphasizes the attainment of a child as per one's desires. Shefali chanted the shloka with full faith, combining affirmations and visualization to manifest her desires effectively. And when Veera was born, to everyone's surprise, so thick were her lashes that they were often mistaken for fake ones, and the cute dimples took everyone's breath away.

2. Logical-mathematical intelligence: This refers to a person's ability to solve mathematical problems effectively, spot trends and patterns with ease and understand relationships, among other vital abilities that are enhanced when this skill set is developed in an individual. The ability to register various changes in our environment and react faster, the ability to be calculative when dealing with life decisions and the ability to judge better, are enhanced with the development of this skill set. If a person possesses logical-mathematical intelligence, it means that order and sequencing feature greatly in their

thinking process.[6] It implies that they can think systematically and conceptually, thus becoming 'logic smart'.

You possess high logical-mathematical intelligence if:

- You are good with numbers and are confident at taking on tasks that involve quantifying things, including math and arithmetic questions.
- You derive great joy in performing experiments and indulging in your own investigations.
- You enjoy playing games that deal with logic and strategy.
- You love to solve puzzles and unravel mysteries.

Great career options are there for people who possess logical-mathematical intelligence. Think of mathematicians, economists, auditors, accountants, scientists, computer programmers, financial analysts and technicians.

C.V. Raman was a famous scientist who gained prominence for his work on light scattering. His son Venkatraman Radhakrishnan was a famous space scientist, who made contributions in the field of radio astronomy. While one should acknowledge his own hard work, one cannot entirely rule out the contribution made by the mother who was constantly surrounded by her husband, whom she would listen to as he talked about his work. The child had a sharp and articulate mind and this, when seen in the light of Garbha Sanskar, could point to the fact that the expectant mother played a large role in unconscious learning and intelligence manifestation.

3. Linguistic-verbal intelligence: This refers to a person's ability to use words effectively. This does not primarily imply learning multiple languages. Instead, being fluent in just one language and possessing the ability to use it effectively to speak, write and practise spoken and written communication also means that one possesses linguistic-verbal intelligence. This intelligence is all about being able to use the right words and expressing what you mean effectively, thus becoming 'word smart'. It is a unique skill that can be utilized in several different scenarios.

You have high linguistic-verbal intelligence if:

- Your choice of words, use of language and manner of expression have a profound influence on the hearts and minds of others.
- You are comfortable speaking as well as writing.
- You are adept at using the right words to persuade, effectively communicate and get your thoughts across.
- You possess a broad vocabulary and can understand when and how to use certain words.
- You love to read and write.
- You have fun playing games that deal with words, such as crossword, scrabble, word games, etc.
- You can easily grasp new languages and/or dialects. However, fluency is not a parameter to measure linguistic-verbal intelligence when it comes to new languages.

People with linguistic-verbal intelligence often have careers as writers, journalists, public speakers, radio announcers, television hosts, YouTubers, lawyers, curators, librarians, politicians, speech pathologists, and also in marketing, sales and advertising.

When mothers are well read, have a love for words and are able to articulate their thoughts and emotions, the probability of bearing children who have a natural flair for words seems high. Padmaja Naidu was the daughter of poet, feminist and activist Sarojini Naidu and her father was a freedom fighter. Padmaja was the co-founder of the Indian National Congress in Hyderabad and was part of the Quit India Movement of 1942. She was later appointed as the governor of West Bengal in 1956. It was all to her credit, but her verbal skill of public speaking and the fervour for freedom were probably imbibed when she was inside her mother's womb.

4. Musical intelligence: This refers to a person's sensitivity to rhythm, melody, pitch and tone, and the ability to understand, create and appreciate music. People who possess this intelligence are adept in creating music effortlessly and music flows through their heads in the same way as we use language. Those who are blessed with musical intelligence are sometimes able to play musical instruments with or without some basic knowledge of it, thus making them 'music smart'.

You are known to possess a high level of musical intelligence if:

- You are adept at understanding the pitch, rhythm, tone and timbre of sounds with ease.
- You can recognize, create or reflect upon music and you love doing so.
- You are comfortable when music plays in the background while you are busy with your other activities.

- You are highly sensitive to sounds and can sometimes hear what others might miss.

People who possess musical intelligence often go on to become singers, musicians, vocal coaches, music teachers, composers, dancers, dance teachers, music therapists and choir directors.

There are great father-son duos in our country like Rakesh Chaurasia-Hariprasad Chaurasia (flute), Rahul Sharma-Shivkumar Sharma (santoor) and Zakir Hussain-Alla Rakha (tabla), to name a few. All of them have a family history of being involved with music and display somewhat of a natural affinity for it, probably because of the music they heard while they were in the womb.

5. Spatial-visual intelligence: This refers to a person's ability to view the world in its three dimensions and perceive and manipulate visual and spatial information, such as maps, charts and diagrams. This involves the following capabilities:

- Mental imagery: When a person can imagine a picture or visualize without any external stimulus, that is, they are able to remember from their memories or past experiences, it is called mental imagery. In other words, it involves the depth with which a person can imagine things.
- Spatial reasoning: The ability of a person to visualize objects in three dimensions and draw generalizations with limited information about the subject is called spatial reasoning. For example, if you mention a

pyramid to a person with spatial-visual intelligence, they will ideally be able to visualize how that pyramid would look based on your description itself.
- Image manipulation: The ability to visualize changes to an image, even before it is actually implemented, is called image manipulation. For example, an artist can visualize how their artwork should look, even before they have begun working upon it.
- Artistic intelligence: It is the ability to create beautiful artworks, including graphic skills.

Spatial-visual intelligence and creativity usually go hand-in-hand. People with good spatial-visual skills can draw on their active imagination to produce an impressive visual piece of art, thus becoming 'picture smart'.

You possess high spatial-visual intelligence if:

- You have an awareness of your surroundings and environment.
- You possess a good sense of direction.
- You love playing jigsaw puzzles and similar games based on visual navigation.
- You daydream a lot.
- You are creative.

People who possess spatial-visual intelligence often become artists, architects, geometry teachers, engineers, surveyors, urban planners, graphic artists, interior decorators, fashion designers, photographers, pilots and cartographers.

Abhimanyu was in Subhadra's womb when Lord Krishna recited the ways and means of entering the Chakravyuh. He learnt the art while inside her womb. However, she fell asleep while Krishna explained how he should escape the Chakravyuh. Years later, during the battle of the Mahabharata, Abhimanyu was equipped with the knowledge to enter the Chakravyuh but had no clue how to escape it. This shows the impact of spatial and visual intelligence and throws light on the fact that what the mother actually listens to is not only heard but also learnt by the child within.

6. Naturalist intelligence: This refers to the ability of a person to explore, understand and bond with nature by showing sensitivity and appreciation for the natural world, including the ability to recognize and categorize living things, patterns in nature and environmental interactions. When a person is sensitive towards nature and all kinds of elements, including plants, animals and the five elements—earth, water, fire, air and ether—they are considered 'nature smart'.

You have high naturalist intelligence if:

- You love and integrate with nature and look forward to spending time outdoors.
- You can easily bond or integrate with animals, birds, plants and other nature elements.
- You are empathetic and are good at taking care of animals, plants and the five elements of nature.

People who possess naturalist intelligence often go on to become botanists, oceanographers, camp counsellors, scout troop leaders, gardeners, farmers, astronomers, meteorologists, geologists and landscape architects.

Looking back on the story of Shakuntala, she raised Prince Bharat to be in complete sync with Mother Nature and all her attributes. This can be seen when he, as a little boy, was playing with a lion with his hand inside its mouth. Throughout her pregnancy, Shakuntala remained in the midst of nature and unconsciously gifted the love and oneness she felt with nature and all its creatures to her son, King Bharat, while he was in the womb itself. King Bharat was not afraid of nature but respected every aspect of it.

7. Interpersonal intelligence: This is the ability to understand and interact effectively with others, including empathise, communicate and be social aware, thereby becoming 'people smart'.

You have high interpersonal intelligence if:

- You are good at understanding differences among a group of people in terms of human nature, ideologies and perceptions.
- You are a part of a wide circle of friends and are extremely comfortable with meeting new people.
- You can gauge the mood levels of people around you and know how to modulate your behaviour accordingly.
- You have the ability to view things from different perspectives while understanding other people's points of view as well.

Great careers for people with interpersonal intelligence can be built in human resources, counselling, management, psychology, public relations, social direction, teaching and social work.

When it comes to interpersonal skills, most of our celebrities are clear examples. It is all about nurturing confidence that comes out in the form of great performances, public-speaking skills and the like. If we look at history, kings and queens raised their children with the skill sets to adapt to the throne and have, by default, inculcated in them the ability to talk freely and with confidence around strangers, have empathy towards their countrymen, and be the next flag bearers of their kingdom.

8. Intrapersonal intelligence: This refers to having an awareness of your own feelings and responding to them appropriately. Have you ever properly understood your own feelings and the real cause behind them? Do you know how to respond to your own emotions appropriately and effectively?

Intrapersonal intelligence involves appreciating and respecting your inner feelings and responding to them according to the situation at hand, through self-awareness, engaging in self-reflection and having an understanding of one's own emotions, motivations and goals, thereby becoming 'self smart'.

You possess high intrapersonal intelligence if:

- You are self-motivated and can put yourself first when required.
- You are independent and strong-willed.
- You have clarity in your thoughts and act without bias based on your thoughts and feelings about a specific event.

- You enjoy taking time off for reflection or to simply be in your own company.

People who possess intrapersonal intelligence tend to gravitate towards roles like psychologists, writers, therapists, counsellors, social workers, theologians, entrepreneurs and poets.

Mata Sita was a princess, and when she was in exile the first time, she was under the care of her husband. However, the second time, she was pregnant with Luv and Kush, and for the entire duration of her pregnancy, she chose to use her solitude to introspect and self-reflect. In spite of the reasons why she had to leave, she decided to raise her children in the likeness of their father Lord Rama—the epitome of maryada (Maryadapurush) and greatest of the great among all men (Purushottam)—which was not an easy task. She was self-aware and knew of the skill sets that she needed to inculcate in her children so that they would be worthy heirs to the kingdom of Ayodhya. Thus, she lived her life in exile with immense dignity, valour and peace. She used the solitude of her exile to empower herself and her children. She chanted mantras and listened to the preachings by Rishi Valmiki while she stayed in his ashram. The sons she bore were, thus, the mirror images of Lord Rama, both in valour and values.

In today's time and age, many women are also prescribed bed rest which is almost like being on house arrest for them. However, if we look at the brighter side and use this solitude to work towards enhancing our intrapersonal skills, initiate self-empowerment, engage in self-introspection and work towards a larger goal, that time will be the best months spent with yourself and with your child within.

9. Existential intelligence: This is all about understanding the real meaning of life and the purpose of one's own existence. It is indeed one of the most complex of the nine types of intelligence proposed by Dr Gardner. People with existential intelligence are 'life smart' as they are absolutely comfortable talking about serious, sensitive and thought-provoking questions regarding their existence, and also strive to find answers to them in their own ways.

You have high existential intelligence if:

- You are deeply interested in finding answers to questions such as, 'What is the meaning of life?' or 'What happens after death?'
- You have clarity about the purpose you serve on earth and what you strive to achieve.
- You demonstrate high understanding and interest on matters related to human existence.

People with existential intelligence can have careers as gurus, inspirational speakers, philosophers, spiritual healers, counsellors, motivational speakers and life coaches.

Bhakt Prahalad—the greatest bhakt ever—was blessed with bhakti by his mother when he was in her womb. Queen Kayadhu was at the ashram of Sage Narada, during the tenure

of her pregnancy. She learnt the value of the Beej Mantra and instilled all those qualities in her son. She blessed Prahalad with existential intelligence that helped him reach salvation at the tender age of five. Thus, a bhakt was born from the genes of a demon—Hiranakashyap—by the persistent efforts of the mother during her pregnancy.

Sonal's Intelligence Model for Holistic Development©

According to Sonal's Intelligence Model for Holistic Development©, these nine intelligences can be broadly categorized under the four quotients, namely, PQ, IQ, EQ and SQ. This model will provide mothers with a step-by-step, comprehensive and structured approach towards the holistic development of the baby in their womb. By working simultaneously upon the nine intelligences, mothers can ensure the balanced development of all-round well-being for their babies and manifest a holistic child in the womb.

A holistic child would be one who is ideally equipped with these four quotients and can demonstrate the nine intelligence levels. Although the proficiency levels might differ in each of the intelligences, the child will definitely demonstrate a good understanding of all the nine intelligences.

When a mother can visualize all these attributes in a structured manner, she can focus on them individually and manifest the same in her child. This can only be achieved when there is complete clarity about our manifestation. This model will inspire mothers to discover innovative ways to envision their child and achieve a complete understanding of their unborn child based on their intelligences.

UNDERSTANDING	DOING
EXISTENTIAL LIFE SMART	**KINESTHETIC** BODY SMART
SQ SPIRITUAL QUOTIENT	**PQ** PHYSICAL QUOTIENT
EQ EMOTIONAL QUOTIENT	**IQ** INTELLECTUAL QUOTIENT
INTERPERSONAL — PEOPLE SMART **INTRAPERSONAL** — SELF SMART	**MATHEMATICAL** — LOGIC SMART **VERBAL** — WORD SMART
NATURALISTIC — NATURE SMART	**VISUAL** — PICTURE SMART **MUSICAL** — MUSIC SMART
FEELING	THINKING

4 QUOTIENTS — HOLISTIC DEVELOPMENT — 9 INTELLIGENCE

SONAL'S INTELLIGENCE MODEL FOR HOLISTIC DEVELOPMENT ©

Quotient	Intelligence
PQ	Bodily-kinaesthetic intelligence
IQ	Logical-mathematical intelligence Linguistic-verbal intelligence Musical intelligence Spatial-visual intelligence
EQ	Interpersonal intelligence Intrapersonal intelligence Naturalistic intelligence
SQ	Existential intelligence

In these four broad categories, we have summed up the ideal attributes that must be inculcated, manifested, affirmed and meditated upon, in order to give birth to a child who bears all the desired attributes right from birth.

Now you may ask, how do we impart these skills to the unborn? Let me give you a step-by-step guide on how to make this happen.

Practical Strategies for Nurturing Intelligences in the Womb

1. PQ: As mentioned before, PQ mainly deals with the bodily-kinaesthetic skillset and aims primarily at our physical well-being, our ability to perform physical activities and how confident we are in our body. It is all about how well we can command and use our body to perform various life tasks and more. In all, PQ is mainly concerned with 'doing' or action.

The factors that help in enhancing PQ are:

- Nutrition: Expectant mothers must indulge in positive life-force and energy-boosting foods that are highly nutritious, provide the right amount of energy and vitamins, and aid digestion. You will find details about what, when, how and why with regard to the right kind of foods in the chapter on physical well-being.
- Exercise and breathwork: Formulating and practising a workout or yoga routine, breathing exercises and stretches that fit your condition are all various ways in which you can teach the unborn child a lot about the value and importance of exercise! In the past, kings and queens in India used combat training routines as their exercise rituals. Many Indian queens like Queen Madalasa and Jijabai would practise sword fighting to ensure that their sons were born with an expertise in the art. Even today, women who are into sports still take part in their discipline despite being pregnant, and there are many such women who have daughters who take up the same sport. Irina Lenskiy of Israel is a national record holder in relay races at 40, while her daughter Olga is also following her footsteps at just 18 and has won national titles at the 200-m relay race.
- Sleep and relaxation: Along with nutrition and exercise, adequate rest is also important. A mother must know that her body is creating a new life. It all comes from within her and, thus, she must give her body the rest it needs. A minimum eight hours of sleep is a must for a healthy pregnancy and healthy baby. Chapter 3,

which talks about one's physical well-being, also delves into the importance of good sound sleep.
- Brain–body coordination: The mind and the body work in tandem and are partners. Thus, in order to improve the body's responses, one needs to do brain exercises, engage in the performing arts (dancing and acting), get involved in sitting sports activities, involve oneself in developing fine motor skills (art and craft, knitting, stitching, etc.), focus on building coordination between the five senses, break away from addictions of any sort, and protect oneself from toxins in the environment.

Thus, if the mother engages in the healthy behaviours described here and also follows the in-depth guidance provided in Chapter 3, then she can ensure that a good development of kinaesthetic skills, with high physical quotient, is manifested in her child.

2. IQ: The IQ is the rational and logical reasoning aspect of intelligence. It is primarily data-driven, makes active use of the left brain, and improves our technical know-how, logical reasoning ability and presence of mind. When a person is intellectually driven, they acknowledge only that which can be scientifically measured. Intellectual quotient is skill-based and lays focus on the thinking ability of a person. It includes four intelligence levels, namely:

- Linguistic-verbal intelligence
- Logical-mathematical intelligence
- Musical intelligence
- Spatial-visual intelligence

Below are the factors that help increase the IQ of a child while it is in the womb.

- The expectant mother can hone her language in the hopes of passing it to the baby while it is in the womb, by engaging in creative writing, expanding voabulary or learning a new language. She can include regular reading to her routine and learn new words every day or by doing simple things like solving crosswords or playing scrabble. Linguistic skills are also enhanced when the mother establishes a bond with the baby within her womb through conversations, which is also known as *Garbha Samvad*. This could be as simple as saying, 'I wonder what's going to happen next in this book.' Or, 'This music is nice, isn't it, my baby?' Or, 'Let's watch this movie and learn from it.' These conversations can vary depending upon the alertness of the mother and the targeted skill set that she has in mind for her child.
- Logical skills are mainly developed when the mother engages in activities that involve the left brain. These include solving puzzles, brain teasers, brain games, mathematical calculations and strategy games such as chess.
- By listening to her favourite music or involving herself in singing or learning a musical instrument during her pregnancy, the mother can impart musical knowledge and intelligence to her child in the womb. She can calm her nerves and spend some quality time with the child while also developing an interest in music by listening to soft, soothing and peaceful music. Singing

to the baby also helps create a strong bond between the child and the mother.

- Spatial skills can be inculcated through activities that involve thinking, ideation and creating one's thoughts in the form of sketches. This could include drawing and painting, creating three-dimensional models with building blocks, and developing the ability to decipher maps and finding the desired location easily. Such exercises will enhance the brain's power to visualize within the mother and the child.

These skills together help in the overall development of the brain, enhance thinking capabilities and lead to an increase in the IQ of the foetus.

3. EQ: The EQ is the attribute of a person to be emotionally sound and to be able to understand, recognize and respond appropriately to not only one's own emotions but also those of others. It is all about feeling rather than thinking. Emotional intelligence makes use of the right brain and is closely associated with emotions, feelings, creativity and intuition.

The expectant mother can enhance the emotional intelligence of her child in the following ways:

- Self-awareness: The mother should be self-aware and ensure that she is mindful about her own needs and requirements.
- Self-regulation: It involves regulating one's emotions towards a thoughtful action. Strong self-regulation necessitates that one first understands their own emotions by being self-aware. The best way for the mother to understand whether she is achieving this is

by simply checking her level of bliss—a state of extreme happiness, joy and contentment that is marked by a profound sense of inner peace and fulfillment. When the expectant mother is completely at bliss, she has regulated her emotions very well and has, indirectly, taught her unborn child the power of bliss.
- Empathy: Being empathetic to people by stepping into their shoes and viewing things from their perspective is important. It reflects the skill to understand how others feel and to communicate emotively and effectively.
- Social skills: Social skills refer to the skills that are needed to handle and influence other people's emotions effectively. Having good social skills facilitates healthy and confident interactions with people from time to time.

Thus, with high EQ, one can express their thoughts, emotions and opinions freely, clearly and directly. A person with good EQ has complete awareness of their emotions (self-awareness) and can respond appropriately towards it (self-regulation).

Once you can understand and manage yourself, you can begin to understand the emotions and feelings of others (empathy) and are finally able to influence them (social skills).

A person with a sound EQ shows proper understanding and empathy towards oneself, his fellow human beings and the world at large. It thus includes the following:
- Interpersonal skills: When the expectant mother can forge healthy relations with others around her through forgiveness, gratitude and unconditional love, then the

child in the womb also learns to build and nurture healthy relationships.
- Intrapersonal skills: The child in the womb is directly connected with the emotions of the mother. When the mother can connect well with her own emotions and feelings by always staying in a blissful state irrespective of what's going on around her, this leads to the development of the intrapersonal skills of the unborn child as well.
- Naturalistic skills: When the show of empathy and concern is not limited only to the human race but covers the entirety of creation, including plants, animals and the five elements (earth, water, fire, air and ether), then the naturalistic skills start developing in the unborn child.

4. SQ: Spiritual intelligence is all about awareness at the level of the soul. A spiritually intelligent person has complete understanding of their purpose in life and every intent or action taken by them is in response to a bigger purpose. They are motivated by long-term goals rather than short-term feats.

Spiritually active people will want to understand the 'true cause' of a particular behaviour without judgement and serve the 'true needs' of others until they are empowered to fulfil their own needs. They are inherently forgiving and patient and selfless in their service of others. The spiritual quotient is enhanced when the mother behaves with wisdom as the base of her actions. She has to be compassionate and maintain peace within and around her by focussing on the inherent question, 'Who am I?', and meditating on the answer, 'I am neither the mind, the body, nor the emotions, but the soul.'

A mother can inculcate spiritual intelligence in her child by:

- Focussing on the soul level of her and the child's existence.
- Finding her purpose in life and trying to answer the question, 'Who am I?'
- Focussing on resolving and not just responding to problems.
- Understanding the true cause of emotions and not just bearing the brunt of it.
- Knowing that emotions are created within; they are intrinsic and not extrinsic.
- Being conscious about the universe and the magnanimity of it all.
- Developing a deep understanding of oneself, the laws of karma, the purpose of life, the cycle of life and the journey beyond.

When the expectant mother meditates on these philosophies, she lets such thoughts seep into the mind of the child as well.

Meditation, chanting mantras, praying, sitting in silence, doing selfless service and listening to scriptures are ideal ways to ensure that there is peace in the mother throughout her pregnancy. These divine acts release her karmas and raise her vibrations, thus enhancing the vibrational frequency of the child within. By raising her consciousness, she gets connected with the true self residing within herself, and unveils and understands the deep truths about her own existence.

Acharya Sushruta reaffirms this belief by saying:[7]

देवताब्राह्मणपरा: शौचाचारहिते रता: ।।
महागुणान् प्रसूयन्ते विपरीतास्त निर्गुणान ।।35।।

It states that during pregnancy, if the expectant mother is engaged in the service of God and His creations, then a divine, virtuous child is born. This highlights the development of the SQ in the womb.

By going beyond the aspects of 'doing, thinking and feeling', the SQ helps us deal with and 'understand' the powers that reside within us. Now, one is not reacting or responding to something but is resolving the issues on an inner level.

One should know that each of the stages—PQ, IQ, EQ and SQ—is equally important and irreplaceable. As we have understood, PQ is about 'doing', IQ is about 'thinking', EQ is about 'feeling' and SQ is about 'understanding'. Each of these quotients acts as a building block over which the next block is placed.

The Divine Womb: First and Most Influential School

The divine womb of the mother serves as the first and most influential school, laying the foundational groundwork for intelligence development in the brain. A mother can holistically pave the way for a child who is born with all the above attributes and shape the future of her child. By engaging regularly and methodically in the activities that have been discussed, the mother can impart invaluable traits to her child within the womb. However, simply reading this will not be enough. The mother must make a structured routine with the right practices and, on a daily basis, work holistically on the well-being of the four areas: physical, mental, emotional and spiritual. The four well-being areas focus on the holistic cleansing by doing *sharir shuddhi* at the physical level, *mann shuddhi* at the mental level, *bhav shudhi* at the emotional level and *karma shuddhi* at the spiritual level. In the next chapters we will go through each of the four well-being areas and work on a step-by-step approach to achieve it.

Practical Implementation through the DreamStar Baby App

DreamStar Baby is an online app that has been created on the basis of Sonal's Intelligence Model for Holistic Development© wherein mothers are provided with questions, tasks or activities for developing each of the nine intelligences daily so that the focussed and holistic development of the baby can be achieved in the womb. You can scan the QR code available at the end of the book and register to avail of a rich repository of free resources and daily activities that can help you to manifest your dream child.

Like a sculptor creating his masterpiece, the mother has all the power to materialize her dream baby by creating the right neural pathways. She just has to focus her energies into herself and her child at every moment by working holistically upon the four well-being areas, ensuring that she is disciplined about it and has only the best intentions and interests at heart.

Envisioning Clarity: The Nine Intelligences

Develop clarity on the nine different intelligences, while assessing the kind of effort you are ready to make in order to achieve them. Grade the skills on a scale of 1 to 10 depending upon the intelligence levels you wish to incorporate within your child, and based on those grades, take part in activities that will help to develop those skills in your child within nine months.

Tracker Sheet for Creating Intelligence in the Womb

Intelligence	Rating out of 10	Description of Desired Skills	Action Monitor Activities to Develop Desired Skills
Bodily-Kinaesthetic			
Logical-Mathematical			
Linguistic-Verbal			
Musical			
Spatial-Visual			
Interpersonal			
Intrapersonal			
Naturalistic			
Existential			

Description (please make it as detailed as possible)

3

Maintaining Physical Well-Being

'The lifestyle choices a mother makes during pregnancy shapes the future lifestyle of the child within her womb.'

Maharani Kaushalya was the epitome of bhakti, discipline and virtue. She was the woman who would bear the Supreme Almighty in her womb. She was someone who was very aware of the divinity of the child she was to give birth to, and thus adopted a strict and stringent lifestyle to enhance her journey with her baby while he was still in her womb.

Although she was the queen of Ayodhya, she was very careful about what she would eat during her pregnancy because eventually that is what she would be feeding her son while he was residing within her. She knew that the purity of the ingredients she ate would affect the purity of the mind as well. She was aware that the money used to buy the ingredients also impacted the energies of the baby residing in the womb. Finally, she was ever so aware that the thoughts of the people who cooked the food also seeped into the meal and that had a deep and long-lasting impact on the body and soul of the person consuming the food. She was a pious lady and knew that the food prepared in the kitchen of the palace was procured with money from the taxes and had the varied emotions of the people.

Keeping this in mind, Maharani Kaushalya requested Maharishi Vasishtha that for the entirety of the nine months of her pregnancy, she would eat all her meals at his ashram—free meals were not something she would accept. Hence, for nine months, the maharani chose to mentor all the girl pupils at the rishi's ashram in return for his kindness.

The discipline, dedication and sheer devotion of Maharani Kaushalya was rewarded when she held her son Lord Rama in her arms for the first time.

People often quote the aphorism 'you are what you eat', by which they mean that the ingredients used in your food and the nutrition your body attains from it directly impacts your energy levels. This, in turn, has a large bearing on the quality of your physical health, thoughts and emotions. It boils down to the most minute details: the emotions of the cook while preparing the meal, the quality of the ingredients, the money used to buy the ingredients, and the methods of preparation. All of this has a strong bearing on overall human health.

These considerations become a lot more important when we look at the delicate biology of a mother and her unborn or young child. While in the womb, and even immediately after birth, the child is completely dependent on the mother for its internal growth. Our ancient scriptures, written thousands of years ago, have detailed the growth process of the foetus in the womb, and it is a surprising revelation that the journey captured by our sages is absolutely in sync with modern scientific findings. Thus, it is important for the mother to improve her food habits, lifestyle and daily activities in order to facilitate the growth process. A detailed description of the month-by-month journey of the foetus with lifestyle guidance has been covered in an in-depth manner in the Appendix, which should be followed by the mothers for best results.

Such a mammoth growth—that of a microscopic embryo growing into a full-fledged baby weighing a few kilograms in just nine months—is only possible when the foetus is nourished well, primarily through the mother's diet. However, one must keep in mind that maintaining physical well-being is not just limited to food but also encompasses the complete lifestyle of the expectant mother, which has to be in tune with Mother Nature.

The Seven Pillars of Physical Well-Being as Prescribed by Mother Nature

1. A nutritious, balanced and positive life-force energy diet
2. Ample intake of positively charged, energized water
3. Adequate and good-quality sleep and relaxation
4. An adequate and mindful exercise regime
5. The right breathwork through pranayama practices
6. Staying away from addictions
7. Protection from environmental hazards and toxins

When a woman is pregnant, she and her family must ensure that the seven practices mentioned above are followed diligently. She should holistically focus on her overall lifestyle because such practices will fill her with positivity, assisting her and the baby by giving them the desired life-force energy to grow and prosper.

Nutritious, Balanced and a Positive Life-Force Energy Diet

We know that food has a long-term impact on our health, more so during pregnancy, as the foetus needs enriched nourishment.

According to the National Institute of Nutrition (NIN), the first 1,000 days of life are crucial in shaping a child's future. This period includes the time from conception to the birth of the child (270 days) and from birth to the child's second birthday (365+365 days). During pregnancy, the embryo in the mother's womb grows rapidly and relies on the mother's nutrition. Therefore, the mother should be healthy and well-nourished at the start of pregnancy to provide the necessary vitamins, minerals, fatty acids, amino acids and energy in adequate amounts to maintain her own health and to nourish the developing immune system, brain and other organs of the foetus, as well as to support the child's growth.

Poor nutritional status of pregnant women, along with inadequate intake of calorie-, protein- and micronutrient-rich foods, or consumption of high-fat, high-sugar, high-salt (HFSS) diets, can adversely affect the growth and development of the foetus. Undernourished women are at a higher risk of giving birth to babies that are small for gestational age or have low birth weight (less than 2.5 kg). They may also deliver preterm. These babies are at a higher risk of childhood infections and short stature (stunting: low height for age) and, as adults, they are more likely to develop metabolic diseases such as diabetes, hypertension, and cardiovascular diseases (heart attack, stroke, etc.).

Pregnant women who receive a balanced diet and gain an appropriate amount of weight during pregnancy (10 to 12 kg) have a higher chance of giving birth to healthy babies.[1]

A correctly planned diet will not only help in nourishing the mother's body and developing the embryo during pregnancy, but also help in improving both the quality and quantity of breast milk post delivery. This is very well explained in the words of Acharya Charka:[2]

स्त्रिया ह्यापन्नगर्भायास्त्रिधा रस: प्रतिपद्यते स्वशरीरपुष्टये, स्तन्याय, गर्भवृद्धये च।

But what are these foods that help in nourishing both the mother and the foetus and what kind of impact do each of them have on our body? On the basis of energy, all foods can be classified into three main categories. They are:

1. Positive Life-Force Energy (*Sattvic*) Foods

Positive life-force energy foods, known as sattvic foods in Ayurveda, are those that are considered pure, clean and conducive to physical, mental and spiritual well-being. These foods are believed to promote clarity of mind, emotional balance and overall vitality. These are primarily all the natural foods from plant-based sources, such as vegetables, fruits, seeds, etc., and from dairy products made from the milk of indigenous cows (A2 milk). These foods are rich in fibre, protein and vitamins, and are full of life-force-renewing energy. However, the rampant use of pesticides and other harmful chemicals has led to these foods becoming devoid of the benefits they once promised.

Thus, care must be taken to grow these organically or to source them from trusted organic suppliers. The elemental part about these positive life-force energy foods is that they start to decay from the moment they are plucked. The longer one delays consuming them, the more the decay advances. In order to delay the decay, suppliers inject them with preservatives that are harmful to the body. So, in order to minimize the intake of these chemicals, it is strongly recommended that one consumes local and seasonal produce only.

Spicy food can be detrimental to the foetus, so care must be taken to avoid the same. Thus, a simple and pure diet will go a long way in making you and your child healthier.

According to NIN, a pregnant woman should eat a wide variety of foods to ensure that her nutritional needs, as well as those of her growing foetus, are met. It is important to focus on the quantity, quality, diversity and frequency of foods consumed. Grains (240 g) such as cereals and millets are major sources of energy and can provide about 45 per cent of the total daily energy requirement.

Consuming pulses (80 g) helps meet the recommended daily allowance of proteins and contributes to fibre and micronutrient intake. Nuts and oil seeds (40 g) offer essential fatty acids, micronutrients and fibre. Combining cereals and pulses in a 3:1 ratio provides good quality protein.

Mineral and vitamin requirements are met by consuming a variety of beans, seasonal vegetables (450 g) comprising a one-third portion of green leafy vegetables, and fresh fruits (150 g). Foods like beans and nuts are excellent sources of iron. The bioavailability of iron can be enhanced by consuming fermented and sprouted grains, along with foods rich in vitamin C, such as guava and oranges, during meals.

Dairy (400 ml) is the best source of biologically available calcium, though it is a poor source of iron. Adequate sunlight exposure for 15 minutes is essential to meet the requirements of vitamin D.[3]

However, it is important to note that the nutritional

requirement of each individual is different and so any dietary planning by an expectant mother should be done in consultation with a gynaecologist or a nutritionist.

While there are many options available, you must be vigilant in what you consume. Accordingly, we have drawn up a diet chart of sorts as suggested by Dr Balaji Tambe, a renowned Ayurveda expert.[4]

Vegetables: Vegetables that are easily digestible and suitable for all body types include bottle gourd (*lauki*), ridge gourd (*dodka*), smooth gourd (*ghosali*), ash gourd (*kohala*), okra (*bhindi*), red pumpkin (*laal kaddoo*), potatoes (aloo), bitter gourd (karela), gherkins (*tondli*), white goosefoot (*chakavat*) and leafy vegetables like spinach (*palak*) and fenugreek (*methi*).

The expectant mother can eat cucumbers, tomatoes, carrots and beetroots daily in small quantities in salads. It is best to avoid vegetables like sweet potatoes, mushrooms, corn and elephant foot yam (*suran*) as they are difficult to digest. Capsicums, eggplants, spring onions, cluster beans and *gawar* should also be used rarely, as they generate excess heat in the body.

Though onion and garlic have great medicinal properties, Ayurveda points to the *taseer*, or nature, of these foods to be hot, advising that when consumed in excess they can have a thermogenic effect on the body, possibly adversely affecting body functions.

Fruits: It is recommended that a colourful platter of fruits be consumed every day as they are rich in antioxidants. It is best if at least one seasonal fruit is eaten every day during the pregnancy from the following list of must-haves:

- Figs, pomegranates and apples are known to nourish the blood directly.

- Sour fruits like oranges, sweet limes, tangerines, amlas, etc., are rich in vitamin C. They indirectly aid the development of blood. The mother-to-be must drink half a glass of undiluted orange, sweet lime or tangerine juice with no additives on a regular basis, as it provides nourishment to both the mother and the foetus, and improves lactation post delivery.
- Seasonal grapes are recommended, but should be avoided during the third trimester as they can generate heat in the body. Care must be taken to wash them thoroughly. They can be soaked in salt water for a few hours before eating. In other seasons, 10–12 raisins, soaked in water for a few hours, should be consumed as they nourish the blood and ensure proper bowel movements.
- Fresh coconut water is very healthy and helps to ensure adequate amniotic fluid. The coconut's tender pulp (*malai*) is easily digestible and nutritious, reduces heat in the body, and is very beneficial, especially during summers.
- Mangoes, one of the most-loved fruits out there, are also highly nutritious. However, they must be eaten in moderation. If one does not adhere to this rule, it can lead to digestive imbalances such as diarrhoea. Mangoes must be soaked in water for two to three hours before consumption.

There are a few other fruits that should be eaten occasionally and with caution:

- The intake of raw mangoes and tamarind should be limited. (Just enough to satisfy the taste buds.)

- Sour fruits such as pineapples, strawberries, wood apples (*bael*) and jujube (*bor*) should only be consumed occasionally.
- Custard apples, guavas, pears, chikoos, rose apples, blackberry (*jambhul*) and watermelon may be eaten occasionally during pregnancy.

Some fruits, like papaya (particularly the raw or unripe variety), are associated with uterine contractions and can induce miscarriages. Thus, it should be avoided by pregnant women.

Some caution points when eating fruits:

- Freshly cut fruits and fresh fruit juices should be consumed immediately, since the nutritive quality diminishes quickly.
- Non-seasonal and non-local fruits should be avoided as they might be full of preservatives.
- Fruit should always be eaten during the day and avoided after sunset.
- Canned juices are stale, contain chemical preservatives and have only artificial flavouring instead of real fruit juice, and thus should be avoided.
- You may be asked to avoid overdosing on fruit salad and milkshake because they would be high in fructose, causing a spike in blood sugar, pushing the endocrine system towards insulin resistance and an eventual case of gestational diabetes.

Nuts and Seeds: Apart from one's regular diet of fruits and vegetables, a handful of nuts and seeds can add a lot more nutritional value to our diets.

- Three or four almonds soaked overnight, peeled and

eaten in the morning are necessary for expecting mothers as it improves health and also nourishes the brain of the developing foetus.
- Dates contain vitamin B folate, an important nutrient that prevents serious birth defects like spina bifida during pregnancy. It also provides potassium that can control vomiting in the first trimester. It also helps in shortening of first stage of labour before delivery, if consumed well in the last trimester. Furthermore, it can act as a substitute for white sugar, which hampers the brain development of the foetus. One dried date (*kharik*) should be eaten or a teaspoon of dried date powder added to a glass of milk should be consumed every day. Alternatively, one or two fresh dates consumed with two teaspoons of pure, homemade ghee, on a daily basis, helps the foetus gain adequate weight.
- Dry figs are rich in folates, help in foetal development and the prevention of neural tube defects, and can be consumed directly or after being soaked in water. The high fibre content also helps in maintaining a healthy digestive system.
- Apricots provide nourishment to the growing baby's brain and may be eaten from time to time.
- Walnuts are heavy to digest but are nourishing and may be eaten occasionally.
- Cashew nuts, pistachios and *charoli* tend to increase heat in the body and may be eaten but only rarely.
- Chia seeds and flax seeds are good sources of polyunsaturated fatty acids with many health benefits. However, they should be consumed in moderate quantities (1–2 tablespoons or 10–20 g per day).

Grains: Grains comprise majority of our diet. Rice, wheat and *jowar* (sorghum, a type of millet) are easily digestible and should be consumed daily as part of a balanced meal. It is strongly recommended in Ayurveda that the grains should be about a year old and should be roasted before grinding as this makes them easier to digest.

It is suggested that one should avoid commercially available packaged flour and, instead, buy grains of good quality—preferably organic—and have them coarsely ground in a mill or at home. Care should be taken that the grain is not sieved too much, and it should be as coarse as possible for better digestion.

Jowar has cooling properties and is best when mixed with *bajra* (pearl millet)—another millet variety which is hot in nature—as a mixture of these flours (from the two grains) turns out very healthy. Among other grains, *jav* (barley) and *nachani* (red millet) improves the digestive capacity.

Pulses and Legumes: Proteins are basic nutrients and should be consumed in adequate quantities for the development of the foetus.

- *Tur* (pigeon peas) and *mung* dal (split green gram) are very nourishing, easily digestible, and thus should be consumed daily.
- Some legumes and pulses are very heavy to digest and may be eaten only occasionally, if at all. This list includes *urad* (black gram), *chole* (chickpeas), *rajma* (kidney beans), *vatana* (dried green peas) and *masur* (red gram). Seasonal fresh peas can be consumed once in a while.

- Soya bean is hard to digest and should be avoided entirely.
- Sprouts of the lighter pulses like mung, *matki* (moth bean), etc., should be steamed or cooked and consumed at least once a day, preferably with the mid-day meal. Nowadays, salads are made with raw sprouts. These, when tested in a lab, may show very high vitamin or mineral content and are thus assumed to be nutritious. However, they have an adverse effect on the digestive system as they are very heavy to digest and the body is unable to absorb nutrients from them.

Dairy Products: Milk is one of the best sources of naturally-available proteins and calcium. It is also an important carrier of vitamins B and A. It naturally facilitates the physical, mental and intellectual development of the baby. It also provides a strong foundation for the development of bones in the foetus. A glass of milk in the morning and one in the evening, throughout the pregnancy, can help relieve back aches and joint pains post delivery. Care should be taken that the milk consumed is A2 only. However, in commercially available milk, pasteurized milk is the only safe option. Homogenized, skimmed, vitamin-enriched or ultra-heated milk is not recommended at all. Homemade butter, fresh buttermilk and pure ghee are essential components of a balanced diet. Pure ghee boosts life-force energy and immunity and is considered as one of the best amongst all oils and lubricating nutrients. It is said to help strengthen the sense organs, particularly the eyes and ears, increase one's memory capacity, and boost the intellect, grasping power and overall intelligence.

Always ensure that the food you consume ticks the following conditions:

1. Vegetarian: plant-based
2. Safe dairy (made with A2 milk)
3. Organic
4. Mildly cooked with less spice
5. Local and seasonal
6. Rich in fibre
7. Easily digestible

2. Zero Life-Force Energy (*Rajsik*) Foods

When the food is devoid of nutritional value but is mainly consumed to satiate the taste buds, it is known as a zero life-force energy food or *rajsik* food according to Ayurveda. This includes heavily cooked food that is rich in spices, oils, salt, sugar, dressings, gravy, etc., that kills the nutrition levels in natural foods. When such foods are consumed, they induce not just ill health, delayed digestion and fatigue, but also lead to thoughts such as insatiable desire for material growth, a distracted mind, ignited lust, excited passion and lethargy. Zero life-force energy foods must be consumed in minimal quantities and only occasionally.

3. Negative Life-Force Energy (*Tamsik*) Foods

Negative life-force energy food, or *tamsik* food as per Ayurveda, primarily includes heavy, stale, overly processed, pesticide-infested or deep-fried food that is extremely sour, spicy or salty. They are filled with negative energy as they are breeding grounds for bacteria and decaying microbes and infested with germs that will harm the human body. These foods are believed to dull the mind, create imbalance of energies and hinder spiritual growth.

Non-Vegetarian Food

According to Ayurveda, non-vegetarian food in any form should be avoided by expectant mothers because of its tamsik nature. Moreover, life-force energy is present in animals only while they are alive, so in order to delay the decay of the meat before it reaches its consumers, it is injected with preservatives and other additives. Consumption of these substances can have serious health implications. So, it is advised that expectant mothers should minimize the consumption of non-vegetarian food to ensure a balanced, nutritious, easily digestible and sattvic diet. However, individual dietary needs may vary depending on health status and cultural practices.

Pesticide- and Preservative-Infested Food

Even though positive life-force energy foods are the ideal ingredients for good health, the current food chain is deeply contaminated due to the use of chemicals, fertilizers and pesticides that are used to grow them. This does more harm than good. There is a constant decline in the nutrient levels of non-organic food. They only satiate hunger while not meeting the nutrient requirements of the body. One might be consuming small doses of toxins that are harmful for the baby, so it is important to consume organically grown food or create a small kitchen garden which can take care of one's basic everyday requirements.

In order to increase shelf life, loads of chemical preservatives are injected in the food, making it hazardous. I strongly advise expectant mothers to stay away from these harmful substances by consuming seasonal and local produce.

However, for best results, it is important that all foods should be washed well, but not repeatedly, before cooking or consumption to remove contaminants like pesticide residues, parasites and other extraneous material. Vegetables and fruits should be washed thoroughly with potable water before peeling or cutting. However, certain precautions need to be taken to minimize the loss of nutrients:

- Avoid repeated washing of food grains like rice and pulses, as it will result in loss of certain minerals and vitamins.
- Cutting vegetables into small pieces exposes a greater surface area of the foodstuff to the atmosphere, resulting in loss of vitamins due to oxidation.
- Cut vegetables and fruits should not be soaked in water, as water-soluble minerals and vitamins tend to get lost, and should be consumed as early as possible, as their shelf-life and nutrient contents reduce drastically.[5]

Stale Food

Consumption of any food four to six hours after it has been cooked not only lessens its nutritional value, but also accumulates negative energy because it becomes a breeding ground for bacteria and other harmful microorganisms. It is in the best interest of the expecting mother that the food is consumed while it is fresh.

However, even if anyone wants to consume within

the aforementioned time window, it is important that the refrigerated cooked food should be heated thoroughly before consumption. Note that repeated heating of stored, cooked food should be avoided.[6]

Refined Food and Oil

Refined flour (like *maida*, which is refined wheat flour) is devoid of fibre and takes a long time to digest. The pizza or burger that you ate last evening might take longer to digest than food that is prepared with more wholesome ingredients. Instead of using packaged flour, grains should be ground in a mill or at home and not be sieved too much, thus preserving more of the fibre. Similarly, refined oil loses all its goodness and nutrition in the preparation process. So, the expectant mother is advised to switch to healthier options like cold-pressed oils (*kachi ghani*).

Cold pressed oils also contain undesirable compounds, similar to crude oil. However, nutrients such as antioxidants and phytonutrients are preserved, as these oils are obtained without altering the nature of the oil by mechanical procedures (such as expeller pressing), without the application of heat.

Moreover, NIN strongly prohibits the use of reheated oil, as the practice of reusing vegetable oils, which have been repeatedly heated during food preparations, is very common for cooking both at home and in commercial establishments. Repeated heating of vegetable oils or fats results in the oxidation of polyunsaturated fatty acids, leading to the generation of harmful or toxic compounds that may increase the risk of cardiovascular diseases and cancer.

At the household level, vegetable oil that has been used for frying should be filtered and can be reused for curry preparation. However, using the same oil for frying again should be avoided. Additionally, such oils should be consumed within a day or two. Storing used oils for a long time should be avoided, as the rate of deterioration is high in such oils.[7]

Refined Sugar

According to the World Health Organization (WHO), limiting sugar intake to 25 g per day is better for health.[8] Ideally, added sugar should be completely eliminated from one's diet, as it provides no nutritive value other than calories. Calories are beneficial only when they come with vitamins, minerals and fibre. Refined sugars lack these nutrients.

It is best to consume naturally occurring simple sugars found in foods like fruits and milk. If there is a craving for sweets, switching to more natural options like dates is advisable. Additionally, using jaggery in the winter and candy sugar in the summer is recommended, but in limited quantities.

Sugar substitutes such as aspartame, saccharin, sugar alcohols and stevia are used to sweeten foods and beverages. These substitutes are lower in calories compared to regular table sugar. However, studies indicate that long-term consumption of non-caloric sugar substitutes can lead to overweight/obesity, diabetes, hypertension and other non-communicable diseases (NCDs). They may also disrupt beneficial intestinal bacteria. Therefore, pregnant and lactating women, as well as children, should avoid sugar substitutes.[9]

Table Salt

It is important to consume iodine fortified salt for dietary requirements. However, expecting mothers should restrict salt (sodium chloride) in their diet as high intake of salt is associated with high blood pressure and related cardiovascular diseases. The current Indian as well as WHO recommendation is 5 g (1 teaspoon) of common salt per day.[10] Moreover, salt should always be added while cooking as uncooked salt is difficult for the gut to absorb. It has been found that for cooking, rock salt is a healthy substitute for regular common salt as it is purer and richer in minerals, but still its consumption should be limited as the sodium content in both is almost similar.[11]

Packaged Food and Aerated Drinks

Packaged foods, while convenient, often come with several drawbacks that are important to consider for expectant mothers. These are highly processed and can lead to a loss of essential nutrients such as vitamins, minerals and fibre. Processing can also introduce additives like preservatives, artificial colours and flavours, which may not be beneficial for one's health. Moreover, snacks and ready-to-eat meals tend to be high in added sugars, sodium (salt) and unhealthy fats like trans fats and saturated fats. Excessive consumption of these can contribute to health issues such as obesity, diabetes and cardiovascular diseases. Packaged foods often have a longer shelf life due to preservatives and processing, but this can result in a loss of freshness and natural flavour. Fresh foods are generally higher in nutrients and offer better nutrition.

Moreover, the gas in sodas and other carbonated drinks not only weakens the digestive fire in the body but also provides more calories from added sugars and should thus be replaced with healthy homemade drinks.[12] Regular consumption of heavily processed and packaged foods and drinks has been linked to various health risks, so it is important to read labels carefully, choose minimally processed options, and balance packaged foods with fresh, whole foods to maintain a healthy diet and lifestyle.

Right Cookware and Serving Utensils

A variety of cookware used in the kitchen are made from different materials such as aluminium, iron, brass or copper. Small amounts of these materials that may leach into the food while cooking or storing are generally not a cause for concern. However, storing acidic foods like pickles, chutneys, sambar and khatta dal in aluminium, iron, untinned brass or copper vessels for prolonged periods can make the consumption of such foods unsafe.

Non-stick pans coated with Teflon pose a risk if they are heated to temperatures greater than 170°C, which might occur if an empty pan is left on a burner. In such cases, the coatings can release irritating or poisonous fumes, which, when inhaled over long periods, could potentially lead to health hazards.

Earthen pots are the safest cookware. They require very little oil, are environmentally friendly and preserve the food's nutritional content. Heat circulates effectively through food in earthen pots, helping to maintain nutrition.

Furthermore, stainless steel cookware is generally considered safe for cooking when used properly. It is widely used in kitchens around the world due to its durability, resistance to corrosion and non-reactivity with foods. Stainless steel does not leach or react with acidic or alkaline foods, making it unlikely to impart metallic flavors or harmful substances to cooked foods.[13]

Importance of a Balanced Diet during Pregnancy

Myth Busting: You Are Not Eating for Two!

Our elders often remark—perhaps out of fondness—that an expecting mother should eat well and should do so for two people! Well, according to NIN, the daily diet of a pregnant woman of normal weight for her height should include an additional 350 calories of energy from the second to the third trimester. An additional 8 g of protein is required during the second trimester and 18 g during the third trimester of pregnancy.[14] The ideal weight gain suggested for pregnant women is 10 to 12 kg. Anything more than this only adds to your body weight, which becomes very difficult to lose post delivery. In fact, when expecting mothers eat more than what is required, they suffer from severe digestive disorders.

Our stomachs are quite small—about the size of a fist. During pregnancy, as the foetus starts growing, the uterus begins putting pressure on the stomach, making effective digestion a challenge. This is why most expectant mothers suffer from problems such as acidity, heartburn and constipation. Therefore, it is important to eat food in moderation and at regular intervals when one is pregnant.

There is another common misconception: that vegetarian diets lack protein. However, a balanced vegetarian diet—one that includes dairy products, grains, pulses, legumes, fruits, vegetables and dry fruits in adequate quantities—is rich in protein. Moreover, animal-based protein-rich foods may not be entirely beneficial since these are difficult to digest and are, therefore, not absorbed easily by the body. Thus, it is better to get your proteins from easily-digestible plant-based food.[15]

A great balanced diet, from a nutrition standpoint, must include:

1. Easily digestible, high-fibre cereals sourced form healthy energy sources to meet the body's carbohydrate needs
2. Low-fat legumes and pulses for adequate protein consumption to build muscle
3. Fresh fruits and vegetables for vitamins and minerals to boost the body's immunity
4. Dairy products made from A2 milk to ensure that the body gets enough calcium for strong teeth and bones
5. Nuts and seeds for healthy fats

Along with balancing nutrients, it is important to balance the six tastes—sweet, sour, spicy, salty, bitter and astringent—which should be included in meals in moderate proportions. According to Acharya Carak, the excess of any of these can develop ailments in the child.[16]

Effect of Overindulgence in the Six Tastes	
मधुरनित्या प्रमेहिणं मूकमतिस्थूलं वा।	Overindulgence in sweets can make the child diabetic or obese, or they may be born mute.
आम्लनित्या रक्तपित्तिनं त्वगक्षिरोगिणं वा।	Overindulging in sour food like tamarind, tomatoes, sour yoghurt or fermented foods may cause the child to suffer from skin or eye diseases as well as bleeding disorders.
लवणनित्या शीघ्रवलीपलितं खलित्यरोगिणं वा।	Overindulgence in salty foods or the addition of too much salt in food can result in the premature greying of hair, balding and early wrinkling of the child's skin.

कटुकनित्या दुर्बलमल्पशुक्रमनपत्यं वा।	Overindulgence in spicy food leads to the birth of a weak baby and also causes reproductive disorders later in life.
तिक्तनित्या शोषिणमबल. मनुपचितं वा।	Overindulgence in bitter food can result in birth of a weak, underdeveloped baby with stunted growth and low weight.
कषायनित्या श्यावम् आनाहिनमुदावर्तिनं वा।	Overindulging in food that is astringent can cause constipation and abdominal distention in the baby.

In short, the dietary preferences of the expecting mother should be accommodated while ensuring that all nutrients as well as flavours are balanced and not present in extreme quantities.

Nutritional Requirements and Proper Supplements

During pregnancy, the mother must ensure the adequate intake of all necessary nutrients prescribed by the doctor, in appropriate quantities for the proper growth of the foetus. However, it is advisable that these nutrients are consumed in their natural form as much as possible as the chemical supplements might not be accepted and absorbed by the body properly. The important nutrient requirements include:

1. Calcium (1,000–1,300 mg): For the bone development of the baby and to ensure the proper bone health of the mother too. The best source of calcium is dairy products from A2 milk derived from indigenous cows.
2. Iodine (220 mg): For the development of the baby's brain and nervous system. It is found naturally in A2 milk and its products and iodized salt.

3. Folic Acid (64 mg): To avoid birth defects, promote brain cell development and a healthy spine for the baby. In fact, if taken in pre-pregnancy and the first 28 days of pregnancy, it reduces the risk of anaemia. Folates are present in green leafy vegetables such as spinach, legumes, etc.
4. Iron (27 mg): For the synthesis of haemoglobin and the prevention of anaemia as well as the brain development of the foetus, as iron deficiency during pregnancy increases maternal mortality and may decrease the birth weight of infants. Plant-based foods such as green leafy vegetables, pulses and dry fruits contain iron.

    A mother as well as the growing foetus need additional iron as well as folic acid to meet the high demands of erythropoiesis (red blood cell formation), so NIN advises them to take daily supplements of iron and folic acid (IFA) tablets from the twelfth week of pregnancy up to six months of lactation. Note that beverages like tea bind dietary iron and make it unavailable, therefore tea should be avoided before, during, or soon after a meal, as well as when taking iron and folic acid supplements.[17]
5. Vitamin C (80–85 mg): Helps absorb iron from plant-based foods and thereby builds stronger teeth and bones and boosts immunity. It is naturally found in oranges, grapefruit, gooseberry, cauliflower, broccoli, coriander, etc.

Eating the Right Way

During pregnancy, one should not eat large portions in a go, but should consume smaller quantities at intervals of every two hours. This is done to ensure that there is no added pressure on the digestive system. Ideally, human beings should eat half the size of their stomach, a quarter of the stomach should be filled with water, and the remaining quarter space kept empty. This is called '*mitahar*' or moderate diet. This is important as it aids in proper digestion. Furthermore, moderate eating increases positivity and energy levels in our body, thus helping in the advancement of our spiritual practices.

Food is energy and it nourishes our body when eaten with an attitude of gratitude. Moreover, by chewing food at least 32 times, we aid partial digestion because of the digestive juices in our mouth which reduces the load on the stomach. Thus, general problems of acidity and heartburn can be taken care of when we chew well and eat slowly in moderation with an attitude of gratitude.

Correct Food Timings

At night, the digestive system is weak as the body is constantly engaged in repairing cells and growing new ones, but these vital activities take a back seat when we eat heavy meals and keep our organs engaged in digestion and its associated functions. The body then tries to digest the food when it should ideally be focussing on rest and repair. Furthermore, it experiences problems such as heartburn and acid reflux that arise out of the horizontal position of the body after a heavy meal. Early dinner, however, gives the body time to wind down and rest. Late-night dining could potentially affect a person's metabolism, cause weight gain, impact overnight blood pressure and raise the risk of heart attack. When we dine less than two hours before going to bed, the body is put on 'high alert'. A healthy person's blood pressure drops by at least ten per cent when they go to sleep. However, when one has a late dinner, the blood pressure doesn't fall properly. I strongly recommend that the expectant mother should eat a light meal by 7.00 p.m.

Ample Intake of Positively Charged Energized Water

People do not often give water the credit it deserves. The average human body is made up of 60 to 70 per cent water. It forms one of the major sources of energy as well. Japanese scientist Dr Masaru Emoto has proved that if we speak words of love, kindness and gratitude to a vessel full of water, the water molecules rearrange themselves to form divine, beautiful structures.[18] But when we curse or ill-treat water, then the opposite effect occurs. This implies that water has memory and changes its molecular structures according to the vibrations it receives. Thus, ideally, we should energize the water before drinking it. This involves boiling the filtered water for minimum 15 to 20 minutes to make it germ-free, else these microorganisms may deprive the body of important nutrients, especially iron. Once boiled, it is advisable to store the water in earthen pots in summer and copper vessels in winter. This will neutralize the water's energy that might have been contaminated due to flowing through taps, etc.

As the human body is alkaline, consuming water with a pH of 9–10 keeps the internal environment of the body healthy. Nowadays, alkaline water machines are available, which can increase the pH of filtered water. Additionally, chanting mantras or saying words of gratitude and love over water will enhance and energize it.

Dehydration can lead to lower levels of amniotic fluid, which can influence the baby's development, result in pre-term labour, affect lactation, and cause a deficiency in nutrients that are vital for the health of mother and foetus. Staying hydrated really helps in a number of ways—it aids digestion, helps form the amniotic fluid around the foetus, circulates nutrients and removes waste from the body.

Expecting mothers should have a minimum of 3 L of water every day. Along with this, I recommend fluid-rich foods like tender coconut, watermelon, cucumber, bottle gourd, buttermilk and lime water with Himalayan salt to improve electrolytes.

Adequate and Good-Quality Sleep and Relaxation

Sleep is restorative and regenerative as it not only provides rest to the physical, mental and emotional body but also helps in the growth and repair of diseased and decayed cells. The growth of the foetus happens best when the mother is at complete rest. Therefore, when an expectant mother does not give proper importance to the quality and quantity of sleep, the health and growth of the foetus are seriously affected.

That said, we do know that a growing belly, frequent urination, heartburn, etc., decrease sleep quality. However, mothers need to ensure good rest for themselves, else it might lead to pregnancy complications such as high blood pressure, gestational diabetes and difficult labour.

The recommended amount of sleep is between seven and nine hours, but this can vary based on an individual's lifestyle. What is important is that one wakes up fresh and energized. However, it should be noted that excessive sleep is also not desirable and would pass on lethargy and dullness to the baby within the womb. It might also affect the brain development and slow down the child's metabolism. Mothers who are advised complete bed rest should remember that rest is advised for the body and not the mind. This can be a blessing in disguise as engaging in enriching activities can help keep the mother mentally active and facilitate the brain development of the foetus.

Early to Bed and Early to Rise

It is not just about when or how much you sleep but also about its quality. Circadian rhythm disorders, also known as sleep-wake cycle disorders, are problems that occur when your body's internal clock—the one that tells you when it's time to sleep or wake up—is out of sync with your environment. The circadian clock cycles every 24 hours and triggers a natural healing process where the energies repair and grow cells while the body is asleep. However, these healing energies are only active from 9.00 p.m. to 3.00 a.m. and, therefore, the human body needs sleep, especially during these six hours. Any sleep before or after this time wouldn't add much to the quality of sleep. Thus, going to bed early (9.00 p.m.) helps keep the body clock intact, and waking up early (between 3.00 and 4.00 a.m.) or before sunrise adds divinity to our lifestyle.

During the hour before sunrise—referred to as Brahmamuhrat—the divine energies are at their peak. If people wake up and connect with these energies, their manifestation and materialization become stronger. However, as explained earlier, the expectant mother is undergoing a lot of physical, emotional, mental and hormonal changes. So, she can adjust the timings according to her health conditions.

Quality of Sleep

The harmful waves emitted by electronic gadgets, especially before bed, seriously affect the secretion of the sleep hormone—melatonin—by the pineal gland, thereby depriving the person of sleep altogether. So, in order to improve the quality of your sleep, I advise that you put away all electronics and spend quality time with your family so that positive hormones are released in you. Bathing before bed and changing into fresh clothes can also do wonders for your sleep quality.

In order to get high-quality sleep, the mother should engage in positive activities like meditation, chanting mantras, recalling affirmations, visualizing the mental movie of her baby, reading a good book, spending quality time with family, etc. In fact, she should declutter her mind by running through the events of the day in her head and seek forgiveness from, or offer forgiveness to, all the concerned people or situations to release the burdens of her heart.

Sleep Posture

The expectant mother should try to sleep in the left lateral position as when the stomach is on the left, it is harder for acids to get into the oesophagus at this angle. It is best to put pillows in between the bent knees while sleeping to support the stomach.

Massage Therapy

Massage therapy during pregnancy gives a sense of wellness, aids relaxation and better sleep, reduces anxiety, decreases symptoms of depression, and relieves muscle aches and joint pains. However, the therapist should be very well trained. They should massage very gently and mildly without applying too much pressure. Moreover, they should not apply any pressure to the sensitive pressure points located on the wrists, ankles or between fingers as this may trigger contractions or potentially induce labour. The belly should never be massaged and expectant mothers should gently get their back massaged while sitting and not lying down.

Adequate and Mindful Exercise Regime

Physical exercise is not just a way of keeping fit and building muscle, but also a way to release toxins from your body. By exercising, you can improve your muscle strength and boost your endurance. Exercise delivers oxygen and nutrients to your tissues and helps your cardiovascular system work more efficiently. When the health of your heart and lungs improves, you have more energy to tackle your daily chores. Moreover, the secretion of positive hormones—like endorphins—reduces stress, anxiety, depression, and induces happiness in us, thereby increasing the quality of our life.

Thus, maintaining a regular exercise routine throughout your pregnancy can help you stay healthy and feel your best. It can also improve your posture and decrease some common discomforts like backaches and fatigue. There is evidence that it may prevent gestational diabetes (diabetes that develops during pregnancy), relieve stress and build more stamina needed for labour and delivery.

It is important to note that if you were physically active before your pregnancy, you should be able to continue your activity with some modifications. You can exercise as you used to as long as you are comfortable and have your doctor's approval. Your heart rate should not exceed 140 beats per minute.

On the flip side, if you have never exercised regularly before, then you should be very cautious when beginning an exercise programme during pregnancy. It should be done only after consulting your doctor. Do not try new, strenuous activities. The American College of Obstetrics and Gynaecology recommends at least 30 minutes of moderate exercise every day, unless you have medical or obstetric complications.[19] Some of the most common and helpful exercises are listed below.[20]

1. Walking: It is a very safe choice for almost all expectant mothers. A 30–45 minutes walk can help reduce weight, decrease chances of cardiovascular diseases, improve blood circulation, strengthen bones and muscles, and also boost the body's immune system. However, it should be only attempted upon approval from your gynaecologist.
2. Swimming: Swimming is advisable during pregnancy if the expecting mother practised it during her pre-pregnancy. It is good for blood circulation, improves muscle tone, increases endurance and helps to sleep better. However, it should be restricted after the sixth month due to the increasing size of the belly.
3. Yoga: During pregnancy, when the expectant mother mindfully performs yoga, it provides numerous benefits for both the mother and the developing baby, contributing to a healthier and more positive pregnancy experience. Yoga promotes physical fitness, flexibility and strength, which are essential for supporting the changes happening in the body and also in preparing for childbirth. However, during pregnancy, the expectant mother should be very cautious while performing yoga poses. Any *asana*s which put pressure on the stomach should be avoided. Moreover, because of the increase in body weight, it is important to stay away from balancing postures. Thus, it is in your best interest to consult your doctor before you begin. If you are not a regular yoga practitioner, then I recommend that you do so only under expert supervision.

In some cases, expectant mothers are advised bed rest by doctors. However, **post consultation with the doctor**, one can do 'subtle' exercises focussing on various joints like neck, shoulders, elbows, wrists, ankles, etc. This will help blood circulation and thereby control the swelling of these joints that might happen otherwise.

Examples of Subtle Exercises (*Sukshma Vyayam*)

1. Exercise 1 (Eye Rotation): Sit straight and move both the eyeballs up and down. Do this five times. Now move both eyeballs to the left and right. Do this five times. Then rotate both eyeballs in circles—clockwise and anticlockwise—five times.
2. Exercise 2 (Neck Rotation): Sit upright and slowly tilt the neck laterally to the right and then to the left. Do it five times. Then rotate the neck five times above and below, left to right and clockwise and anticlockwise.
3. Exercise 3 (Shoulder Rotation): Fold both hands and put your fingers on respective shoulders. Now rotate both hands clockwise and anticlockwise. Do this five times.
4. Exercise 4 (Wrist Rotation): Sit upright and keep both hands forward with fingers curled inward. Rotate the wrist clockwise and anticlockwise in small circles. Do this five times.
5. Exercise 5 (Toe Stretching): Sit upright and stretch both legs forward. Now, move your toes down and up. Do this exercise five times.
6. Exercise 6 (Ankle Rotation): Sit upright and stretch both legs forward. Now, stretch your ankles towards the front and back. Repeat this exercise five times. In the same position, rotate your ankles clockwise and anticlockwise.

Please note that you can increase the number of counts as per the advice of your gynaecologist.

Right Breathwork through Pranayama Practices

Pranayama is the ancient practice of breath regulation by controlling the timing, duration and frequency of every breath and is meant for physical and mental wellness. In Sanskrit, '*prana*' means life force energy and '*yama*' means control. According to Sage Patanjali, 'Cutting the speed of inhalation and exhalation is pranayama.'

तस्मिन्सतिश्वासप्रश्वासयोर्गतिविच्छेद:प्राणायाम: ॥49॥

The goal of pranayama is to connect your body and mind. It heals the internal organs by supplying oxygen to them while removing toxins. There is a very deep synergy between our mind and our breath. For example, when we are angry, our breathing becomes rapid; when we are afraid, our breathing becomes shallow; when we are at peace, our breathing is stable; when we live in a state of pure bliss, our breathing is continuous and rhythmic. Thus, in order to calm our mind, the simplest, most accurate and permanent solution is to regulate our breathing through the practice of pranayama. It is very important for a pregnant woman to do this because the minds of the mother and child are completely connected. They are in constant harmony and, thus, if the mother remains in a state of bliss, then the child also becomes blissful.

Importance of Prenatal Pranayama

During pregnancy, the foetus depends on your body for oxygen and nutrients. Through conscious inhaling along with mindful exhaling, one can ensure the supply of oxygen and the expulsion of carbon dioxide from the blood. This purifies the blood, rids it of toxins and supplies the foetus with fresh oxygen and nutrients. Supplying the baby with adequate oxygen contributes to its development—both cognitive and physical—in the womb. By practising pranayama, you can also reduce your own anxiety by fuelling your body with oxygen.

During the initial stages of labour, the body releases adrenaline due to the stress and anxiety experienced by the mother which further delays the release of oxytocin, a chemical compound in the body that aids in the delivery process. This can be taken care of by the mindful practice of pranayama by the mother during labour.

Yogic Breathing

A form of pranayama that is highly recommended for expectant mothers is yogic breathing. It is done by inhaling and completely filling up the abdomen, thorax and clavicular space to their full capacity and then exhaling slowly with the same intensity. This breathing technique offers several benefits to the body like reducing blood pressure and heart rate, improving relaxation and increasing lung capacity.

To practise yogic breathing, first fill the abdomen with air completely and expand it while inhaling (abdominal breathing); the chest expands as it gets filled with air (thoraxic breathing) and finally there is an expansion in the shoulder region (clavicular breathing). This has great effects on the physical as well as mental health of the mother and the child. As she breathes out, at first the shoulders drop, then the chest relaxes, and finally the stomach moves in.

A 2017 study shared that yogic breathing reduces the secretion of cortisol—the stress hormone—in the body.[21] I too feel that yogic breathing may help alleviate symptoms of stress and anxiety. The expectant mother should train herself well enough that yogic breathing comes naturally to her. So, whenever you are seated, be attentive to how you breathe and make it as deep and complete as possible.

Some of the pranayama techniques that are safe during pregnancy—which even those on bed rest can perform—are:

1. *For Balancing—Nadi Shodhana Pranayama:* Nadi shodhana is made up of '*nadi*' meaning 'flow' and '*shodhana*' meaning 'purification'. It is basically alternate-nostril breathing and helps to get rid of toxins, infuses oxygen into the blood, and restores hormonal balance. It is a very effective method for balancing and purifying the *ida*, *pingla* and *sushumna nadi* (which is dealt with in greater detail in Chapter 6). This must be done on an empty stomach.

   - Take a full, deep breath and follow it with a gentle exhalation.
   - Repeat the breathing cycle several times until you feel your breath becoming rhythmic and naturally paced.
   - Close your right nostril with your thumb and inhale through the left nostril.
   - Then, gently close your left nostril with your little and ring finger and exhale through the right nostril.
   - Now, inhale through the right nostril, close it and exhale through the left.
   - Alternate nostrils and repeat this exercise three to five times every day. Remember, the first inhalation should be from left nostril and final exhalation should also be from the left.

2. *For Sensitizing—Ujjayi Pranayama:* Ujjayi detoxifies the mind, promotes mental clarity and the free flow of prana

throughout the body, thereby increasing energy and self-awareness.

- Close your lips and breathe in and out through the nose slowly and deeply several times till your breathing becomes rhythmic.
- Inhale slowly and deeply through your nostril.
- Constrict the muscles at the back of the throat and exhale slowly through your nose making a hissing sound. This sound is called ujjayi.
- Repeat the above for five to 10 rounds according to your comfort.

3. *For Cooling and Developing Awareness—Shitali* and *Shitkari Pranayama:* Shitali translates into 'cooling' and it reduces the fight or flight response in the body by relaxing the parasympathetic system. It also lowers blood pressure and acid reflux symptoms in the body.

- Sit comfortably while aligning the neck, spine and head.
- Do deep breathing while keeping your eyes closed till your breathing becomes rhythmic.
- Open your mouth and curl your lips into an 'O'.
- Inhale deeply as if you're drinking through a straw.
- Direct your focus towards the cooling sensation of your breathing.
- Pull back the tongue and close your mouth, while you exhale completely through the nostrils.
- Repeat the steps of inhalation and exhalation for five to 10 rounds.

'Shitkari' consists of 'sheeth' (meaning 'coldness') and 'kari' meaning ('that which arises'). A sound of 'si' or 'sith' comes out while doing this form of breathing. This breathing technique cools down the mind and the body.

- Sit comfortably with your spine erect and take a few deep breaths.
- Bring the upper and lower teeth together while keeping the lips open as much as you can and inhale through the closed teeth, while making a soft hissing sound.
- Release the teeth and close the mouth as you exhale through the nose.
- Repeat this for five to 10 rounds, allowing the cooling effect to bring ease to your body and mind.

These pranayama techniques should be done regularly during the summer, but not during the winter.

4. *For Expanding Awareness—Brahmari Pranayama* and *Omkar:* Resembling the typical humming sounds of the bee, the brahmari pranayama is relaxing and helps calm the mind while regulating emotions. It relieves sinuses and hypertension and makes delivery comfortable. It also relieves stress, tension and anxiety during pregnancy.

- Sit in a comfortable position.
- Close your ears with your thumbs.
- Place your index fingers lightly above the eyebrows and close your eyes with a gentle pressure with the rest of your fingers.
- Apply gentle pressure to the sides of your nose.
- Focus your mind on the area in between the eyebrows, also called the *Ajna Chakra*.
- Inhale deeply through the nostrils.
- Exhale through the nose and, while doing so, hum the

'om' sound while keeping the mouth closed.
- Repeat five times.

'OM' is the primordial sound of the universe. It is the original vibration of the universe from which all other vibrations were manifested. By chanting it we can align our frequency with that of the original universal frequency, which has the power to transform our mind and the senses and take us to an elevated state of consciousness. 'AUM' is the sound of 'OM' when broken up into three syllables—A, U and M—which stand for the creation, sustenance and destruction of the universe, respectively. 'A' and 'U' together form the 'O' sound. So, when we are chanting Omkar, then two-thirds of the time should be focussed on 'O' and one-third on 'M'. Chanting 'OM' during pregnancy is said to directly affect the body's digestive, circulatory and nervous systems. If the mother is filled with the energy of the positive vibrations, the lives of both the mother and the child are positively affected and this ensures maximum energy absorption.

Follow these steps to correctly chant 'OM':

- Turn your left palm up and keep it close to your navel. Place the back of your right hand onto your left palm. Maintain this position for the rest of the steps.
- Close your eyes and get into a relaxed mode. Make sure both your body and mind are at ease. Feel the energy through the body.
- Once you have paid attention to the sounds and vibrations in your body, breathe in and count to five. As you exhale, count to seven. As you practise more, you will be able to inhale and exhale for longer durations. This should be repeated thrice.

- Utter 'AUM' or 'OM' as you breathe out. Two-thirds or 66 per cent of the chanting must be focussed on 'AU' or 'O' by feeling the vibrations from your abdomen to chest, and only one-third or 33 per cent should be devoted to the 'M' sound, as you feel the vibrations from your throat upwards.
- The chanting of 'OM' should initially be done three times. Slowly, you can work your way up to nine times.
- As soon as your meditation ends, start breathing normally and spend some time concentrating on your breath and absorbing the energy.

Important Pranayama Techniques for Expectant Mothers

- Balancing: Nadi Shodhana
- Sensitizing: Ujjayi
- Cooling and Developing Awareness: Shitali and Shitkari
- Expanding Awareness through the Body: Brahmari and Omkar

Note: It is important to practise yogic breathing (deep breathing) as much as possible at all times.

A Note of Caution

Expectant mothers should perform the pranayama very gently and slowly. I strongly advise that expectant mothers should avoid those pranayama techniques which require rapid breathing and put pressure on the stomach, like *kapalbhati*, *bhastrika*, *agnisar*, etc. *Bandha*s and *kumbhak*, which focus on restraining and holding of breath, should also be avoided.

Stay Away from Addictions

The crux of physical well-being is all about being disciplined. It involves being regulated and motivated from within and not by coercion. A very important aspect of good physical well-being is staying away from addictions.

Addiction is a disease and has a range of psychological, physical and social effects that can drastically reduce a person's quality of living. It changes the brain at the physiological level, alters the way it works, and rewires its fundamental structure. It reflects a lack of control over your mind as the brain comes under the control of the addiction. Intoxication of any kind is not good for pregnancy as it disturbs the functioning of your brain.

- The most common intoxicant is caffeine, which is present in coffee and tea. Caffeine is not good for pregnancy and if required, less than 200 mg per day can be consumed.
- Smoking, directly or indirectly, has a detrimental effect as tobacco causes problems that can lead to miscarriage and premature delivery, and can put the baby at a high risk of sudden unexpected death in infancy (SUDI).[22]
- When the expectant mother consumes alcohol, it passes from her blood through the placenta to the baby and can lead to a serious life-long condition called foetal alcohol spectrum disorder (FASD), which can cause problems with learning and behaviour, managing emotions and social skills, and hyperactivity and impulse control, as well as impair communication skills, especially speech, and affect the functioning of joints, bones, muscles and some organs. Furthermore, it increases the risk of

miscarriage, premature delivery, and low birth-weight.[23]
- The most serious addiction in today's times is the use of electronic gadgets. We are all severely addicted because it has become a part of our lifestyle requirement.

    One must be aware that all electronic gadgets emit very harmful radiation which is not good for the health of either the expectant mother or the foetus.[24] It is strongly advisable that the mother use electronic gadgets in moderation. It is equally important to keep them far away while sleeping and also during the day when not in use.

Environmental Hazards and Toxins

We are surrounded by chemicals and toxic substances. These include pesticides in the garden, flame retardants on furniture, lead, mercury and some cleaning products. Heavy metals such as lead and mercury, organic solvents, alcohol and ionizing radiation are environmental teratogens, and exposure could contribute to hazards during pregnancy.

Most chemicals that you come across in your daily life won't harm your baby. But if you are exposed to large quantities of chemicals for long periods, it is possible that your child will be at an increased risk of congenital disorders or future health problems. If you breathe in or swallow some chemicals, they can enter your bloodstream and pass to your baby via the placenta.

The negative health effects that may be caused by exposure to these hazards include miscarriages, still births, delayed foetal growth, birth defects and increased risk for certain illnesses in the baby.

Chemicals to Avoid When You Are Pregnant or Breastfeeding

Pesticides and herbicides	Pesticides (bug killers) and herbicides (weed killers) are known to affect both the foetus and newborn babies.
Mosquito repellent	Mosquito repellents have chemicals like diethyltoluamide (DEET) or picaridin that might enter the skin, and it is advised that one should avoid this during their first trimester. Choose a repellent with a low to moderate concentration of the chemical—between five per cent and 20 per cent—and consider other ways to avoid mosquitos.
Mercury	Being exposed to high levels of mercury can damage your health and increase the likelihood of brain damage and hearing- and vision-related problems in a developing baby. Some fish contain mercury, including shark (flake), broadbill, marlin and swordfish. To be on the safe side, pregnant women should limit eating these species of fish. If you need a dental filling, then check for options that don't contain mercury.
Arsenic-treated timber	Outdoor wood is often treated with copper, chromium or arsenic to protect it from dry rot, fungi, mould and termites. From diabetes and cancer to miscarriage and stillbirth, this treatment has been said to be the cause of human health hazards. It gives the wood a greenish tinge, which fades over time. You can protect yourself and your baby by not putting food on arsenic-treated timber and washing your (and your child's) hands after they play on it.
Nail polish and other cosmetics	Formaldehyde is a chemical used in nail polish, some cosmetics and hair-straightening products. The amount of formaldehyde in nail polish is very small and quickly broken down by the body. However, adverse effects on the baby cannot be ruled out. So, it's best to use cosmetics that don't have formaldehyde.

Flame retardants	The chemicals used to make household furniture less flammable can impact the child's brain development. To minimize their impact, wash your hands frequently, use a vacuum fitted with a HEPA filter and mop the floor regularly.
BPA	The chemical bisphenol A (BPA) is found in most plastics and can pass from a mother to her baby in the womb. It could cause brain and behaviour problems in some children. It is, therefore, advised that one stays away from BPA during pregnancy and infancy to avoid childhood asthma.

If you are exposed to a toxic product while you are pregnant, don't panic as a one-off exposure is highly unlikely to cause any harm. Remember, it's only long-term exposure to large quantities of chemicals that could potentially harm your baby, so be alert!

The Dos and Don'ts in Lifestyle during Pregnancy

The condition of an expectant mother is delicate and it is important for her to be careful at all times. Acharya Carak has given some valuable advice for the expecting mother and she must make focussed efforts to follow these recommendations as much as possible during her pregnancy.[25]

उत्कटविषमकठिनासनसेविन्या वातमूत्रपुरीषवेगानुपरुन्धत्या
दारुण अनुचितव्यायामसेविन्या: तीक्ष्णोष्णातिमात्रसेविन्या:
प्रमिताशनसेविन्या गर्भो म्रियतेऽन्त: तथा अभिघातप्रपीडनै:
श्वभ्रकूपप्रपातदेशावलोकनैर्वाऽभीक्ष्णं मातु: प्रपतत्यकाले गर्भा:
तथाऽतिमात्रसंक्षोभिभिर्यानैर्यानेन अप्रियातिमात्रश्रवणैर्वा ।

Go through the following recommendations very carefully.

- The expectant mother should not sit on hard, irregular or uncomfortable surfaces or on chairs that are not

flat. Such sitting positions could force her to sit in a slanted or oblique posture or with her legs apart. Rather, she should sit with her spine straight at all times without hunching, so that the foetus can take its appropriate position in the womb.
- Natural urges such as urination, bowel movement or flatulence should never be suppressed as this could cause problems over time. Suppression of the urge to urinate can lead to an increased risk of urinary tract infection and increases pressure on the uterus. Holding back intestinal gases might trigger nausea, heartburn and belching. Suppression of natural bowel movement can lead to a loss of appetite and anorexia. It is essential that bowel movements be regular to prevent the formation of intestinal gases and prevent the need to exert pressure during bowel evacuation, which might affect the uterus in an undesirable way.[26]
- Indulging in intensive and extreme forms of physical exercises and weightlifting can harm the foetus. The expectant mother should avoid anything that involves too much twisting, turning and bending, which can hamper the growth of the foetus.
- Food in general should not be too spicy, hot or pungent. Moreover, if the pregnant woman eats less or more than required and consumes unhealthy food, then she will not receive adequate nutrition.
- She should sleep on her side and avoid sleeping on her back (supine position) as the latter can increase the probability that the umbilical cord twists itself around the foetus's neck.

Maintaining Physical Well-Being

- She should not look into the depths of a well or down a steep cliff or into a valley, as these could cause fear or physical jolts, which might harm the baby.
- The expecting mother should not listen to disturbing noises such as loud music, discordant sounds, burst of fireworks or any sounds that can unsettle the baby inside.
- Pregnant women should not travel long distances during the first and last trimesters of pregnancy. In the second trimester, they should only travel when it is necessary and comfortable. It is important to ensure that the bumps and jerks while travelling are minimum, as any kind of direct injury or impact to the abdomen can injure the foetus. So, during pregnancy, travelling on potholed roads or vehicles that shudder should be avoided.
- Expecting mothers should wear loose and comfortable garments as tight-fitting clothes can impede circulation. Jeans, skirts and petticoats that tend to tighten around the abdomen should be avoided.
- Wearing high-heeled shoes or sandals may cause backaches and, as the foetus grows, it becomes more difficult for the expectant mother to maintain a straight posture and she can lose balance easily while wearing them. Hence, she should always wear flat, comfortable footwear conducive to her present condition.
- It is a scientifically proven fact that smoking during pregnancy can have a devastating effect hampering the mental, physical and intellectual development of the baby. So it is important for expecting mothers to refrain from smoking.

- Resting in the afternoon is acceptable but it is certainly not advisable to sleep deeply during that time or stay up late at night. In fact, sleeping more than 8 to 10 hours can cause laziness, listlessness and developmental delay in the child, and can even slow down its metabolism.[27]
- It is strongly advised that the pregnant woman should not roam aimlessly or stay in, or even visit, unprotected places or deserted areas that are unknown to her for the duration of the pregnancy.
- During pregnancy, the vagina and uterus are extra sensitive and prone to injury. Thus, sexual intercourse must be performed only with a doctor's approval, especially in the first trimester, when the embryo is not yet stable, and during the final trimester, when the foetus has grown considerably.
- The expecting mother should not get involved in things that are unpleasant, irritating and disturbing to her. The home environment should be harmonious and no undue stress arising out of family feuds should be put on the mother. Under no circumstances should she have to shout or get angry or irritated.
- Expectant mothers should not read books that induce excitement, or watch horror films which could generate fear as the unborn child is very sensitive and could easily get affected. They should also avoid watching television programmes that show deceit, stressful situations, unhappiness and immorality. Books and films have a deep impact on the subconscious mind and those that have negative effects must be avoided. Such influences on the unborn baby could result in the

- child being weak or fainthearted and, in extreme cases, the excitement caused may even lead to miscarriage.
- Feelings of grief, anxiety, worry and overthinking can make the child inside the womb fearful, apprehensive, anxious and, in the worst cases, can even shorten the life span of the child. Jealousy, anger and negative thinking can make the unborn child envious, corrupt or unethical.
- The expecting mother should always live in a clean, tidy environment and not visit places that harbour obnoxious or unsavoury odours.

These list of do's and don'ts might seem overwhelming, but if you are conscious and careful enough, you will be amazed to find the benefits experienced by you and the child growing inside you.

Enhance your Kinaesthetic Skills through Brain-Body Coordination

It is important to increase the responsiveness of the body and the brain–body coordination by engaging in various activities like:

Brain Gym

It is a set of activities and movements designed to connect both hemispheres of the brain. They are performed to improve brain functioning, create mind–body coordination, balance the effects of daily stress, and help in achieving an optimal state of mind. It is a series of exercises that helps people stay in shape, think and learn efficiently, and increase concentration for longer durations. The basic premise is how fast our body can respond to the neural signals. The faster the response time, the better the kinaesthetic skills. The expectant mother who is following the seven pillars of physical well-being properly will be able to respond faster, thus attaining a better brain gym performance.

Brain gym was created by the pioneer of brain research, Dr Paul Dennison. He based his work on educational kinesiology (kinaesthetic psychology) and learning psychology on the principle that we can educate a person through movement.

A consistent use of the brain gym movements help awaken neural connections in the brain and the body, making one feel safe and emotionally centred.

This concept is based on the idea that physical movements stimulate different parts of the brain, improving neural connections and facilitating learning and retention.

Performing simple, easy and neurologically specific movements can actually release stress. Brain gym activities also help improve vision, coordination, cognition and behaviour. It helps us coordinate, organize and filter sensory information, while also allowing tasks to be performed with maximum efficiency.

When the expectant mother does brain gym exercises, the coordination and communication between the left and right parts of the brain become very strong. This increases the physical well-being of the mother and the child, while also simultaneously impacting emotional and mental well-being.

Another interesting version is Brain Dance. Developed by Anne Green Gilbert, BrainDance©2000 is an effective, full-body/brain warm-up exercise based on eight developmental movement patterns that humans move through in the first year of life to wire the central nervous system.

Many of us might have missed a pattern, but by moving

through these patterns weekly or daily we re-pattern our brains, align our bodies, develop better focus and concentration, and strengthen social and emotional skills. This exercise prepares everyone for learning.

However, it will be wise to consult your gynaecologist before engaging in any physical activity.

You can access a range of Brain Gym and Brain Dance activities through the DreamStar Baby App.

Performing Arts and Sports

Engaging in performing arts like dancing and acting, various sports and yoga will help the mother develop kinaesthetic skills and pass these to their unborn child. However, all these activities should be performed with great caution. It is preferred that these activities are conducted while seated, without any jerky movements. It is best to consult your gynaecologist before doing any physical activity.

Art and Craft

Creating a beautiful piece of art requires a lot of brain and body coordination, especially of the fingers and the hands. Activities like cutting, pasting, folding, knitting, stitching, etc., involve fine motor skills and increase the dexterity of the hands.

Five-Sense Coordination

It is our five senses that collect information from the outside world. The information is then processed by the brain, which in turn communicates with the body. So, in order to improve one's kinaesthetic skills, the mother should work upon each of these senses—sight, sound, smell, taste and touch—and their related organs for better coordination.

All these activities are aimed at facilitating foetal brain development and can be accessed daily through the DreamStar Baby app by scanning the QR code at the end of the book.

Love Your Body: It Is a Temple to the Child inside You

During pregnancy, the body undergoes a lot of physical changes due to high fluctuations in hormones, adversely impacting the beauty of the expectant mother. This includes weight gain, stretch marks, breakouts on the face, itching, breast sagging, etc. One should be aware of these changes and try to limit their impact, and maintain a good lifestyle by incorporating the best practices as discussed earlier. Stretch marks and body itches can be controlled by applying oils as they lubricate the body and increase skin elasticity. Under no circumstances should the expectant mother scratch her body harshly and unnecessarily as this might lead to permanent marks.

The expectant mother should know that these changes are transient and accept them with grace. She should always think of the bigger happiness knocking at her door, and these lifestyle adjustments will seem miniscule. Through mindful eating, holistic living and staying close to Mother Nature, the expectant mother can automatically nourish her child in the best possible manner. She must strongly adhere to the seven pillars of physical well-being to build a body that is a temple to the child within.

Hence, dear mother, I highly encourage you to choose to commit to this pregnancy with all the happiness and love that your heart can muster, all the commitment and faith that your mind can ignite, and all the divinity and desire that your soul yearns for. Use it all to manifest the holistic, divine child of your dreams. If you feel overwhelmed, then just motivate yourself by saying, 'It is a matter of nine months only. And the benefits will be enjoyed for eternity.'

Tracker Sheet for Maintaining Physical Well-Being

	Present Rating Where you are (on a scale of 10)	**Desired Rating** Where you want to go (on a scale of 10)	**Action Monitor** (steps taken to achieve it)
Nutritious and Balanced Diet			
Energized Water			
Quality Sleep			
Adequate Exercise			
Right Breathwork			
Refraining from Addictions			
Avoiding Environmental Hazards			

4

Developing Mental Well-Being

*'An expectant mother has the power to manifest
in her child whatever she is focussed on.'*

One sunny afternoon in 1671, Christopher Wren saw three bricklayers on a scaffold—one crouched, one half-standing and one standing tall—all working very hard to achieve their targets. He went to the first bricklayer and asked, 'What are you doing?' to which the bricklayer said, 'I'm laying bricks to feed my family.' The second bricklayer, when asked the same question, replied, 'I'm building a wall.' But when he asked the third bricklayer, he excitedly responded, 'I'm building a great cathedral for the Almighty.'

The three bricklayers were doing the same work but their purpose was different. The focus of the first one was just to earn his daily wages, the second one only wanted to complete his assigned task, but the third one was working with a higher purpose—the divine task of building a cathedral to house the Lord. So who would be able to deliver the highest-quality work? The one with vision and purpose. So my question to you, dear mother, is this: how will you deliver the best baby?

Have you ever noticed how when we focus the sun's rays over a piece of paper through a magnifying glass, the paper catches fire? This happens because the lens converges the rays to such an extent that when all of them are focussed on a paper, it burns.

The power of the human mind is similar. When we focus and converge our thoughts positively, we can achieve anything and everything we desire, and the reverse is also true. That's why a popular saying goes, 'Your mind is your greatest friend as well as the worst enemy.'

While the human mind has tremendous capacity, unfortunately an average human being uses only 4 to 5 per cent of their mind power. Einstein could use up to 8 per cent and that is what made him a genius. Thus, the million-dollar question is: How can we give birth to another 'Einstein'? How can we instil 'genius' in our child?

If you are still wondering about this, then, my dear mothers, the answer is yes, you can. This can be made possible when you are carrying your child in your womb.

According to Acharya Caraka:[1]

तत्र पूर्वं चेतनाधातुः सत्त्वकरणो गुणग्रहणाय प्रवर्तते।

(The foetus creates an individual mind of its own from the moment fertilization occurs and the embryo is formed.)

He further states:

सत्त्ववैशेष्यकराणि पुनस्तेषां तेषां प्राणिनां मातृपितृसत्त्वान्यन्तर्वर्त्याः
श्रुतयश्चाभीक्ष्णं स्वोचितं च कर्म सत्त्वविशेषाभ्यासश्चेति॥

(This mind of the foetus is totally synchronized with its mother and develops as per her preferences and choices.)

Therefore, during pregnancy, the mind of the expectant mother and foetus are always perfectly aligned. By tapping into the powers of the subconscious mind through affirmations and visualization, the expectant mother can manifest the child of her dreams within the womb itself. This was exactly what Jijabai did when she resolved to give birth to one of the bravest sons on earth. It was this affirmation that helped her give birth to Shivaji Maharaj—the epitome of courage and bravery.

This chapter will provide step-by-step instructions on how one can really create the power within to visualize and act upon their thoughts to bring forth a child who is manifested with all the traits that the mother envisions.

But before we move on to understand 'how to manifest', it is important to note that the mother should have complete clarity of 'what to manifest'. So, as a starting point, dear mother, use Sonal's Intelligence Model for Holistic Development© to create a complete wish-list for your dream baby because unless you have full clarity, you won't be able to manifest effectively.

Suhasini was always apprehensive about any changes in her body after her first miscarriage the previous year. She went to her mother-in-law, who had stood by her, and said, 'I am feeling very sick, Maa.' She had been feeling dizzy and thought it could be the blood pressure playing skip in her system. 'Why? What happened? I noticed this yesterday. You skipped dinner last night, too. If you continue doing this, you will spoil your health, beta,' her mother-in-law said, empathetic and worried at the same time.

'I will take care, Maa. I just don't know what's going on. I think my blood pressure is low. I will have it checked tomorrow.'

The following day, Suhasini felt the same dizziness and decided to go get herself checked. Somewhere deep down, she was excited that she could be pregnant again. But immediately the thrill changed to worry and then agony as she recalled her experience from the last time.

'You are right. You are pregnant, Suhasisni!' Her gynaecologist beamed at her. 'That is wonderful news. Thank you, doctor. But please tell me everything that I need to do and everything that I must not repeat from last year. I want this baby, doctor,' Suhasini said, teary-eyed.

'This time, I am going to recommend something spiritual, aside from all the medical advice that I give you. I need you to go and look up Garbha Sanskar and the methods associated with it. Last time, you pursued your usual way of life. But certain things have been practised for ages and have been proved over and over again by the sages,' said her doctor.

'Suhasini, you will read some works that I will list. This includes the Bhagvad Gita, the Ramcharitmanas, some mantras and some more spiritual works,' the doctor continued. 'I'll give you a reservoir of activities for the holistic development of your baby and you will never be bored. Trust me—try this and you will raise a child who will be everything you dreamt of.'

Suhasini listened, speechless, worried, excited and nervous, all at once. Yes, she wanted all those things, but was she capable of raising a child like that?

'You need to keep envisioning your child and talk to them. Once you believe that you are doing all this for the life that you will create, you will automatically find the strength, motivation and urge to walk on the path that I show you.'

'I will do everything that you tell me to do, doctor,' Suhasini said, her eyes moist.

Suhasini was a devotee of Lord Krishna and, as she returned home from the clinic, she put up a big picture of the deity right in front of her bed that her mother-in-law had got from Vrindavan a few months ago. She kept internalizing and meditating upon this form of Krishna that was big-eyed, had dimpled cheeks and a naughty smile, such that she started addressing her baby in the womb as 'KB'—Krishna Baby.

She started following the spiritual path of waking up early every day, bathing and meditating upon what she wanted in her 'KB'. She prepared her meals herself and included only fresh produce and lentils. She would hum her favourite chant of 'Hare Krishna, Hare Krishna, Krishna, Krishna, Hare, Hare,' while cooking and eating.

She read about various entrepreneurs, Indian kings and freedom fighters who had epitomized virtue, and also followed the reading list and activities that her doctor had prescribed. Throughout her pregnancy, she realized that she barely had an acid reflux, her skin glowed, and her heart sparkled. She was a symbol of happiness for every member of her family.

The day finally arrived; Suhasini gave birth as she had envisaged. Lovingly, and with a lot of gratitude, she held her KB in her arms with happy tears flowing from her eyes. To everyone's amazement, she gave birth to a son who was the exact replica of the little Krishna she had put right in front of her bed.

'Oh, he is perfect!' Suhasini said, as her husband looked at them adoringly and whispered 'thank you' to his wife.

This exemplifies that the mental well-being of the mother goes hand in hand with physical and emotional health. When a mother makes a decision for her child, she becomes unstoppable. From this, we clearly and precisely understand what mental well-being truly is. The power to manifest one's dreams, aspirations and desires lies within one's mind. And we have the power to reprogramme our mind and achieve what we desire through two important tools—affirmations and visualizations. But before delving into its implementation, it's crucial to grasp the workings of the human mind. Understanding the mind's mechanisms lays the foundation for effectively reprogramming it and achieving the desired outcomes.

Understanding the Human Mind

The human mind is like an iceberg where the tip constitutes the 'conscious mind', which is only 10 per cent of that iceberg. The five sense organs—ears, nose, eyes, tongue and skin—receive the signals from the external world which are then processed by the conscious mind and help us make our day-to-day decisions, react to various life situations, and also guide us in critical and logical thinking.

But then, like we said, it is only the tip of the iceberg! The remaining 90 per cent of the human mind is where the real mind power lies. This constitutes, in post-Freudian studies, what we know as the 'subconscious mind' which always responds to the conscious mind positively in the form of affirmations. It works on an auto-pilot mode and is all about dealing with tasks such as beliefs, emotions, habits, values, intuitions, imagination and long-term memory.

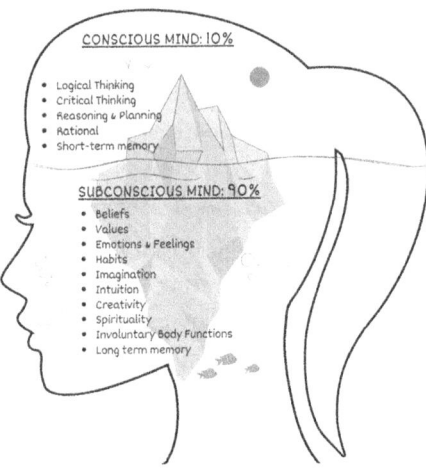

So how are these two minds related? The conscious mind is objective and can think, rationalize and reason. It is the centre of reasoning and has the ability to define the choices of a person and impact their decisions. It is all about facts. It collects sensory inputs from the environment and has the power to either accept or reject it on the basis of its past experiences, knowledge and information. However, once an input is accepted by the conscious mind, it processes it further and sends the processed output to the subconscious mind. The conscious mind, thus, has a large impact on the subconscious mind and both work in collaboration.

Every conscious thought sends a programming message to the subconscious mind. These thoughts are then repeated in the subconscious mind over and over again like a tape recorder, and thus establish the foundation of all the beliefs, behaviour and habits that you may have.

Let us understand this with the help of a simple example of an elephant which we might have witnessed in our lives. When the elephant was a baby, it was tied to a tree with a strong rope by its mahout. The baby elephant, being weak, could not break free and, after multiple attempts, it gave up. However, the baby started growing and gained in strength, while the rope stayed the same. The elephant, now a grown marvel, was still conditioned by its conscious mind that the rope was very heavy, and it could not be broken. This message was programmed into the subconscious mind of the elephant to such an extent that it never even dared to yank it away! Had the elephant tried, it would have realized that it had enough power to uproot the tree along with the rope. Alas! It never attempted this.

Don't we behave like the giant elephant who lived a life of bondage, unaware of our true potential? We fail to assess the hidden powers of our subconscious. The subconscious mind does not have the ability to logically differentiate between good or bad, right or wrong, fact or fiction. It behaves according to what is fed into it and is unable to differentiate between the positive and the negative. It replays the thoughts that go into it like a recorder. Anyone could have laughed at the elephant's plight—enslaved by a tiny rope. But more than the rope, the elephant was enslaved because of his conditioning. Thus, the subconscious completely operates on auto-pilot according to the information it is fed by the conscious mind.

Characteristics of the Subconscious Mind

The subconscious mind is the epicentre of all emotions, habits and all involuntary behaviour. Any thought which is wrapped with high-intensity emotions from your past impressions and is felt strongly through the five senses, gets accepted and stored within the subconscious mind more strongly. This is the reason why you can remember life's special moments vividly as if they were etched into your heart forever. If I ask you to recall your day from a week ago, you might struggle to remember, but if I ask you to recall your wedding day, it would be absolutely clear and vivid in your mind.

While recalling your wedding day, you might have realized that there was no set script in your mind for that day that played out. The special day actually plays in your mind like a movie. This is because the subconscious mind uses visual imagery effectively to store and process information related to experiences, memories and learned patterns. Moreover, those visuals that are emotional and sensory (involving all the five senses) create a stronger imprint on your subconscious mind. The subconscious mind understands the language of emotionally-charged visuals very effectively and quickly. Thus, when one communicates with the child in the womb through emotionally-charged, sensory, visual language (like a movie scene), the child responds in amazing ways.

Moreover, the subconscious mind is beyond time and space and lives in the present moment only. It has the power to focus on any memory and traverse its neural pathways as if it were happening in the present moment. Didn't you realize that when you recalled your wedding day, you actually relived it as if it was happening right then?

It works with full faith and trust, and a drop of doubt or lack of faith can poison it completely. So, the moment a mother starts doubting whether she will be able to create that 'genius' or not, she might not be able to at all!

Again, if I ask you that you shouldn't recall your wedding day under any circumstances, then what happens? The mind is bound to recall, and maybe even more strongly. This is because the subconscious mind does not understand 'no'. It simply deletes 'no' from the input that is provided to it. The subconscious mind thus responds more effectively to positive and affirming language. Instead of using negations like 'don't' or 'no', it's often more effective to frame messages in positive terms. For instance, instead of saying 'don't forget to do meditation,' you can say 'remember to do meditation.'

Just like weeds start growing when a farm is not tended properly, when the subconscious mind is not anchored to anything positive, it automatically attaches itself to negative emotions like fear, doubt, anxiety, etc., justifying the age-old saying 'an empty mind is a devil's workshop.' This is why when the expectant mother is not kept engaged, she keeps worrying over the growth of her child, her delivery and all the various aspects of her pregnancy. This actually make her doubts come alive because of the power of her mind. The mother should instead engage herself in activities as guided in Sonal's Intelligence Model for Holistic Development© which will help her to channelize her entire energy into the holistic development of the child in the womb.

Characteristics of the Subconscious Mind

- Does not focus on logic and rationality
- Does not base its decisions primarily on facts and factual data
- Influenced by emotions, sensory experiences and visual imagery
- Triggers negative self-programming when not engaged
- Lives in the present moment
- Responds better to positive and affirming language
- Only works on trust and responds negatively to doubt

Science has proven that many diseases we suffer from are psychosomatic or have taken birth first in the mind and then affect the body.[2] Such is the power of the mind! Thus, my dear mothers, visualize your baby equipped with all the desired intelligences, imagine them happening for real, and then witness them materializing. The programming of the mind is such that the mind creates and the body responds.

Maharani Madalasa knew this really well and so with great confidence, she would announce the traits of the child taking shape in her womb. Let us now understand how Maharani Madalasa programmed her mind, which actually created her baby in the womb.

Programming the Subconscious Mind

We have understood that the conscious mind is like a doorkeeper and is all about facts and figures. So, the moment we present our wishlist, it will be rejected instantly. We need to access the subconscious mind. However, we cannot really reach the subconscious mind without tapping into the conscious mind first. If one wants to programme the subconscious mind independently, then one has to come up with a way of bypassing the conscious mind and entering into the domain of the subconscious directly, which is actually an impossible task but we can trick our mind and achieve it very easily.

The brain works on different frequencies. Beta is the active frequency that the conscious human mind works upon and it is this frequency (between 14 and 40 Hz) that helps deal with all worldly matters.[3] While you are reading this, you are in the beta mode. This is the usual 'awake' state of mind where you are conscious of your surroundings, activities, people and places.

But the subconscious mind works on the meditative or alpha frequency (between 7.5 and 14 Hz). When you meditate and focus on your breathing, when you are engrossed in the silence and feel a peace that makes you smile from within, or when you become deeply engrossed in your favourite activity and do not notice the passing of time, you have quietly entered into the alpha mode. This mode is also active when you are at rest mentally, and during this time, your subconscious mind is completely open to any instructions that you wish to give it. This is exactly the reason why a pregnant woman is told to refrain from watching negative content as her mind completely absorbs all the negative aspects from it and seamlessly transfers it to her womb.

Thus, when we switch from the worldly beta mode to the peaceful alpha mode by lowering the frequency levels, we can easily bypass the conscious mind and get in touch with the subconscious mind. We can enter alpha mode by doing yogic breathing, chanting mantras, doing meditation and practising silence. The 'how to' for doing this effectively is discussed in depth in Chapter 6. And now, once we have entered the realm of the subconscious mind, we will use the tools that follow to strengthen the neural pathways to manifest our dream baby effectively.

Tools for Strengthening Neural Pathways for Effective Manifestation

Visualization

Visualization is the process of creating and reinforcing a mental picture of the kind of qualities and intelligences you want to develop in your baby. Our brain is made up of millions of neurons, and when we visualize something, neural pathways are formed. These neural pathways get strengthened every time the mind visualizes. Again, the subconscious mind does not differentiate between the neural pathways created due to actual occurrence of any incident or through imagination. The same neural pathway is used in case of visualization or the real occurrence of the incident. This way, one can trick the mind into believing that a mental visualization is a real occurrence. As one visualizes countless times, the neural pathway becomes exceptionally smooth, free from any resistance. The neural pathways can be further strengthened when the visualization is done with full trust and commitment, using the five senses and powerful emotions. When that particular incident which we have been visualizing for so long actually occurs, then the materialization happens like magic as if it had been waiting to happen.

For Powerful Visualization

- Create neural pathways
- Five senses
- High emotions
- Full trust and commitment

Affirmations

While the visualization is happening, we need to feed the subconscious mind with statements we want it to believe and act upon. These statements are called affirmations. They are positive statements that we want to bring to fruition.

Affirmations are positive self-talk statements that are consciously chosen and repeated to oneself, with the intention of reinforcing a desired belief, mindset or outcome.

The words we use for affirmations are critical as they will determine what we programme into our subconscious mind. There are certain rules for writing affirmations so that we can trick the mind to believe that they are facts or genuine occurrences happening at the current moment. It is, in fact, all about using the limitations of the subconscious mind in our favour. There are a few common rules for writing affirmations:

- Affirmations should be simple statements written in present tense as if the desired outcome is already happening or true. This helps to reinforce a positive belief system in the subconscious mind. For example, instead of saying 'I will be healthy', say 'I am healthy'.
- They should be framed in positive terms, focussing on what you want to achieve or experience, rather than what you want to avoid or eliminate. For example, instead of saying 'I am not afraid of my delivery', say 'I am confident about giving birth to my baby'.
- They should have positive intentions.
- They should be personal and only related to you and your baby in the womb. You can write affirmations for your baby only till the time it is in your womb and not after it has taken birth.
- There should not be any comparison with any other human beings.
- They should be as specific as possible.
- There should not be any doubts about their achievement.

- They should be filled with very high emotion and felt through all the five senses (emotional and sensory).
- They should be repeated regularly, preferably daily, to reinforce positive beliefs and thoughts in your subconscious mind over time. Repetition helps to strengthen neural pathways associated with the desired outcomes.

Dear mother, a whole reservoir of sample affirmations for the development of PQ, IQ, EQ and the SQ of the baby and for the overall well-being of the mother has been shared in the Annexure 2. You may use them for your reference and create affirmations that are suitable to your requirements.

Creating a Vision Board

Once the expecting mother has complete clarity about the child of her dreams and begins to manifest by writing affirmations for each of the intelligences and the quotients, she should strengthen the neural pathways further by creating a vision board. A vision board is like a dream board that visualizes your affirmations for all development areas as described in Sonal's Intelligence Model for Holistic Development©. It is made up of a collage of images, drawings, doodles, quotes, etc. It should be placed in front of the eyes of the mother, where she spends maximum time so that constant watching will help create the necessary neural pathways in the brain and also aid visualization and manifestation.

There are no rules when it comes to making vision boards. Perhaps the only condition for the success of a vision board is that it should be a projection of the mind of the mother depicting her desires effectively and should be visible to the mother. The more the mother sees the board, the stronger will be the neural pathways that are created.

A sample vision board is shared here which can be used as a reference for making one for your dream baby.

Playing and Replaying the Mental Movie

The strength of the neural pathway increases exponentially if we engage all the five senses in the process and combine it with very high emotions as if we were watching a movie. By engaging in the mental activity of visualization and creating a mental movie of the child we want, the pathways become strongly imprinted into the subconscious mind. Dear mothers, make it a rule that every morning, immediately after you wake up, and every night before you go to sleep, you run this mental movie in your mind as these are times when the subconscious mind is fully alert and active. Do not forget to make the mental movie emotional and sensory.

Forming a Habit

It is proven by scientific research that a consistent, repetitive practice in affirmations and visualizations strengthen the neural pathways and gets it into an auto-pilot mode.[4] Thus, through consistent affirmation and visualization, a mother can internalize a habit and create neural pathways to create the image of the child of her dreams in the subconscious mind. Now, to strengthen these neural pathways, the mother needs to take action by practising the skills that she has been envisioning, e.g., singing, art, dramatics, calculations, etc., and it will help the baby absorb the traits that she has envisioned for it. However, it should be noted that only those skills suitable to pregnancy conditions should be practised.

Moreover, it is important to note that in the entire process the mother should act like a true *karmayogi* and work without any expectation of results. As Lord Krishna teaches us in the Bhagvad Gita:[5]

कर्मण्येवाधिकारस्ते मा फलेषु कदाचन ।
मा कर्मफलहेतुर्भूर्मा ते संगोऽस्त्वकर्मणि॥

(Just stay focussed on your action plan but do not get deterred by the expectation of results.)

The expectation of the desired results is the root cause of anxiety in our mind which acts contrary to the functioning of the subconscious mind. So, dear mothers, refrain from getting anxious or doubting the results. Just have complete trust in the power of your mind. Do what you are supposed to do with full faith, determination and dedication, and surrender the rest at his holy feet.

Get Set Go!

While there are at least 3,50,000 babies being born on the planet every day, each one is undeniably special. Yet, only a select few tap into the divine realm, embodying the essence of pure potential and greatness. For your child to be among these chosen souls, it is vital that they are manifested from your deepest desires and intentions.

Your thoughts, emotions and intentions are not merely personal; they transcend to shape the very fabric of your child's prenatal experiences. By consciously monitoring your inner world—your thoughts, beliefs and emotions—through the right tools and interventions, you create a harmonious sanctuary within, one that resonates with the purity and brilliance you wish to instill in your child.

So, dear mother, with full confidence, trust and surrender, take charge of your subconscious mind. Immerse yourself in this beautiful journey of manifestation, birthing your dream baby—your little genius.

i. Tracker Sheet for Developing Mental Well-Being

Set a minimum of three affirmations in the following areas:
Physcial
Intellectual
Emotional
Spritual
Self

ii. **Make a vision board.**
iii. **Create a mental movie of your child using emotions and the five senses.**

5

Ensuring Emotional Well-Being

'Only a happy mother can give birth to a happy baby.'

'I love the way you are so dedicated to your pregnancy, Deepali, but you also have to remember to take care of yourself.'

Deepali was 26 weeks into her pregnancy, and she was ecstatic. Listening to her mother's concern made her smile as she tried to push the anxiety away. Seven years into her marriage, she was carrying her first child after two soul-wrenching miscarriages. Her entire family—maternal and paternal—had been on guard from the moment they had found that she was pregnant. She, being spiritual by nature, left no stone unturned in making sure her baby was safe within her. Two-and-a-half months more, and she would be ready to hold her baby in her arms.

'I know, Mumma, and trust me, I have been taking care of myself. The baby shower was tiring, that's all.'

'It was tiring but I think you need to get a sonography done. I will only go back to Mumbai when I know that you and the little one are doing fine,' her mother said. Deepali smiled, 'Okay, let me book an appointment then.'

'I have already take care of that. We have to be there in an hour,' her mother said, one step ahead of her.

'I just hope I can be half a mother as you are,' she said. Deepali held her belly fondly.

They left for the hospital. Fifteen minutes into the examination, Deepali was told that the amniotic fluid level was below the acceptable mark and thus the baby's growth had slowed. This meant that if the fluid level went lower, the baby would need to be delivered immediately. Deepali did not get alarmed by this news because she was very aware what emotional turmoil it would bring to her baby.

'What should I do to make this right, doctor?' she asked as calmly as she could.

'You need to stay hydrated and relaxed. I need to keep you under observation and would recommend that you come in tomorrow.' Mother and daughter looked at each other as the doctor waited for them to acknowledge what she had said.

'Alright. We will do that. Thank you. But there is nothing to worry at the moment, right?' her mother asked.

'It will be all right, ma'am. Just don't stress over it. Drink plenty of water and rest. I will see you tomorrow.'

They left for home and Deepali's mother cancelled her flight. Deepali slept through the night. She slept deeply after chanting the Hanuman Chalisa—it had helped her stay calm. It was 5.00 a.m. and she was up and meditating. She was chanting the mantras when she realized her phone was vibrating. Her father's face flashed across the phone screen. Going against her rule of not pausing between meditations, she followed her instinct and answered the call.

'Where are you?' came her father's voice from the other end. He sounded tense and worried.

'I am at home, papa. What happened?' She broke her rule of talking before completing her meditation, after listening to the fear in her father's voice. 'I need you to pack and leave, right now. Ask your family members to leave as well. But you need to leave now!' There was an urgency in his voice that left Deepali unsettled.

'Okay. I will leave right now,' she said.

She stood, packed her things and walked out of her room. She knocked on the door of her sister-in-law and mother-in-law. She told them about her father's call and asked them to leave as well. She was aware that no one would worry her by relaying stressful news. She also knew that becoming anxious was bad for the baby. Deepali left instantly to a friend's place and switched off the mental exertion in her head.

'Are you at Surbhi's place?' her mother asked on the phone.
'Yes.'

'Okay. We will go to the hospital by 10. Will you be ready by then? I will come and pick you up,' said her mother. 'There is a strike at the factory. In case things go out of hand, I need you to be safe and away from a stressful environment,' her mother replied.

'I know there is more to it. As long as everyone is safe, I am going to focus on this,' Deepali said, placing a protective hand over her womb.

She and her mother arrived at the hospital. The sonography revealed that the fluid level was still low and she was asked to get admitted so that she could be closely monitored.

The next week was spent in the hospital. She had turned off the phone and her mother did not let her watch the news. She was busy chanting her Durga Kavach along with her regular meditations and following the doctor's instructions. Both Deepali and her baby stayed absolutely calm and composed, in a complete state of bliss oblivious to the chaos outside.

The next week, the doctor seemed puzzled after looking at her sonography results.

'What is it, doctor?' her mother asked.

'This is unreal. I haven't seen something like this happen ever,' said the doctor.

'Is everything okay?' they asked in unison.

'Yes! More than okay! The amniotic fluid level has actually increased and the baby's growth has started improving. I thought we would be operating on you tonight and here,' said the doctor pointing at the monitor in a rather dramatic manner, 'Deepali, whatever it is that you are doing is just right. Continue it and we shall not have to worry about you or the baby at all. At today's development, the baby is quite out of danger!'

The simple declaration filled their hearts with wonder and gratefulness. 'Thank God,' they said and laughed at the intensity of their words.

This is a real-life example of a mother who decided that nothing was more important to her than the baby residing in her. She had valid reasons to panic and become anxious, but she decided to do otherwise.

Prenatal maternal stress is a form of stress that the pregnant mother experiences but should be avoided by her under all circumstances. From the shooting up of blood pressure levels to physical damage to the development of the baby, a lot can happen that can cause losses we don't want to even think about. Prenatal stress can be *chronic* (linked to ongoing events in a woman's life) or *acute* (linked to a sudden change in a woman's daily routine or environment).

Stress in Pregnancy International Research Alliance (SPIRAL) has divided prenatal stress into two components: objective stress and subjective stress.

- Objective Stress refers to the external factors or events that typically cause stress. These can include things like work deadlines, financial pressures, relationship conflicts or health problems. Objective stressors are measurable and observable by others, regardless of how different individuals may subjectively respond to them.
- Subjective Stress refers to an individual's personal experience and perception of stress. It's how someone feels and reacts to stressors based on their thoughts, emotions, and interpretations of events or situations.

So, objective stress is the stress that exists in the environment and subjective stress is how it is being internalized. It is important to note that there is no direct correlation between the two stresses as it totally depends on the stress-bearing capacity of the mother.

Deepali had a very high level of objective stress but with her wisdom she reduced the subjective stress to a bare minimum level and thus controlled any negativity from being passed on to her child. However, below is another real-life example where the objective stress was not high, but the expectant mother was too naïve and created a high level of subjective stress, which may have been the cause of her premature delivery.

We now know that the mind is a powerful tool and that emotions can be overpowering. But Sanaya was oblivious that her mind was capable of creating such chaos in her life. Sanaya married into a kind-hearted family and believed in enjoying life to its fullest. She married young, and was soon welcoming a new life into the family! She (and everyone around her) was thrilled. They held festivities in her honour and she spent the initial months of her pregnancy with a lot of adoration and charm. Once the initial phase of the first trimester was over, the agony and nausea came to an end. From her second trimester, she went out, had fun, ate whatever she wanted, and lived a happy life, ready to welcome her newborn.

It was the seventh month and, as traditional customs prevailed in her family, she was pampered with a ceremony called Godh Bharai. Sanaya enjoyed the celebrations and was exhausted by the end of the day. As she got home, she saw the chaos of the things that had been strewn about because of the preparations. In the process of getting things back in order, she asked her staff to give a helping hand. However, they refused and said, 'We will do this tomorrow.'

Sanaya was agitated and her hormones were acting up. She was furious and insisted that they do as they were told. The whole process got her highly agitated and she ended up heading into her room, angry and with an elevated heartbeat. While the matter was trivial, it agonized her, and since she had acted contrary to her nature, she felt a lot of anger and self-remorse. That night, she simmered in her own anger. The following morning, Sanaya woke up with a severe burning sensation in her abdomen. The pain was intense and she felt dizzy like never before.

Her family rushed her to the hospital. They found that her blood pressure was extremely high, and that this had resulted in the foetus having low oxygen supply. Sanaya would have to deliver the baby that day itself, or her life would be in danger, too. She ended up having a surgery and the baby was delivered, all of 800 grams. He was immediately taken to the NICU. The journey was full of guilt and remorse, and the family struggled to keep faith and persevere. The child finally beat the odds and developed. Soon, he was fine and discharged into the arms of his mother, who then dedicated every living moment towards caring for him.

Sanaya never thought that a small outburst could almost cost her the life of her son and also endanger her own. It was a life lesson that she took to heart.

Time flew by and soon, the boy was going to turn five. It was then that Sanaya realized that she was expecting once again. The past ordeals screamed through her mind, and she promised herself that this time she would be highly devoted to bringing her child safely into the world. She researched the norms of Garbha Sanskar and lived by them. She maintained a low-salt to no-salt diet to ensure that her blood pressure was under control at all times. She would chant mantras, exercise, eat right and eat only home-cooked meals, and also woke up and slept according to a proper timetable.

Once again, when she was two weeks into her seventh month, the memories of the last pregnancy rekindled and caught her off guard, making her take extra efforts to avoid feeling fear. However, one day, she ended up having a tiff with her staff once again. This time it was another person, another small matter. Sanaya was determined that she would not react and meditated towards not responding. She stayed silent and closed herself in her room. She stewed, trying to not think about it but, in the process, ended up storing all the agony inside her. As fate would have it, her blood pressure shot up once again and this time, the doctor said that, no matter what, they had to remove the placenta, and that meant delivering the baby immediately.

Sanaya was shattered, all her hard work and perseverance was acting against her. Yet, she was not willing to give up. Just then, the doctors informed her about the option of a steroid injection that could enhance the baby's development, brain functioning and lungs protection, but these injections had to be given in two doses and needed a gap of 12–24 hours between each dose and that they could only be administered when the blood pressure of the mother was normal. But such a timeline could be dangerous for Sanaya.

Sanaya's family, especially her mother-in-law, sat by her side and tried calming her down. Kind words, prayers and a warm heart helped her relieve Sanaya's anxiety and brought her blood pressure level down. The steroid injection was given and everyone waited with bated breath. Every hour was a prayer and a lifetime. After 15 hours, the doctors felt it was safe to administer the second dose of the injection to help the baby strengthen and survive a premature delivery.

However, the following morning, Sanaya's heart rate was high, and her blood pressure had shot up to 100 again, and this set off alarm bells. She was taken to the operation theatre but then, through the grace of God, the two injections had already worked and the baby had enough time to strengthen its lungs and brain. She was born and Sanaya was out of danger. The baby was taken to the NICU for one-and-a-half months until she was all right. Sanaya broke down but held on to her crippled yet strong faith. She took care of her daughter, and her son watched and cared for them in his own six-year-old way. He made sure that his sister was not disturbed and his mother was not troubled.

The child in the womb has nothing to do with objective stress. No matter how stressful the situation (objective stress), the foetus only gets affected when the mother internalizes this stress (subjective stress).

Effect of Prenatal Stress on the Foetus

Stress levels are directly associated with negative consequences in foetal and infant development. Understanding how prenatal maternal stress is transmitted to the foetus requires some understanding of the human stress response system.

When a person is exposed to an event that is perceived as stressful, the brain triggers a cascade of reactions that ultimately leads to the release of stress hormones such as cortisol. These stress hormones help prepare the individual to cope with the stressful situation.

During pregnancy, women possess naturally elevated levels of cortisol, which, under stressful conditions, can reach abnormally high levels. However, it has been demonstrated that in pregnant women, these hormones can pass from the mother to foetus via the placenta. This is supported by studies that have found that high maternal cortisol levels are often mirrored with high foetal cortisol levels, which can then have negative consequences to the developing foetus and might also prove fatal.[1] Moreover, it has been demonstrated that in utero exposure to high levels of cortisol also affect postnatal development. Research has proved that when the foetus experiences very high-level stress, any growth activity of the foetus stops for a considerable time.[2]

Susceptibility and the Solution

In pregnancy, timing is everything. In fact, the baby develops every moment from conception to delivery at an enormous rate and the expectant mother needs to adapt to the massive changes that are happening in her body. The first trimester is highly sensitive because that is when the foetus is actually settling down and getting implanted in the womb, leading to a lot of physical and emotional upheaval experienced by the expectant mother. The second trimester is marked by a massive growth phase where the development of the brain, the senses and all the internal organs takes place. The final trimester is where the foetus actually takes the shape of a complete baby that is ready to come out of the womb and independently experience the world. The whole process of preparing herself for delivery is accompanied by numerous physical, mental and emotional challenges that the mother would have to undergo. Thus, every stage of pregnancy is marked by its own needs that require a lot of emotional strength and for which the expectant mother should be completely prepared for.

Although every day of the pregnancy is important and care needs to be taken at all times, doctors often highlight two periods as the most crucial, and stress at all levels must be eradicated around the mother during that time.

- At week 10, the embryo becomes a foetus and begins to move. The vital organs now have a solid foundation. During this time, the brain will produce almost 250,000 new neurons every minute. This is called neurogenesis. Stress during this time can hinder or completely disrupt foetal growth.

- During weeks 24 to 30, the nerve cell connections occur. Thus, this time is vital and there should be no stress around the mother. Guided by chemical signals, the nerve processes seek out their target and establish contact and the communication between neurons begin. A formation of synapses (a point of contact between neurons to pass information from one to another) between the neurons in the nervous system occurs. This is called synaptogenesis. At birth, there is an excess of nerve connections, and those that are not used degenerate.

Exposure to extreme stress during these critical periods of pregnancy influences the developing structures of the foetus and, therefore, determine the physical, cognitive or behavioural outcome. Such children may show difficulties while paying attention and may possess aggressive attitudes. In addition, they may show an increased risk for other mental health disorders such as autism and depression. Recent research findings have demonstrated that obstetrical complications, low birth weight and delayed physical development may all be influenced by prenatal maternal stress.[3]

Despite being subjected to it, the human mind has the potential to distance itself from the stress if it wishes to. As we have already discussed, subjective stress refers to an individual's perception of stress and the way they interpret and respond to various challenges, pressures or demands in life. However, if the expectant mother meditates on the fact that she will not be moved by stress or such situations, the game is already won. It is possible for an expecting mother to have high objective stress but low subjective distress. This means that there is a lot of external stress but the expectant mother does not internalize it. Even if there is a lot of stress in the environment, as long as the mother does not internalize the stress, it does not get passed on to the baby and the baby continues to stay in a state of bliss. On the other hand, if the mother starts reacting to even the slightest of pressures, then the baby absorbs it instantly and becomes stressed. So it barely matters whether stress is present or not, what is important is how the mother feels and responds to the whole situation. It should be noted that the baby in the womb feels exactly what the mother is feeling. We saw how Deepali removed herself from the situation and simply focussed on her child. She was well aware of what could happen if she let the situation overpower her. Thus, she chose to step away, emotionally, mentally and physically, until the situation was under control. On the other hand, Sanaya absorbed stress far more than what was present; the baby suffered. So, the only emotion that the expectant mother should absorb is that of bliss. She should not have a choice. Thus, we can understand that the exposure of an expectant mother to acute stressful situations can be reduced by creating a relaxing environment or by simply stepping away from the situation entirely. The goal of these interventions is to remove the anxiety and provide a sense of control.

Emotional Well-Being: It Is All about Making a Choice

Physically, the baby is connected to the mother through the umbilical cord, but they are emotionally and mentally connected in more ways than you can imagine. The minds of the mother and baby are constantly synchronized. That means, the mother and the baby go through the same emotions and have the same thoughts. Thus, the only emotions that the mother should ideally have are love, bliss and happiness. The idea is not to run away from our emotions or thoughts, but to acknowledge them and handle them constructively.

If people keep a constant check on their thoughts and emotions, they can avert mental and emotional issues way before they affect them at a physical level. The key to good health is, after all, bliss. As discussed earlier, staying in a state of bliss is a choice and the expectant mother should continuously try to achieve this state of mind. In the best interest of her baby, any state other than a positive one is not ideal. As the mother puts in her best efforts, it is paramount that those around her—her spouse, parents and relatives—ensure that they maintain a peaceful environment. As we saw in Deepali's story, her family's prompt support and care enabled her to sail through the crisis safely and efficiently.

This is because, when one is blissful and happy, they secrete hormones such as dopamine, oxytocin, serotonin and endorphins (also called the happiness DOSE hormones), the daily dose of which will keep all our diseases at bay. The placebo effect works because any illness can be easily cured if we simply believe that we will get better. Emotional well-being is cultivated through behavioural adaptations and lifestyle choices. The following are some of the ways that can help mothers experience bliss and strengthen their emotional well-being.

- A safe and loving family environment: The responsibility of the child is not just of the mother but also of the entire family, and it is important that the entire family ensures a loving environment for the mother and child. The family should know that they are sowing seeds that will reap fruits for generations to come. The mother faces a lot of physical, mental and emotional challenges, and with her hormones fluctuating uncontrollably, she needs a lot of support and comfort from her family and especially her husband. It is of utmost importance that her family pays attention to her emotional well-being, so that she can learn to let go of negative emotions and live happily.

Moreover, the love given to the mother is felt by the baby and this helps it create strong bonds with the family members even before they are able to hold the baby in reality.

Acharya Caraka has very clearly explained the importance of a loving family environment in the following verse.[4]

विमानने हास्य दृश्यते विनाशो विकृतिर्वा ।
समानयोगक्षेमा हि तदा भवति गर्भेण केषुचिदर्थेषु माता।
तस्मात् प्रियहिताभ्यां गर्भिणीं विशेषेणोपचरन्ति कुशला: ॥ 15 ॥

When a pregnant woman experiences happiness, fear or anxiety, the effects of those emotions are directly felt by the foetus. Therefore, wise and caring individuals should treat pregnant women with special care and attention, ensuring their well-being and happiness; otherwise it will have a detrimental effect on the growth of the foetus.

According to psychiatrist Dr Thomas Verny, the role of the husband is the most important as, during this stage, the bond that he feels and shares with his wife and the child in womb has a deep, long-lasting impact on the child. It is important for him to give quality time by talking to the baby and expressing his love, act like a strong support by ensuring his availability and being patient enough to handle the insecurities and emotional fluctuations that his wife is undergoing.

- Unconditional love: The child should grow in a healthy and loving environment even when it is in the womb of the mother. However, the greatest challenge is to ensure that a permanent loving environment is made available to the child, and this is something that might not be practically feasible. It is tough to control and regulate the emotions of the world towards oneself or the child. It is difficult to be in one state of emotion at all times because, after all, we are living a life and that has its ups and downs. But then, if you train your mind in a way that nothing affects your inner peace, happiness or calm, you have already achieved a state of mind which is unaffected by day-to-day situations. The child experiences all the emotions through its mother; if the mother can filter her emotions and ensure that only the loving emotions are being sent to the baby in the womb, then the child remains very healthy, calm and peaceful.

  Everyone has taken birth to fulfil their own purpose, and by judging them, you are questioning that and interfering in their karmic cycle. Thus, the advice for the expectant mother is to not judge, compare or complain, and focus only on her ability to determine the good in the situation. When you start appreciating everyone as they are, and do not pressure them with expectations of who you want them to become, then everything gets resolved.

- Forgive and forget: The greatest problem in any relationship is that people are unable to forgive and, even when they do, they are unable to forget. This is because forgiveness has happened only superficially and not from within their heart. Real forgiveness comes when you delete the sour emotions attached with the incident. Both the aspects are equally important—seeking forgiveness, as well as giving forgiveness. By doing this simple gesture, the mother can resolve the karmic baggage of the child in the womb itself. So, it is suggested that the expectant mother does a forgiveness meditation just before she sleeps so that any karmic transaction that happens during the course of the day gets resolved.

Three-Step Forgiveness Meditation

1. Focus on all those you might have hurt consciously or unconsciously and seek forgiveness.
2. Focus on all those who might have hurt you consciously or unconsciously and forgive them.
3. Focus on the self and seek forgiveness from the self.

- Gratitude: It is important for us to possess an attitude of gratitude directed at everything and everyone. Life is a circle and what you give will come back to you multifold. Therefore, always be grateful and accept whatever someone has to offer to you with sincere and deepest gratitude. When an expectant mother sincerely does a gratitude exercise in the morning, she fills her womb with positive energy. The child will be in the spirit of thanksgiving every moment and will create an energy that is loved and supported by the whole world.

Morning Gratitude Meditation

1. Thank God for everything that you have and desire.
2. Thank your soul for what you truly are.
3. Thank your body for making everything possible in this mortal world.
4. Thank your parents, who were your first teachers.
5. Thank your Guru for giving your consciousness a rebirth.
6. Thank your family and friends for supporting you through thick and thin.
7. Thank your competitors and critics for getting the best out of you.
8. Thank your experiences for making you what you are today.
9. Finally, thank the baby in your womb for choosing you as its mother.

Every morning start your day with positivity by doing a Gratitude Meditation by THANKING from the core of your heart.

- Bond with the child through Garbha Samvad: Garbha Samvad refers to communicating with the foetus through various means such as music, chanting, reading and talking. This practice is believed to have positive effects on the development of the foetus and create an everlasting bond between the parent and the unborn child.

Of all the sound information that impacts a baby during pregnancy, the mother's voice stands out above all others. During this time, the baby is in the uterus, and the mother's voice reaches it both as ambient sound through the abdomen and internally through the vibration of vocal chords. As these vibrations are felt by the little one, the mother–child bond strengthens.

When you talk to the baby in your womb, it can feel the positive vibrations that are radiated, and it starts responding to these. While you are talking to your child, use the sense of touch by warmly holding your womb; love it, feel it, just as you would if the child was in your arms. So, when you want to have a special time with your baby, caress your belly, sing a song, read aloud, say 'good morning', tell them what you observe in the world, and all this will create a strong bond even before birth.

You can also read scriptures such as the Bhagvad Gita or those you believe in, and also narrate to the child stories about great people. Listening to these can create the desired neural pathways, and the desired qualities will shine upon the child. You should tell the baby about the strengths of every family member and how much it is being loved by them. This will help create a loving bond between the baby and the family members in the womb itself, much before they are born.

In fact, it is important for the father also to spend some time doing Garbha Samvad with the baby as that will help the baby recognize the voice of the father and develop a strong bond with him. Furthermore, on a daily basis, share all the affirmations that you have created for your child, explain the vision board that you have made, and let them know about the nine intelligences and the four quotients and how well they are performing on that. This will make the child feel loved and wanted and also strengthen the brain by creating the desired neuropathways.

- Listen to Garbha Sanskar music: Music is a language that can touch the soul, and a repetitive, rhythmic pattern of music has a calming effect on both the mother and the child. It can help relax the brain and take it into the alpha mode, where the subconscious mind is highly activated and becomes very receptive towards affirmations. Music has amazing healing capabilities and helps soothe emotions, de-stress, relax and uplift mood. Hence, the day you get to know about the good news of your pregnancy is the best day to start listening to music. Good hormones rush through your placenta and make the baby happy, even though it will take a while to develop its listening skills. It is proven that music has a role in the brain development of the foetus as it facilitates neuron connections in the brain.[5]

  In fact, a peaceful melody reduces the chances of a low birthweight, a lower head circumference and a preterm birth. It also helps maintain the blood pressure in women with pre-eclampsia or pregnancy-induced hypertension.[6] However, one should avoid loud and aggressive music like rock and metal, as prolonged exposure to higher frequencies can potentially cause hearing loss and induce stress.

  Most of the mantras, when chanted rhythmically or even when the mother keeps listening to these continuously, provide a lot of positive energy to her as well as the baby in the womb. Listening to auspicious chants and peaceful music, even if it is purely instrumental, can bring peace and enhance the concentration abilities of the child, all while supporting its holistic growth.

  Scientists at the Institute Marques in Spain played

different kinds of music to babies in the womb and found that foetuses prefer classical music, with Bach and Beethoven triggering much happier responses than any contemporary music.[7] According to Girija Devi, an eminent personality in Indian classical music, 'Ragas like *Malkauns, Shaant, Bageshwari, Yaman* and *Bhairav* are also considered to be very good for a child's growth because they have a very soothing effect on the mother.' Rhythm in Indian classical music excites the various cognitive areas of the brain and stimulates the motor cortex part, thereby facilitating new neural connections.[8]

A study conducted by European scholars in 2013 found that newborns could remember lullabies that were played to them in the womb.[9] Thus, it has been found that the music that is played continuously to the child remains in its memory after birth. It also acts as a wonderful tool for the mother, even after delivery, to soothe the baby when it is cranky and unsettled.

- Engage in creative activities: The more the expectant mother engages in creative activities, the stronger the functioning of the brain becomes, and this fosters positive emotional health for the baby. It also helps the child in developing and honing many creative traits. Thus, if the mother is fond of painting, music, writing, cooking or any other creative activity, she will inevitably pass these interests to the child. On the other hand, if the mother does not have any such interests, but wishes that her child has such creative abilities and spirit, she can indulge in the activities herself with interest and sincerity throughout her pregnancy. It is observed that the child will inherit those traits and interests as well.

When a person indulges in activities that interest them, they often become passionate about the same, which results in a state of heightened happiness and bliss. Doing what one's heart desires creates a sense of self-actualization and awareness and gives almost meditative results. Therefore, igniting a creative spirit in oneself will not just make the child creative but also enhance the state of bliss and happiness within the child and the mother.

Summing It Up

For a mother to be tested again and again on her valour, to be pushed towards the edge and yet to come back with strength that only she knew she had, is what motherhood is all about. It is hard to even imagine, but when a woman feels the existence of life within her, she gives her all to bring that life into her arms. The struggle and emotional upheaval within her throughout the nine months are mitigated by her love for and devotion to her child. This is the ideal motherhood and the undying spirit to nurture its foundation.

When we speak of distress, just think what Maa Devaki must have gone through. A mother who watches her newborn children being thrown to death by the hands of her own brother! The eighth child was none other than Lord Krishna, an incarnation of Lord Vishnu. It is perhaps the ultimate test of the mother's patience, perseverance and faith that she could have had in herself and in the existence of justice by the Almighty. It is only when one is faced with the most extreme circumstances can one begin valuing the blessings that they receive. It is only after going through a zillion hardships that a diamond comes into existence.

As we learn from Maa Devaki, Maa Sita and Maa Shakuntala, one must make sure that the expectant mother is happy from inside as well as outside, and this can be possible only when she mentally resolves to be in a state of bliss, come what may. And for that she should care for her baby from the beginning and, in turn, care for herself. Yes, the fact that the people around her must be caring as well would be an added advantage, but if that is not the case, a mother is powerful enough to treat herself and her baby with all the love, tenderness and care that she can bestow. It's finally her own choice.

Dear mothers, remember that only a happy mother can give birth to a happy baby. So exercise only that choice that keeps you in a permanent state of bliss and helps you to manifest your precious, little blessing—your dream baby!

Tracker Sheet for Ensuring Emotional Well-Being

	Present Rating Where you are (on a scale of 10)	**Desired Rating** Where you want to go (on a scale of 10)	**Action Monitor** (steps taken to achieve it)
Loving Family Environment			
Unconditional Love			
Forgiveness			
Gratitude			
Garbha Samvad			
Garbha Sanskar Music			
Creative Activities			

Monthly Check on Stress Levels

	Present Rating Where you are (on a scale of 10)	**Desired Rating** Where you want to go (on a scale of 10)	**Action Monitor** (steps taken to achieve it)
Objective Stress			
Subjective Stress			

6

Imbibing Spiritual Well-Being

'Only the best womb can attract the best soul.'

Diti and Aditi, the daughters of King Daksh Prajapati, were married to Rishi Kashyap, who was one of the Saptarishis. Aditi became the mother of the Devatas, like Surya (the eldest, also named 'Aditya' after his mother), Indra and Vaman. On the other hand, Diti gave birth to the Asuras, like Hiranyakashipu, Arunasara, Holika, to name a few. Despite the fact that the environment and the genetic composition was the same, they gave birth to two different clans—one bore the Devatas and the other the Asuras. One might think that their environment or family background played a vital role, but in this case, both the factors were the same as they were sisters and married to the same man. Yet, they bore children who were poles apart. Aditi was the mother of the Devatas and was known to possess qualities of the divine. She was considered to be a kind, warm-hearted and compassionate soul. Meanwhile, Diti was known to be cruel, both to her husband and her sister. She was the bitter enemy of her sister's sons and was all about getting her sons, the Asuras, in power.

If a mother wants to gift her child a life that is smooth and not obstructed with too many obstacles and roadblocks, then she should focus on spiritual well-being as it is the fulcrum around which all revolves. When the expectant mother is spiritually elevated, her energies vibrate at a very high frequency. She is in a position to make the right choices and attract powerful, divine energies from the universe, which is home to both negative and positive energies. We attract those energies we emit. Despite the fact that both Diti and Aditi were carrying babies from the same man, Diti emitted and attracted the impure energies while Aditi remained connected with the divine powers, thereby giving birth to Asuras and Devatas, respectively. Hence, it is said that everything that you materialize is a function of your consciousness. Here, in this case, the individual consciousness of the two sisters overpowered everything else.

So, my dear mothers, have you ever checked where your consciousness is going? Do you really know who you are? Have you ever focussed upon the powers that you possess? Truly speaking, as Dr Avdhoot Shivanand always says, we are all delivered but never truly installed. My dear mothers, it is time to identify your real self—read your manual, install your applications, and manifest the child of your dreams in the womb.

We know that the human body is far more supreme and divine than what we give it credit for. We are only aware of our physical body which is made up of complex organs that perform complex tasks in the simplest of ways, such that we are not even aware of what each and every cell in our body is working on. We do know about the physical or tangible aspects of the human body but there are subtle energy patterns that we are totally oblivious of. The human body is connected with the universe and can understand and respond to these subtle energy forces. It has the powers to manifest, create and expand things beyond our imagination.

Thus, it is important to first understand the spiritual realm of the human existence and how to ignite the consciousness to a level where we can become spiritually active and benefit by engaging in spiritual practices. When we start understanding and connecting with the subtle energy patterns, we learn the art of materialization. We attract the right frequencies in the universe, connect with them and finally materialize what we desire. We all know about Einstein's law of mass and energy where he proved that the sum total of mass and energy are fixed, and that they can be converted from one form to the other using the formula $E=MC^2$. The whole universe contains both gross or tangible bodies as well as the subtle energy forms, and both are interchangeable. We believe in gross or tangible forms as they have mass and can be perceived by our five senses, but we don't even know the existence of all the subtle powers that remain as energy, away from our sensory perceptions. But the power of subtle entities is much higher than that of the tangible ones and we actually need to tap into that power.

I Am Not This Body, I Am a Soul

The image that you admire in the mirror whenever you get an opportunity is your body. But is your existence limited to the image that you see in the mirror? The image in the mirror is one that you can touch, feel and perceive through your five senses and is actually your physical body. As this is the only body that is perceived by our senses, we spend our entire lives serving it and, effectively, become slaves to its desires.

We are not this body but the soul. The body is transient, but the soul is permanent. The body is just a covering within which the soul resides. Just like we keep changing our clothes every day, similarly our bodies change in every lifetime. The child in your womb is actually a soul who has chosen you as its mother to get incarnated as a human to discharge all its purposes and responsibilities.

It is very important for you to know that it is not you who has chosen your child, but the other way around. When the souls in the astral world decide to reincarnate as humans, they decide on their life script—agendas, purposes, learnings and experiences, and for that they need a family and parents; they need a mother who can support them through their life. Thus, they choose a womb whose vibrations match the frequencies they are vibrating at. So, dear mother, if you want to have the best child, then you need to become the best mother. Remember: only the best womb can attract the best soul.

Nandini was 32. She had been married for seven years and was finally pregnant after trying for three years. Her happiness knew no bounds. It was nothing short of a miracle.

Her doctor had advised complete bed rest. This was a great challenge for her. As a woman who was always keen on being on her feet, ticking off errands and working as a human resource head for her husband's business, she was all about keeping busy.

Challenges were what gave her an adrenaline rush and motivated her to push herself to the limits. No, she wouldn't sit idle, and was committed to make the most of this time.

Nandini's family members were ardent worshippers of Lord Shiva, and so, they decided to have Rudrabhishek performed every single day at dawn and in the afternoon for the entirety of the nine months. She was blessed to have a family that was so considerate and followed the divine path. Nandini wanted to give birth to a child that had all the qualities of Lord Shiva— she wanted him to be someone who was intelligent, beautiful, compassionate, and knew the value of human life.

Thus it began. Eleven brahmin pandits would religiously begin the Rudrabhishek every single day. Nandini's room was adjacent to the temple within her home, and she would listen to the mantra chanting, doing her bit by meditating through it all. Yes, she had the opportunity to talk to friends or binge-watch television, but she chose to adopt the practices of Garbha Sanskar and invoke the blessings of Lord Shiva for her child.

Months passed, and the day of the delivery arrived. Nishan was born. Looking at the beautiful boy, Nandini and her family were completely in bliss and felt grateful to Lord Mahadev. They soon decided to continue the Rudrabhishek every day and continued their journey towards the spiritual realm.

Nandini would give Nishan to the pandit-ji every morning. He would keep the baby on his lap while performing the Rudrabhishek and would make Nishan touch the shringhee *that was used to offer the milk to the Lord.*

As months passed, Nishan would sit next to the pandit-ji and hold the shringhee with which he would offer the milk and perform the Rudrabhishek. Suddenly, the pandit-ji realized that Nishan would mumble something along with him while the Rudrabhishek was going on. The pandit-ji moved in closer to listen to what he was saying and was surprised to hear that Nishan was chanting the mantras.

This was only the first of many miracles. As Nishan grew older, he developed a photographic as well as an echoic memory. He only had to listen to a Sanskrit verse once, and would be able to recall the chant as if he had always known it. At school, he excelled in every subject and developed a general knowledge that could only be described as prodigious.

Nishan is only ten years old now and many applaud his mental abilities. Only time will tell how Nishan will add to the glory of the world in the coming years! For now, it is his family and friends that are always in awe of him and await his latest feats.

One important aspect that needs to be highlighted here is that though the whole process elevated Nandini's consciousness and increased her spiritual powers, she didn't learn a single shloka. Quite similar to the Mahabharata where Maa Subhadra did not learn the technique to enter the chakravyuh but Abhimanyu in her womb mastered the art. So, dear mother, don't be disappointed if you do not learn the mantras and the shlokas or are unable to master any particular skill that you are trying out. The real learner is the little baby in the womb who is doing its job just perfectly.

Thus, what Nandini achieved was simply miraculous. Nishan had come in her womb as a soul with his set of karmas. But with her commitment, dedication, positivity and spiritual practices, she was able to ignite and dissolve his karmas to a great extent.

Theory of Karmas

Karmas are the consequences of all the actions of a person in their present and past lives, and the cascading chain of cause and effect because of these actions. Whatever we are suffering today is because of the karmas that we have accumulated over our lifetimes. Our present is a result of our past karmas, and our futures will be created in accordance with our present karmas. It is because of these karmas that we face the roadblocks that deter us from achieving our goals and attaining success. So, if a mother wants to reduce the sufferings, obstacles and blockages in the path of her child's life, she should focus on reducing the karmic baggage.

The one and only time when you can achieve the mitigation of karmas for your child is when the child is still in your womb. At this stage, the mother and the child are merged. So the mother, with the help of positive intent and action, can work upon her own karmic load as well as that of the child. But the moment the baby is born, they become an individual entity. So dear mother, without wasting a single moment, get started on your divine journey of reducing the karmic baggage of your child, and the results that you will achieve shall be great.

In order to dissolve the karmic baggage of the child, let us add to our understanding of spiritual development by knowing the *Panchbhootas*, the *nadi* network, the three main nadis, the seven chakras, the power of mantras and the infinite possibilities that they are all capable of.

The Panchbhootas or the Five Elements

Our physical body is made up of five elements: earth, water, fire, air and ether. Acharya Sushruta has very beautifully explained the importance of the five elements (panchbhootas) in the growth and nourishment of the foetus, in the following shloka:[1]

तं चेतनावस्थितं वायुर्विभजति, तेज एवं पचति, आप:
क्लेदयन्ति, पृथिवी संहन्ति, आकाशं विवर्धयति।

The following table clarifies the role of each element in the growth of the foetus, the defects that may arise due to misbalancing of the five elements, and the relationship of each element with the sense organs and the body parts, as explained by Acharya Sushruta.

**Table 6.1
Elements and Their Effects**

Element	Role of Elements	Imbalance of Elements	Senses and Body Parts
Earth (*Prithvi*)	Gives stability and density to the physical body and contributes to its structure.	Causes instability, which could result in miscarriage, underdevelopment of the foetus, brittle bones or short stature.	Sense of smell, nose, general physical structure.
Water (*Jal*)	Imparts moisture and lubrication to the organs, binds them together and helps to nourish the unborn child.	Results in inadequate nourishment of the foetus, decreased amniotic fluid and hydrocephalus (excess water in the cranium of the foetus).	Sense of taste, tongue, fatty tissue, phlegm, muscle, semen.

Fire (Agni)	Provides the necessary energy for the development of the foetal organs and is responsible for the various essential transformations taking place.	Leads to skin defects, allergies, digestive disorders and various eye problems.	Sense of vision, eyes, *jatharagni* (digestive fire).
Air (*Vayu*)	Responsible for all divisions occurring in the foetus, right from the first division of the cells, to the division of all body parts and organs.	Unnatural cell division, leading to various anomalies, such as the growth of extra fingers, the absence of an anal aperture, fused openings of bladder and rectum, etc.	Sense of touch, skin.
Ether (*Akash*)	Provides optimal space for all these changes to take place at the correct time.	Leads to congenital defects, such as openings in the septum of the heart, deformities of the heart chambers or abnormalities of the ear.	Sense of sound, ears, mouth, voice, throat, the hollow organs of the body.

The mother should do *bhootshuddhi* or element balancing meditation to ensure that no defects arise due to imbalances of any element, and that the development of the senses and body parts of the foetus happens properly. The step-by-step method of doing the meditation is explained very clearly later in this chapter and all expectant mothers must practise it every day for long-term benefits.

The Nadi Network

The subtle or the etheric body comprises 72,000 nadis (subtle pipes) that carry the 'prana' (life-force energy) to the physical body, because of which we are physically, mentally and emotionally healthy. The moment the energy flowing through the nadis becomes imbalanced, the part or organ that is not receiving adequate energy becomes diseased. It has been stated that any disease first comes to the etheric body and then starts showing physical symptoms after six months. In a nutshell, in order to have a healthy body and a strong mind, the energy flowing through the nadi network has to be powerful.[2]

Out of these 72,000 nadis, there are three that are most important and powerful—Ida, Pingla and Sushumna. Ida is the left nadi and is also known as the moon or feminine nadi that is responsible for our mental faculties. Pingla is the right or the male Nadi and is also known as the sun or masculine nadi. It is responsible for the physical aspects of our body. When both Ida and Pingla are balanced, it awakens the third and the most important nadi: the Sushumna nadi.

These nadis start from the tip of the tail bone and spiral upwards, intersecting at various points and ending between the eyebrows. Beyond this, only Sushumna travels and ends at the crown centre. These points of intersections are the seat of 'chakras'.

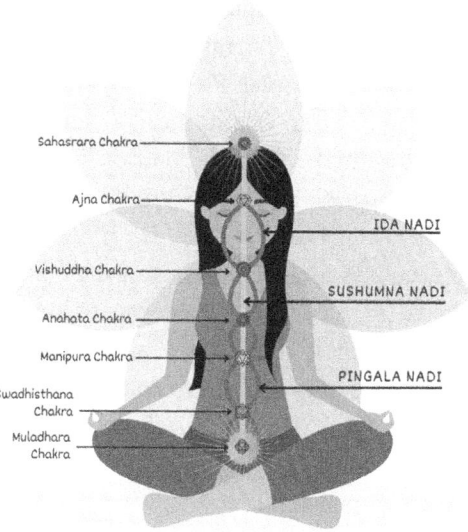

Chakras

Chakras are the receivers, transformers and distributors of the life-force energy. Located subtly along the spinal cord, they are responsible for pumping the life-force energy through the nadi network. The chakras absorb vital energies from a person's surroundings and the cosmos and then transform the absorbed energies into energies with specific frequencies that are distributed by the nadi network. It is important to note that the chakras of the expectant mother and the foetus are always in perfect alignment. So, it is important for the mother to understand each of the chakras individually, the factors that govern them, and how each chakra plays a role in mental and physical health.

There are as many as 114 chakras, out of which seven are the most important. They are located subtly along the spinal cord and are as follows: *Muladhara* or Root Chakra (tip of the tailbone), *Swadhisthana* or Sacral Chakra (four inches below the navel), *Manipura* or Solar Plexus Chakra (at the navel), *Anahata* or Heart Chakra (at the heart's centre), *Vishuddha* or Throat Chakra (at the throat), *Ajna* or Third-Eye Chakra (between the eyebrows), and *Sahasrara* or Crown Chakra (at the crown centre). Each of the chakras can be visualized as a lotus with a specific number of petals in their unique colour, which are listed in Table 6.2. Moreover, each chakra has a sound frequency that is represented as the mantra for that chakra. Furthermore, it is interesting to note that each chakra governs the functioning of the physical organs situated at their location and also plays a role in activating specific feelings and emotions.

Each of the chakras has its own vibrational frequencies. However, due to our karmic baggage, these chakras shift from their natural frequency and are thus not able to absorb the divine energies from the universe. Therefore, the energy exchange between the chakra and the nadi network gets hindered, which in turn fails to energize the physical and the mental bodies, resulting in diseases and suffering. In order to achieve a proper energy flow through the chakras and the nadi network, it is important to balance the chakras by making them vibrate at their natural or optimal frequency.

Balancing of Chakras

In the womb, the entire energy system is completely permeable and open to all vibrations and experiences. Every reborn soul is given the chance to experience and lead a fulfilling life. However, when inside the womb, the child cannot achieve anything by itself. It is completely dependent on the desire, efforts and care of its parents, especially the mother. This presents the parents with a great opportunity and a great task.

As a foetus experiences and perceives its world mostly through its mother, the beginnings of blockages in the energy system can start in the womb if the life growing there feels rejected or the mother lives in a state of continual stress. On the other hand, loving attention to the small being in the womb will provide its energy system with the vibrations that will make it feel loved and secure. If the mother experiences the months of her pregnancy as a happy and fulfilled time, she will provide her child with the very best prerequisites for a happy and creative life.

Furthermore, as the chakras of both the mother and the foetus are in perfect alignment, by balancing her chakras, she can parallelly achieve that for her child as well. This will ensure proper energy flow in the nadi network leading to a holistic development of the child.

The most effective way of balancing the seven chakras is through sound vibrations or mantra chanting. Each chakra has its own natural vibrational frequency, which gets changed due to the chakra becoming imbalanced. When we chant the mantras with the same vibrational frequency, then the chakras get balanced by shifting back to their original frequency of vibration. Similarly, each chakra is associated with a particular colour, which matches the natural vibrational frequency of the chakra. Thus, when the chakra is visualized with its respective colour, it helps in its balancing. The chakras can be balanced in various other ways as well. However, given the scope of this book, we will limit ourselves only to this.

The Swadhisthana or Sacral Chakra directly controls the workings of the reproductive system. It is, therefore, important for the expectant mother to balance the Sacral Chakra through affirmations, visualizations and effective chanting of mantras, thus ensuring a harmonious working of the reproductive system.

However, it may be noted that one should focus not only on Sacral Chakra during pregnancy but also on balancing of all the chakras, and give special emphasis to the Sacral Chakra.

Step-by-Step Meditation to Balance the Seven Chakras (Chakrasadhna) and the Five Elements (Panchbhootshuddhi)

1. Visualize the Muladhara or Root Chakra. It is made of the earth element, located at the tip of the tailbone and is a bright-red, four-petalled lotus. Feel its vibrations. Chant the mantra 'Lam' nine times and, as you chant, feel the connection with your baby in the womb and sense the flow of energy towards your excretory and skeletal system. Feel the increased vibrations giving you stability and the power to materialize your baby.
2. Visualize the Swadhisthana or Sacral Chakra. It lies four inches below the navel, is made of the water element, and is an orange-coloured, six-petalled lotus. Feel its vibrations. Chant the mantra 'Vam' nine times and, as you chant, feel the connection with your baby in the womb and sense the flow of energy towards your reproductive system. Feel the increased vibrations adding creativity and giving virtuous enjoyment to you and your baby.
3. Visualize the Manipura or Solar Plexus Chakra. It is at the navel made of the fire element. It is coloured a bright-yellow, 10-petalled lotus. Feel its vibrations. Chant the mantra 'Ram' nine times and, as you chant, feel the

Table 6.2
The Seven Chakras

Name	Location	Number of Petals	Colour	Element	Mantra	Affected Physical Organs	Affected Feelings and Emotions
Muladhara or Root Chakra	Tip of the Tailbone	4	Red	Earth	Lam	Excretory Organs, Skeletal System, Teeth	Stability and Materialization
Swadhisthana or Sacral Chakra	4 inches below the Navel	6	Orange	Water	Vam	Reproductive Organs	Creativity and Virtuous Enjoyment
Manipura or Solar Plexus Chakra	At the Navel	10	Yellow	Fire	Ram	Digestive Organs	Purpose and Direction
Anahata or Heart Chakra	Heart Centre	12	Green	Air	Yam	Respiratory and Circulatory Organs	Unconditional Love
Vishuddha or Throat Chakra	Throat Centre	16	Blue	Ether	Ham	Thoraxic Organs	Pure Intention
Ajna or Third Eye Chakra	Between the Eyebrows	2	Indigo	Light	Om	Brain, Eyes, Ears, Nose	Clarity and Clairvoyance
Sahasrara or Crown Chakra	Crown Centre	1,000	Violet	Beyond Elements	Om	Brain and Nervous System	Divine Powers

connection with your baby in the womb and sense the flow of energy towards your digestive system. Feel the increased vibrations giving purpose and direction to you and your baby.
4. Visualize the Anahata or Heart Chakra. It is located at the heart centre and made of the air element. It is a green 12-petalled lotus. Feel its vibrations. Chant the mantra 'Yam' nine times and, as you chant, feel the connection with your baby in the womb and sense the flow of energy towards your respiratory and circulatory system. Feel the increased vibrations giving unconditional love to you and your baby.
5. Visualize the Vishuddha or Throat Chakra. It is located at the throat centre and made of the ether element. It is a blue, 16-petalled lotus. Feel its vibrations. Chant the mantra 'Ham' nine times and, as you chant, feel the connection with your baby in the womb and sense the flow of energy towards your thoracic system. Feel the increased vibrations giving pure intentions to you and your baby.
6. Visualize the Ajna or Third-Eye Chakra. It lies between your eyebrows. It is an indigo-coloured, two-petalled lotus and is made of the light element. Feel its vibrations and chant the mantra 'Om' nine times. As you chant, feel the connection with your baby in the womb and sense the flow of energy towards your brain and various parts of your face like eyes, nose, ears, etc. Feel the increased vibrations bringing clarity of mind and clairvoyant faculties to you and your baby.
7. Visualize the Sahasrara or Crown Chakra, located at the crown center and made of the divine element. It is a violet-coloured, 1,000-petalled lotus. Feel its vibrations. Chant the mantra 'Om' nine times and, as you chant, feel the

connection with your baby in the womb and sense the flow of energy towards your brain and the nervous system. Feel the increased vibrations giving spiritual and divine powers to you and your baby.
8. Now complete nine deep breathing cycles. Each cycle must consist of inhaling the breath from Muladhara to Sahasrara and breathing out from Sahasrara to Muladhara. As you breathe deeply, visualize your baby with all the qualities that you desire to develop within it with respect to PQ, IQ, EQ and SQ. Say affirmations and run the mental movie of your child in your mind to manifest your dream baby. Feel the divine energies protecting your womb and giving strength to you and your baby.

This meditation will help balance the chakras and cleanse the five elements (bhoot shuddhi) of both you and your child.

Power of Mantras

A mantra is a collection of celestial or divine sounds that help increase our vibrational frequency and raise our consciousness. 'Man' means 'mind' and 'tra' means 'transport'. In other words, mantra is the instrument of the mind, a powerful sound or vibration, that transports a person to the highest level of consciousness. Mantra chanting not only heals our body but also protects our mind and connects the person who is chanting with the divine supreme being. The importance of mantra chanting has been prominent in our scriptures and witnessed time and again. It is important to note that mantras transcend barriers of religion, caste and creed, and resonate with universal truths. Chanted in any language, the power of mantras has been felt similarly by every religion and region.[3]

Modern science and ancient wisdom agree that the universe is a symphony of vibrational frequencies. Mantras are celestial sounds that, when chanted, have the power to raise the vibrational frequency of the person chanting and help in the healing, transformation, materialization and inner awakening of the person.[4]

Mantras emit sound vibrations or energies and have the power to attract similar frequencies, which helps us in the manifestation of our desires. Therefore, mantras have the power to tap into the desired frequencies in the universe and direct the course of a person's future. The power of the mantras is validated in all our scriptures and do not need any further proof.

Chanting is an ancient practice that calms your mind and soul. Mantras do not fail, and we need to constantly tap their powers into our lives, thus helping us achieve our goals. However, in order to extract the full power of the mantras, some lifestyle corrections are necessary. These include diet, food timing, sleep cycle, exercise and breathing exercises. It also includes the mental strengthening of neural pathways through affirmations and visualizations. These corrections ensure that one is able to tap into the complete power of the mantras that they are chanting.

Belief is the most important element while chanting any mantra. One needs to have complete faith and surrender to this healing system. The moment the subconscious mind creates any doubts about its effectiveness, the healing stops. So, the mantras need to be chanted with full intensity, firm belief and pure intention that one will be healed completely.

There has been enough scientific evidence proving the fact that the chanting of mantras releases positive hormones, including serotonin, which enhances one's well-being and decreases anxiety, negative thoughts and stress. It also releases melatonin, which is an anti-carcinogenic agent and helps with immunity building.[5]

The mantras, when chanted repeatedly in the multiples of 108, in the form of a *japa* for 21 days, brings a shift in consciousness that ultimately leads to the manifestation of our desires.

Scientists believe that embryos listen with their entire bodies. The foetus's ears are completely functional by the sixteenth week and active listening starts by the twenty-fourth week. For the foetus, the mother's voice is clearer than any other voice. Thus, upon chanting of mantras by the mother, the baby listens to it and can feel the calming energy created by this vocalization. Even when the mother is not able to chant, listening with full faith and surrender will also bring positive results to both the mother and the baby in the womb.

The easiest and yet most powerful mantra is 'Omkar' and, when chanted during pregnancy, it helps lower the blood pressure and reduces mental tension and stress. By chanting 'OM' regularly, the mother helps the baby develop spiritually simply with the sound and the vibrations of the chant. 'OM' chanting also gives the mother and the baby better immunity and provides self-healing abilities. It is advisable for the pregnant mother to chant 'OM' three to nine times daily. The right technique of chanting has been shared in Chapter 3 under pranayama techniques.[6]

There has been enough scientific evidence proving the fact that the chanting of mantras, particularly 'OM', releases positive hormones, including serotonin and dopamine, which enhance one's well-being and decrease anxiety, negative thoughts and stress. Furthermore, chanting causes a significant increase in neural connectivity in the prefrontal cortex, thereby improving cognitive functioning, mindfulness and self-awareness. It further induces relaxation, increases concentration, and fosters connectedness with the divine.

However, for more focussed results, the various pregnancy mantras to be chanted by expecting mothers are shared in Annexure 3.

Meditation

Meditation is a practice that involves training the mind to achieve a state of focussed attention, relaxation and heightened awareness. Its purpose extends beyond stress reduction and improved concentration, it also serves as a tool for manifestation, emotional well-being and spiritual growth. Often associated with mindfulness, which emphasizes being fully present and non-judgemental, meditation doesn't aim to empty the mind or suppress thoughts. Instead, it invites a gentle redirection of attention back to a chosen focal point—be it a desired thought, mantra or breath.

Various techniques, such as mindfulness, guided visualization, mantra repetition or breath awareness, can be employed in meditation. The ultimate goal may vary, but for those practising Garbha Sanskar, it's often about manifesting their dream baby and a complete clarity enhances the probability of manifestation.

The Right Technique for Maximizing the Benefits from Mantra Chanting and Meditation

Meditation and chanting form one of the most common ways of activating the various spiritual realms within our body, provided they are done correctly and with the right technique.

1. Emotions: The frequency of the mantras reach you when you are receptive and open to it. Thus, it is important to have faith and belief in the power of mantras. Having emotions that are pure, calm, positive and happy will help the expectant mother in attracting the benefits of both meditation as well as chanting more effectively. As shared earlier, any element of doubt can poison the functioning of the subconscious mind and deter us from getting results. Mantras should be chanted with full trust, devotion and surrender towards the divine.
2. Visualization: While meditating or chanting the mantras, the expecting mother should project all her energies onto the vision board and the mental movie that she has created for her baby in the womb. When her entire focus is on her baby and the qualities she wants to be developed in it, she can manifest her dream baby really fast.
3. Connect with breath: Our mind is very playful. So, in order to stabilize our mind while chanting and meditating, the expectant mother should connect the mantra chanting with her breathing. Anchoring the subconscious mind with the breath slows down the thoughts being created in the mind, thus helping to move away from the unnecessary clutter of the mind and connecting with the self. Moreover, the connection of the breath and mantra should become so strong that even when you are consciously not chanting or meditating, the mantra keeps playing in your subconscious mind like a recorder. This way, the subconscious mind is always anchored to positive mantras and does not drift away towards negativity.

4. Timing: The ideal time for meditation or mantra chanting is during the early hours of the morning right before sunrise, between 4.00 and 5.00 a.m. It is called the Brahma Muhrat, wherein the divine energies are in abundance and thus any divine act performed during this time gets amplified. However, given the physical limitations of the expectant mother, she should try to perform these divine acts in accordance with her health conditions. Always remember, dear mothers, that for you, health comes first!
5. Direction: While meditating or chanting mantras, the expectant mother should face north, east or the northeast direction. This will help get better results.
6. Posture: Mothers should meditate or chant mantras with their spine erect, as energies rise from the Muladhar situated at the tip of the tailbone, traversing through the other chakras along the spine to the Sahastrasar at the Crown Centre. A correct posture helps the smooth flow of energies, thereby raising your vibrations. It is best if one can sit on the floor and chant or meditate, but if that's not feasible, then sitting on a chair with the spine erect will also give great results. The bottom line is that the expectant mother should be still, happy, and have an upright posture while chanting. As Sage Patanjali says, 'Sthiram, sukham, aasanam' (strong, steady and stable). In extreme cases, when the expectant mother is advised complete bed rest, she should continue with her meditation or chanting while lying down only as a special case, but in no circumstance should she refrain from engaging in these divine acts.
7. Silence: Complete silence or *maun* is advisable during meditation or mantra chanting for the divine energies to build in. Along with external silence, it is equally important

for the expecting mother to maintain internal silence by slowing down her thoughts. This will help her feel the vibrations better.
8. Cleansing: It is advised to physically cleanse yourself by taking a shower and wearing fresh clothes before you start with these divine processes. But more than physical cleansing, it is important to do mental and emotional cleansing by harbouring only positive and loving thoughts, emotions and feelings towards all.
9. Food: Our body consumes maximum energy during digestion. Thus, by eating light and sattvic food, the expectant mother can focus her energies on raising her consciousness. A sattvic diet also relieves a person of incessant materialistic desires and helps maintain a positive frame of mind that can channelize the positive vibrations from the universe.
10. Avoid electronics: It is best to stay away from electronic gadgets as the frequencies emitted by them interfere with the receptive frequencies built during meditation or chanting, thereby acting as energy thieves.
11. Personal devotion products: When we meditate or chant, we emit an aura and vibration that is absorbed by our surroundings. Therefore, when we have our own *jap mala*, aasana and devotional books, they absorb that positive energy. When a person meditates or chants repeatedly using the same products, they are further blessed with the absorbed energy.
12. *Sankalp* or commitment: The neural pathway in our subconscious mind gets strengthened every time it is traversed. Hence, when the expectant mother is chanting or meditating continuously, with full faith and devotion,

focussing on and visualizing her desires, she moves very close towards achieving her goals.

13. Seek guidance: When it comes to meditation or chanting, a lot of care must be taken by the expectant mother as these powerful processes help in activating the flow of energy into one's body which should be channelized properly. This is when the required guidance of a guru or an expert should be sought.
14. Complete clarity: Last but not the least, it is important for the expectant mother to have complete clarity on the various attributes of her baby using Sonal's Intelligence Model for Holistic Development©. The greater the clarity, the higher the chances of manifesting her dream baby.

When the expectant mother meditates or chants using the above-mentioned techniques, she is bound to enter the alpha state of consciousness. Here, she can tap into the powers of her subconscious mind and manifest the child of her dreams.

Queen Kayadhu was the wife of the demon king Hiranyakashipu and the mother of Bhakt Prahalad. While the demon king was ruthless, she was an ardent devotee of Lord Vishnu. She had made many failed attempts to make her husband realize the value of the Lord in their lives and tried to make him a devotee, but nothing worked.

When she was pregnant with her son Prahalad, Lord Indra came to know of it. Knowing a son was to be born to the great demon king, he decided to kill the child in the mother's womb itself. He was afraid that the child would also take after his father and then become another threat to the Devatas.

However, Narada Muni was aware of the pure-hearted Queen Kayadhu and knew that the boy that would be born would be a true Vishnu devotee. He decided to save them. He took Kayadhu to his ashram and looked after her as his own daughter. He protected them and told Lord Indra about the boy who would be born.

Later on, Narada Muni gave Kayadhu the beej mantra—Om Namo Narayana—and told her to chant it continuously. She maintained a sattvic diet, lived a simple and disciplined life, and chanted the Guru Mantra at all times.

Soon, the great Bhakt Prahalad was born, and the mother and son returned to their palace. The king doted on his son until he realized that the child was nothing like him. The little boy would always chant the beej mantra and loved Lord Vishnu to an extent that he believed he was everywhere around him. The king tried many ways to kill his son simply because he hated the Lord more than he loved his son. However, at every attempt, Bhakt Prahalad was protected by the Lord himself.

Bhakt Prahalad was all of five years old when Lord Vishnu took the Shri Narsimha Avtar to kill the demon king Hiranyakashipu and save his dear Bhakt Prahalad from the demon's wrath.

There lies a lot of power in bhakti. The simple chanting of a mantra with immense faith blessed Queen Kayadhu with a son who was loved by the Lord himself. Such is the power of Garbha Sanskar and spiritual awakening. No one can ever believe that the greatest bhakt of all times—Bhakt Prahalad—had the genes of the greatest demon king.

Persistence with Mantras

Many times when expectant mothers don't get the desired results, they lose faith and start questioning the powers of the mantras. Mantras never fail and are bound to give results, provided you have chanted properly with full trust and surrender. However, sometimes, if even after chanting for a set duration the desired results are not achieved, it is because the karmic load factor is very high and it takes time to be resolved. Here, instead of giving up, one should take it as a challenge and chant with twice the intensity. So, the most simple and effective solution is to be persistent. Remember that each chant that you are doing is reducing your karmic load and bringing you closer to your desired goals. Mantras transcend religious boundaries as they are universal tools for meditation, focus and spiritual connection. Irrespective of any religion, the mantras are celestial sounds which are used by people of all beliefs to attain inner peace, clarity of mind and spiritual growth. So, whatever your faith might be, you should continue the chanting as prescribed in your scriptures, with full faith, trust and surrender, and direct the energies being created to your desired goal. Do this with affirmations and visualization, and the desired results are bound to manifest. Nobody can stop you from carrying the child of your dreams in your arms.

Increase Your Spiritual Well-Being by Following the 4S Principle!

Every morning, you charge your electronic gadgets by connecting it with the main supply, but when did you last charge yourself? Just like our phones, tablets and laptops, we keep on depleting our energy and eventually get discharged in the hustle-bustle of this materialistic, mortal world. The 4S principles of *Seva*, *Sankirtan*, *Swadhyay* and *Sadhna* are various ways by which we can ensure our connection with the ultimate main supply of the universe—the divine cosmic powers. The expectant mother should incorporate each of the principles in her daily routine so that both the mother and the baby within are continuously connected with the powerhouse of energy.

1. Seva: This is the path followed by the Karma Yogis, wherein one does unconditional, selfless action without any attachment of getting the desired results. A Karma Yogi surrenders all the actions upon His holy feet. As Lord Krishna said to Arjuna in the Bhagvad Gita, '*Karmanyadhikarastu maa faleshu kadachan.*' (You have the right to perform your actions but you are not entitled to the fruits of the actions.) So, the expectant mother should undertake all actions which are important for her unborn child but under no circumstance must she attach expectations to those actions. She should selflessly serve the needy around her—people, animals, birds, etc.—without any expectations, which will raise the level of her and her womb's consciousness.
2. Sankirtan: This is the path followed by Bhakti Yogis, wherein you sing of His glory and connect yourself with His ultimate power, leading to a state of heightened consciousness. When the expectant mother sings and chants the *bhajan*s and mantras, the foetus also gets connected with the raised vibrations. This will help the mother materialize her divine child with all the qualities that she had envisioned.
3. Swadhyay: This is a path of Gyan Yogis who are continuously gaining knowledge and putting it into practice such that the knowledge starts reflecting from one's personality.

The expectant mother who follows this by reading and implementing the divine learnings from the Holy scriptures such as the Bhagvad Gita, Ramcharitmanas, Tatwartsutra, etc., becomes the embodiment of the practised knowledge. The learning that goes into the womb shall get reflected once the child is born.

4. Sadhna: This is a path of Raj Yogis who live a very disciplined life in soul consciousness to achieve self-realization. When the expectant mother lives a value-based righteous life, refraining from pleasures of the senses and focussing on the meditative path, then she gradually shifts from body consciousness to soul consciousness. This way, the unborn child automatically starts to develop soul awareness.

In order to achieve spiritual well-being, one needs to go into an inward journey by following the 4S principle for reaching the alpha state—the heightened level of spiritual awareness and consciousness. In this state, the mother is connected with the universal consciousness and, thus, whatever she desires, she materializes. As discussed before, Queen Madalasa's consciousness was merged with the universal consciousness. So, she always sought what she desired, and thus materialized both a divine monk and a majestic king. The universe recreated her desires exactly the way she wanted it.

However, this cannot happen in isolation and can only be achieved when our physical body is completely at ease (physical well-being), and happy thoughts are focussed on. The mind must have complete clarity about what it wants to achieve (mental well-being), and feelings must be settled in a permanent state of bliss (emotional well-being).

This way, the four well-beings work in unison to take the expectant mother and the baby to a raised consciousness level where even impossible says 'I-M-Possible'.

Tracker Sheet for Imbibing Spiritual Well-Being

	Present Rating Where you are (on a scale of 10)	**Desired Rating** Where you want to go (on a scale of 10)	**Action Monitor** (steps taken to achieve it)
Mantra Chanting			
Seva Activities			
Sankirtan			
Swadhyay			
Chakra and Bhootshuddhi Sadhna			
Meditation			

7

A Miracle Is Born

*'Before giving birth to her little miracle,
a mother undergoes a rebirth.'*

It was a very special day for Diya as she was being showered with love and care. All her friends and family had gathered around her, celebrating the new member to be born, and pampering her for all that she was giving to the family.

It was indeed a hectic day and by night, all the guests had left. Though physically tired, Diya was emotionally charged up remembering the beautiful day it was, when suddenly, around midnight, she felt a lot of discomfort and realized that she was leaking. Alarm bells rang in her head as she was still six weeks away from her due date. She woke her husband and immediately called her doctor, but it went unanswered.

She tried again and when a voice answered, she said, 'Doctor, I am leaking. There is spotting and water is leaking constantly.'

'I need you to come to the hospital right away. I will see you there,' came the doctor's response.

Her husband rushed to pack her things and they sped to the hospital. The moment they arrived, they were taken to a room where her doctor was already waiting for her.

'Why are we here, doctor? Why not in your chamber?' She asked as the doctor examined her.

'Diya, we have to deliver,' the doctor said.

'Deliver? When?' Confusion set in as she looked at her husband and then to her doctor.

'Now,' the doctor said in a raised voice. 'We will be doing the delivery now.'

'But I was waiting for Navratri to start and hoped that my baby will be born then,' Diya said, unable to comprehend what was going on.

'Diya, calm down. Your water bag has a tear and we cannot risk it,' the doctor told her as her husband wrapped a protective arm around her.

She calmed down and prepared for the delivery. She chanted her mantras constantly, trying to prepare herself for the event that would change her life.

'Diya, we have to shift you to another hospital,' said her doctor a little later.

'What? Why? What's going on?' Her nerves were acting up again, and it seemed as if everything was suddenly going haywire. In fact, just two days ago, she was told that everything was normal.

'Since the baby is being delivered six weeks ahead of time, we want the NICU unit to be prepped. Unfortunately, we don't have the facility since there have been a few deliveries today and the babies are in there,' the doctor said. 'Don't worry. We are taking care of this. But we have to rush.'

They acted fast and soon they were on their way to another hospital, which was about thirty minutes away. The moment she arrived, they saw nurses were waiting for her with a wheelchair.

They rushed her in and the moment she reached the delivery room, they helped her change. One checked her vitals, while another was ready with an injection. One put on a catheter and another checked her blood pressure. It was scary and it unnerved her. She prayed and shut her eyes, calming herself and her baby.

Soon, the doctor began the procedure as her husband looked on, holding her hand tight. In no time, the baby was born. It was a boy!

Everything about him was perfect. He was slightly underweight but nothing that a little care and devotion wouldn't sort. The moment Diya saw him, she felt as though he was coming towards her with open arms. The universe had blessed her with her divine little Krishna. Her husband looked at them adoringly, his eyes glistened with happy tears.

All her family members, who had just arrived home, were overwhelmed with joy as they heard the news. 'It is Krishna! It has to be,' they all said on a group call as Diya smiled, looking at her wonderful baby in awe.

She raised her son with a lot of love and devotion. Two years passed and yet she would get overwhelmed every time she thought of her delivery experience. She and her husband wanted to expand the family and have one more child, but the delivery experience had scared them quite a bit. Diya felt as though the entire process of her son's birth was ruled and governed by the 'fear' energy. Every time she thought about her past experience, she would tremble at the sheer memory of it. She decided that she would not let this happen to her again; she wanted to try for another child.

She delved into her perseverance and began praying to God for a miracle. She wanted a pregnancy and a delivery that was nothing like the previous one. She wanted to rewrite the whole experience!

It was during a chance encounter with their family guru that she got introduced to the concepts of Garbha Sanskar. She was told that faith, mantra chanting and leading a right lifestyle would help her become pregnant and also ensure a smooth delivery.

She imbibed the concepts and methods of the ancient science and decided to follow them. Soon, she was pregnant with her second child. She decided that this time only love and peace would rule over every moment of her pregnancy. She practised religious chanting, maintained a sattvic diet, and made sure that her body was nourished and taken care of. She had read about vision boards and affirmations in Garbha Sanskar. She began deploying all happy thoughts into her mind, her baby and her womb. She would read, solve puzzles, create art and a lot more. She started visualizing a blissful, healthy and ideal pregnancy and a perfect delivery.

The day of her delivery approached. She refused to think about her previous experience. She had already visualized a divine celebration in the form of her new baby. It went on in her head like a movie—she would be in a state of bliss, giving timely birth to a healthy baby in contrast to her previous experience, where she had no idea of what was going on. She was lost during her first pregnancy and the overwhelming emotion during that delivery had been that of fear. And now she felt she knew exactly where she had to be. She was rooting for her baby and knew that her delivery would be the exact, beautiful projection of the movie in her mind.

As fate would have it, the date of her delivery was here. She heaved a sigh of relief as her husband, her son, her mother and her in-laws all walked into the hospital with her. She was happy, they were laughing, and her son held her hand tightly as they walked on. They reached the patient room and took a few pictures. The entire process was divine and filled with loving energies. Diya was grateful as she visualized Lord Shiva standing beside her, smiling down at her. She knew that everything was going to be alright.

Two hours later, she held her baby girl in her arms and lovingly breastfed her. With a big smile she chanted in her tiny ears all the mantras she could remember.

Motherhood is the most divine experience one can ever be blessed with and, very soon, you will be holding the child of your dreams in your hands. You are going to be the creator of the most beautiful creation of God. The first cry of the baby is the most melodious music to a mother's ears. It is important to note that the time of delivery is very important for both the mother and the child. On a farm, if the farmer makes the slightest mistake at the time of fruiting or harvesting, then all the hard work they have put in might go in vain.[1]

कालस्य परिणामेन मुक्तं वृन्ताद्यथा फलम्
प्रपद्यते स्वभावेन नान्यथा पतितुं ध्रुवम् ।
एवं कालप्रकर्षेण मुक्तो नाडीनिबन्धनात्
गर्भाशयस्थो यो गर्भो जननाय प्रपद्यते ॥

As the fruits fall from the tree naturally when they ripen, similarly, the mature foetus releases itself from the umbilical cord and arrives for birth. So, childbirth is considered as natural a process as the falling of ripe fruits. Thus, instead of becoming anxious and worried, welcome your baby with lots of enthusiasm, excitement and bliss. After all, the time has arrived to enjoy the fruits of all the hard work that you have put in and the sacrifices you have made over the past nine months.

All the efforts that you have put in to strengthen the baby's PQ, IQ, EQ and SQ will now give results. The mere fact that over 140 million deliveries happen every year across the globe should be enough to give you confidence that you can do it too![2] Every second, four babies are born across the globe. So do not let your thoughts overpower you.[3]

But in this fast-track age, expectant mothers sometimes lack the patience to endure the immense labour pain that accompanies childbirth, which leads to an increasing number of caesareans. This is because, many times, they think that they can avoid labour pain by undergoing surgery. But the truth is quite contrary—often, the labour pains last for a short time while the effects of surgery last throughout one's life. Ignorance creates more worries. What is important here is to know about the care we should take at different stages of delivery. Nature has built the woman strong enough for childbirth. Throw away all the negativity and get ready to welcome your little miracle in your life.

A woman should resolve to have a normal delivery as far as possible, as a natural, vaginal delivery is most ideal.[4] Caesarean section should only be performed if there is a genuine requirement for it. However, ultimate choice rests with the mother, and her autonomy should always be respected.

Natural delivery is beneficial for both the mother and the baby for the following reasons:

- In case of natural delivery, the birth happens very gradually. The baby actively participates in the process.

It completely acclimatizes with the new world outside the mother's womb as opposed to a caesarean baby who is abruptly taken out and enters this world in a state of shock.[5]
- Babies born vaginally have a stronger immune system and are less prone to allergies because of the hormones released during vaginal birth and the important bacteria that they get in the process.
- With uterine contractions during childbirth, pressure on the cervix from the foetus stimulates the pituitary gland to release oxytocin, which continues until the baby is born. The release of oxytocin in a normal delivery thus has a positive impact on lactation, helping the mother to start breastfeeding the baby immediately after birth.[6]
- After a natural delivery, it is easier for the uterus to contract and slowly return to its normal shape and size, helping in faster healing of the mother.
- In case of a natural delivery, the mother can have a shorter hospital stay and get back to normal movement faster, as opposed to the mother of a caesarean baby who takes much more time to heal because of incision, stitches, blood loss, etc.

These benefits of a natural birth are important for the physical as well as psychological well-being of both the mother and the baby.

However, there is a note of caution as, according to research conducted by Dr Sarnoff Mednik on 170 young men suffering from schizophrenia, it was found that 70 per cent of them were born from a painful delivery.[7] In yet another research conducted by him, it was found that out of America's

16 most brutal murderers, 15 had births that were painful for the mother.[8] While a normal delivery is advisable, it should be noted that a traumatic normal delivery has a very severe impact on the overall well-being of the child, so this decision should be taken with full awareness of the same.

A full-term delivery happens eight days before or after the expected due date (EDD), i.e., within the time frame of approximately 16 days around the EDD. The delivery date is never fixed, so there is no point in being anxious about it. Labour pains that commence naturally are beneficial for a normal vaginal birth. However, the reason and the timing for the commencement of labour pains has never been fully understood. So, there is nothing to get anxious about when it comes to the timing of delivery, but as the time draws nearer, the mother should always have someone around her. She should always be in the company of an experienced and loving woman who is vigilant about the changes happening in the expecting mother's body and has the capability to respond effectively to these changes.

So, dear mother, as you step into your ninth month, you should know that a nine-month foetus is a fully grown baby whose senses are completely developed and is sensitive to all the developments happening around. Some do's and don'ts for the mother to make the delivery process absolutely divine are shared below.

- The mother should mentally prepare herself and her baby for the upcoming birth. She should spend a lot of time bonding with the baby through Garbha Samvad. She should create excitement within the baby by sharing the eagerness of the entire family to welcome it. She should

ease out all the anxiety that the baby might have by sharing how easy and simple the entire delivery process is going to be. Furthermore, encourage the baby to take birth vaginally or naturally as it is the best way.
- In case the decision for a C-section is already taken, start preparing the baby by talking about the birthing process so that it gets mentally prepared and does not feel the shock of suddenly leaving the comfort of the womb.
- Mothers should create a mental movie of the entire delivery process involving all the five senses, with a lot of happy emotions. The delivery process should be nothing less than a celebration where the entire family is involved and excited. This will create the neural pathways for the desired delivery process, which will be strengthened each time it is traversed in the mind by the mother. When the day finally arrives, then the mental movie which was created and visualized repeatedly in the mind of the mother will just get replayed—this time not in mind but in reality.
- She should devote maximum time to her child and stay connected to it through her practices of affirmations, visualizations, meditation, mantra chanting, reading scriptures, listening to healing music, etc.
- She should stay relaxed and not get involved in unnecessary activities. Travelling or leaving the house should be strictly avoided unless absolutely necessary.
- To ensure natural labour, the mother should eat an appropriate diet, be at peace, and perform light exercises as suggested by the gynaecologist. A light diet and

early dinners (by 7.00 p.m.) is most important as this will ensure that bowel movements are regular.
- If the guidelines outlined in the previous chapters for the development of physical, mental, emotional and spiritual well-being are followed properly, then the muscles of the lumbar, pelvic region and the back become supple, lubricated and flexible. All of this will lead to the birth of a healthy and strong child naturally, at full term, without any problems.
- It is strongly recommended that the expectant mother learns and practises controlled breathing techniques for pain management during childbirth from experts. Breathing steadily during labour increases the mother's focus, relaxes the muscles and the mind, distracts from pain and brings much-needed oxygen to her and the baby.
- Mothers should start taking good care of their breasts. They should check for any engorgements, massage them gently to clear the milk ducts, take care of the nipples, and prevent them from cracking by moisturizing them. Give affirmations for breastfeeding and start visualizing the feeding process that will begin after birth.
- Closer to the due date, the mother should always be accompanied by a woman who is loving, caring, experienced and capable of independently taking action if an emergency arises.
- The doctor and the hospital have a vital role to play in the delivery process and so they should be selected carefully.
- It is important for the mother to keep her hospital bag

ready to avoid any delays or stress when emergencies arise.
- In order to achieve a comfortable delivery, it is very important for the expectant mother to do a perineal or perineum massage for better muscle suppleness.
- Last but not the least, the mother should be in a state of complete bliss. Always remember that a happy mother will give birth to a happy child.

Natural Position of the Foetus

The developing foetus floats within the amniotic fluid inside the uterus. Initially, it moves freely in various directions—up, down, sideways, and even turns upside down. However, as it grows larger, its movements become more limited. Prakrut Aasan refers to the natural and ideal position of the foetus in the uterus, as described by Acharya Caraka in the following verse.[9]

गर्भस्तु खलु मातुः पृष्ठाभिमुख ऊर्ध्वशिराः
सङ्कुच्याङ्गान्यास्तेऽन्तःकुक्षौ ॥22॥

The position of the foetus in the womb is usually facing towards the mother's back, with the head facing up and the limbs folded. By the eighth or the ninth month, the foetus assumes its natural head-down position and this position gets fixed till delivery. As delivery approaches, the foetal movements naturally decrease, which might concern the mother. However, this reduction in movement is a normal part of the process and actually contributes to a smoother delivery. There's generally no need to worry about it.

During the end pregnancy, it's beneficial for the expectant mother to maintain a routine of regular walks as guided by the gynaecologist. This helps the baby's head descend and fit into the pelvic brim, making delivery easier. Additionally, practising deep yogic breathing between contractions can help control the speed of the baby's descent and manage contractions. So a consistent practice of walking and pranayama throughout pregnancy, under professional guidance, can significantly ease the delivery process.

Any change happening in the natural position of the foetus (Prakrut Asan) is known as *moodhgarbha* in Ayurvedic literature, which can create complications in the process of natural labour.

Some of the causes for moodhgarbha are listed below:[10]

- Too much physical work
- Lifting heavy objects
- Too much travelling
- Inappropriate or excess exercise
- Trauma to the abdomen due to a fall or injury
- Severe jolts, possibly due to the swinging of the legs while sitting, swinging on a swing, or travelling on bad or potholed roads
- Sitting incorrectly or squatting
- Attempted abortion
- Suppressed natural urges (urination and bowel movements)
- Eating very dry or very spicy or any other gas-producing food
- If the placenta is attached to the lower rather than upper part of the uterus

When Is C-Section Recommended?

Normal delivery is most beneficial for both the mother and the baby. The probability of a natural childbirth is said to increase for women who religiously follow the principles of Garbha Sanskar from the very beginning. However, there are certain situations where a vaginal delivery is difficult and the mother and the family must make judicious decisions under the guidance of their doctor. One can opt for a caesarean delivery if the doctor expresses concerns for any of the reasons cited below. What is ultimately important is that both the mother and the baby should be safe and healthy.

Chances of a C-section increase when:[11]

- The buttocks, knees or legs emerge before the head. This situation is called a 'breech'.
- The foetus lies horizontally (perpendicular to the vaginal opening) in the uterus. This position is called *parigh* and it is the most difficult for labour.
- The low-lying placenta partially or completely covers the cervix (placenta previa).
- There is some irregularity in the baby's heartbeats.
- The mother's previous delivery was caesarean.
- The pelvic region size is smaller than the baby's head.
- The baby's head gets tangled in the umbilical cord.
- The baby has passed stool in uterus.
- The mother-to-be is carrying twins.
- The cervix is not opening despite strong contractions for several hours, in case of stalled labour.
- The mother is not comfortable with a normal delivery.
- The doctors feel that the health and safety of the mother or baby are at risk. It is of utmost importance

for the mother and the family to trust their doctor. It is strongly recommended to know all your options before choosing and finalizing your doctor. However, once you have decided, trust your doctor completely.

Signs that You Will Go into Labour

When the woman approaches labour, she starts showing typical signs which are expressed in the following verse in the Sushruta Sharirsthan:[12]

जाते हि शिथिले कुक्षौ मुक्ते हृदयबन्धने ॥
सशूले जघने नारी ज्ञेया सा तु प्रजायिनी ॥6॥
तत्रोपस्थितप्रसवाया: कटीपृष्ठं प्रति समन्ताद्वेदना भवत्यभीक्ष्णं
पुरीषप्रवृत्तिर्मूत्रं प्रसिच्यते योनिमुखाच्छ्लेष्मा च ॥7॥

(Emptiness on both lateral sides of the abdomen, lessening of pressure around the heart, and onset of pain in the pelvic region are indications that the mother is going to deliver her baby very soon.)

With the approach of labour, the baby moves down into the pelvis, a process known as 'lightening', which alters the shape of the abdomen. This downward shift eases pressure on the upper abdomen, allowing the mother to breathe more comfortably. However, she may feel heaviness in the lower abdomen due to increased pressure on the urinary bladder and nearby organs. This often results in more frequent urination or bowel movements. Walking or sitting on the floor may become challenging and her thighs may feel heavier.

For first-time pregnancies, these symptoms typically arise about a week before delivery, while in subsequent pregnancies, they occur just three to four days before delivery.

What Labour Feels Like

According to the Caraka Sharirsthan, the following is a description of the process of labour:[13]

> तस्यास्तु खलु इमानि लिंगानि प्रजननकामभितो भवन्ति, तद्यथा क्लमो गात्राणां, ग्लानिराननस्य, अक्ष्णो: शैथिल्यं, विमुक्त धनत्यमिव बहस, कुक्षे अवस्नंसनम्, अधोगुरुत्वं, वंक्षण-बस्ति कटि कुक्षि-पार्श्वपृष्ठ निस्तोद:, योने: प्रस्नवणं, अनन्नाभिलाषश्चेति ।

(Exhaustion in the body; tiredness on the face; flabbiness of the eyes; reduction of pressure from the chest; heaviness in the lower part of the body; pain in the back, waist and lower abdomen; onset of vaginal discharge; loss of appetite.)

The period between the beginning of these symptoms until the time the placenta is delivered encompasses three distinct stages of labour or delivery.

Stages of Labour

There are three main stages of childbirth. Usually close to the EDD, if there is a discharge of blood or water from the vagina, then you should go immediately to your doctor because it may be the beginning of the first stage of childbirth. Each process of labour varies in its duration. The mother and child go through the different stages from the onset of pains to the actual birth of the baby.

First Stage

The initial stages of labour are from the onset of contractions to the dilation of the cervix. For first-time mothers, this phase may last up to 12 hours, while subsequent deliveries might shorten to four to six hours. Contractions are typically felt in the abdomen or pelvic region, with back pain radiating toward the inner thigh and buttocks, sometimes extending to the middle of the abdomen, being common symptoms.

During this stage, the time between contractions is around 15–20 minutes, lasting 10 to 30 seconds each. The frequency of contractions increases gradually, leading to further dilation of the cervix as the baby progresses through the birth canal.

Occasionally, towards the end of this stage, mothers may feel the urge to push despite incomplete cervical dilation. It's crucial not to act on this urge, as premature pushing can cause cervical swelling and hinder later stages of labour. Breathing techniques can help regulate contractions and manage the urge to push, promoting proper cervical dilation.

Here are some important considerations for mothers during this phase:

- Focus on deep breathing to prevent muscle fatigue and preserve energy for later stages.
- Ensure regular bowel movement, as irregularity can disrupt contractions and labour progress.
- Stay relaxed, active and accepting of the situation without fear.
- Opt for liquid intake such as soups, fresh fruit juices, and water with salt and sugar to provide adequate energy to the muscles. It's best to avoid solid food as it might lead to constipation. Soft rice, liquid khichdi or pureed rice are suitable for meals.

Second Stage

The period from the point of complete dilation of the cervix until childbirth is the second stage. It lasts for one–two hours for first-time mothers and around half an hour for subsequent deliveries. During the first stage of labour, the woman may still be mobile, but it is advised that she lie down during the second stage. The second phase begins once the cervix is fully dilated. During this stage, active participation from the mother is crucial to push the baby out. Her pushing complements the contractions that also aid in pushing the foetus. Contractions typically happen every two to three minutes and last around one to one-and-a-half minutes each time. During the interval between contractions, the woman should focus on deep breathing to prepare to apply sufficient pressure during contractions. This pressure should be directed from the neck and shoulders, making the exercises practised for these muscles during pregnancy beneficial and practical. It's important for her to push when a contraction begins and continue until it subsides. Applying pressure outside of contractions isn't beneficial for delivery or for the foetus; it only exhausts the mother unnecessarily. Instead, she should concentrate on deep breathing between contractions.

As suggested in the Caraka Sharirsthan, chanting of the following mantra or even meditating upon its meaning with full faith and devotion will help the mother bear the contractions in the second stage.[14]

क्षितिर्जलं वियत्तेजो वायुर्विष्णुः प्रजापतिः। सगर्भां त्वां सदा पान्तु वैशल्यं च दिशन्तु ते। प्रसूष्व त्वमविक्लिष्टमविक्लिष्टा शुभानने।। कार्तिकेयद्युतिं पुत्रं कार्तिकेयाभिरक्षितम ।।31।।

It says, 'All the deities, be it the Earth, Water, Sky, Sun, Air, Vishnu or Prajapati, will protect you and your baby. They will be there to help you have a comfortable childbirth. You may be blessed with a child like Kartikeya. May Kartikeya protect him. The mother should have these emotions while she is in labour.'

Generally, by the end of the second stage, the head, then the shoulders, followed by the hands and the rest of the baby's body exit the womb. The baby's airway will be cleared if necessary, and the umbilical cord will be cut. In the first pregnancy, this stage can last for about two hours, and for about half an hour in subsequent pregnancies. It is important to cover the vaginal area soon after childbirth to prevent dirt from entering the uterus. If required, doctors may perform an episiotomy (make a slit) at the opening of the vagina for a smooth delivery. It is done after administering local anaesthesia so that the procedure is as painless as possible. Normally, the mouth of the vagina is optimally dilated and relaxed at this stage, so that the foetus can come out easily. Stitches given after an episiotomy can restrict the woman's movements while sitting or standing, and, in some cases, may also cause problems during sexual intercourse for a short period.

As guided by Charakacharya in the following verse:[15]

तस्यां च प्रवाहमाणायां स्त्रिय: शब्दं कुर्यु:-
'प्रजाता प्रजाता धन्यं धन्यं पुत्रम्' इति ।
तथाऽस्या हर्षेणाप्याय्यन्ते प्राणा: ॥40॥

(While the mother is straining herself in the process, someone attending to her should say loudly, 'You have delivered a worthy child', and these words will fill her heart with immense joy and bring great relief and happiness.)

The second stage of labour ends with childbirth, leading to the onset of the third stage.

Third Stage

During the third stage of childbirth, the placenta is delivered. As the baby is born, the uterus begins to shrink, causing the placenta, attached to the uterine wall, to loosen. Strong contractions lead to fatigue in the uterine muscles, and the placenta's spontaneous expulsion typically starts after a brief pause of 15 to 20 minutes. Contractions during this phase are usually mild and not excessively uncomfortable. The placenta is usually expelled within 30 minutes after the baby's birth, and if it reaches the vagina, it is manually removed without exerting undue force by pulling the umbilical cord or applying pressure.

Attention then shifts to monitoring for internal bleeding. Your gynaecologist will assess if you need stitches or treatment for any vaginal tears. It's crucial to ensure that the entire placenta is expelled to prevent any from remaining inside. The natural delivery process concludes with the placenta's expulsion during the third stage.

The duration of the entire delivery process can vary, lasting between 12 and 24 hours for first pregnancies and about 4 to 12 hours for subsequent pregnancies. In some cases, a woman's first labour may last only four hours if they didn't experience significant pains during the first stage, perceiving the labour process as comprising only the last two stages.

Many women lack a comprehensive understanding of the birthing process, leading to fear about delivery. However, with proper guidance, they can prepare adequately, gaining the confidence and courage needed to navigate labour more comfortably.

So, dear mothers, now you should shed all anxieties and fears with respect to childbirth and labour. With such detailed explanations, start visualizing your delivery process now; it should be no less than a celebration. Do a very detailed visualization with full emotions using all your five senses, which will make the process easy when it actually happens in reality.

A mother must always be in a state of bliss. When the mother is happy and stays calm during labour, she will be able to support the process. Oxytocin is released in her blood, which helps to contract the uterus. Furthermore, staying calm acts as deterrent to the production of adrenaline in the blood, which stops oxytocin from working. The production of oxytocin also supports lactation post delivery. So, dear mothers, as you prepare yourself for motherhood, do it with a lot of happiness in the heart as it is good not only for your health but also for your baby.

Actions to Be Taken Immediately after Birth (*Jatakarma Sanskar*)

In Ayurveda, Jatakarma Sanskar refers to all the important precautionary actions that must be taken immediately after childbirth. These must be handled simultaneously with the postpartum care for the mother.

As guided by Acharya Sushruta:[16]

अथ जातस्योल्बं मुखं च सैन्धवसर्पिषा विशोध्य

(The mucus or secretions covering the newborn's face, eyes and nose should be promptly removed as the baby takes its first breath independently after birth.)

These deposits on the mouth or nostrils can hinder proper respiration. So, with washed hands and trimmed nails, gently clean the lips, palate, tongue and the inside of the cheeks with a sterile cotton swab wrapped around the finger to clear any obstructing mucus. The baby's first cry marks the commencement of respiration, signifying an important milestone. If the baby appears exhausted from the delivery process, which may delay the cry, gentle measures like fanning, patting the back or sprinkling a little water can help stimulate breathing. If these efforts are ineffective, artificial respiration should be initiated.

The baby's cry, immediately after birth, indicates good health. Once the baby is breathing satisfactorily, recite the following mantra into its right ear:[17]

अङ्गादङ्गात् संभवसि हृदयादभिजायसे
आत्मा वै पुत्रनामासि स जीव शरदां शतम् ।
शतायु: शतवर्षोऽसि दीर्घमायुरवाप्नुहि
नक्षत्राणि दिशो रात्रिरहश्च त्वाभिरक्षतु ॥

This mantra is a prayer for the child to be blessed with a long and healthy life, and that it may stay safe and live for a hundred years.

As guided in Sushrut Saristhana, it is customary to offer pre-lacteal feed to the newborn immediately after birth, even before breastfeeding.[18]

अथ कुमारं शीताभिरद्भिराश्वास्य जातकर्मणि कृते मधुसर्पिरनन्तचूर्णं
अङ्गुल्याऽनामिकया लेहयेत्।

The baby is made to lick either a honey–ghee mixture or just honey applied on a 24-carat gold object—usually a ring or a coin—by the most revered family member whose qualities the parents wish upon the newborn. The person faces the east and feeds this concoction to the baby using the ring finger of their right hand while chanting mantras into the baby's ears.[19]

ओम प्र ते ददामि मधुनो घृतस्य वेद सवित्रा प्रसूतं मघोनाम।
आयुष्मान् गुप्तो देवताभिः शतं जीव शरदो लोके अस्मिन्।।

(I make you taste ghee and honey and as these elements are godsent, they will protect you. May you live for 100 years.)

This process, popularly called 'ghuti pilana', has great scientific significance as the delivery process is very stressful and exhausting for the baby, and the sucrose in the honey helps the baby overcome this stress. It also boosts the immunity. However, due to concerns about the purity of pre-lacteal feeds offered to infants, it is important to follow this ritual post consultation with the doctor.

The Many Firsts

The moment of birth is a milestone in the life of every human being as it creates an impression in the mind of the newborn that lasts a lifetime. Whether we perceive the world as a friendly and pleasant place or as cold, unfriendly and lacking in love, all depends upon our experiences at the time of our birth. At birth, the child leaves the perfect physical security that the mother has provided it, including the nourishment and protection of the womb, for the first nine months of its life on earth. However, it is not prepared to be separated from the mother immediately after birth. As long as it feels the vibrations of the mother's body that it has become accustomed to, and remains embedded within the energy vibrations of the mother's aura, it is willing to open itself up to new experiences in a feeling of trust.

If the newborn is taken from the mother right after birth, it will experience the deep pain of separation and loneliness. As long as the mother can consciously send the newborn child her loving feelings and thoughts and maintains contact with the child, it is not totally cut off from the mother's energy supply. If the mother becomes preoccupied with other things or is too emotionally drained or fatigued due to the medication she has received, this ongoing contact will be disrupted. The newborn child will start feeling helpless and alone in an unknown world without the protective presence of its mother. This experience is so overpowering that the child's energy system is unable to cope with these alarming feelings and the impressions made result in the first blockage of energies. It is interesting to note that fathers also develop more intimate feelings towards their babies and greater intuitive understanding if they are present at the moment of birth and are permitted to touch and hold the baby.

First Touch

The bodily contact between the mother and child immediately after birth establishes a bond. A stream of loving emotions and positive energy automatically and spontaneously flows from the mother to the newborn child and continues without interruption as long as her body feels the baby near her. This flow of love fills the little soul with trust and joy. So, it is of utmost importance that the mother establishes bodily contact with her baby soon after it is born. Immediate skin-to-skin contact helps regulate the newborn's body temperature, normalize respiratory rate, help the baby breathe deeply, and exposes them to beneficial bacteria from their mother's skin.[20] These good bacteria protect the baby from infectious diseases and help build their immune systems. In cases where the baby is born premature or is distressed, the best way to regulate temperature and breathing is by keeping the baby between the mother's breasts and encouraging breastfeeding on demand—a practice popularly known as kangaroo mother care (KMC). Research has proven that KMC reduces the mortality and morbidity in pre-term and low birth-weight infants by providing them protection from infections, and also regulates their body temperature, breathing and brain functioning by increasing the mother–baby bonding.[21] Furthermore, it helps kickstart lactation. Studies have shown that immediate contact with mother increases the chances of effective and seamless breastfeeding, and also improves the rate of exclusive breastfeeding.[22]

However, one should not assume that it is just the baby who needs this intimacy. The mother needs the baby as much as the baby needs her. Pitocin is artificially administered oxytocin given to new mothers to help with the contraction of uterus and reducing post-delivery bleeding. Oxytocin is naturally created during the first hour after delivery, and nipple stimulation accelerates oxytocin production. So, instead of giving pitocin artificially to stop the bleeding, letting the mother and child be together and encouraging breastfeeding might naturally stop the bleeding. Also, oxytocin is amnesic and analgesic, which provides pain relief to the mother, thereby naturally reducing her birth trauma.

First Breastfeeding

मातुरेव पिबेत्सन्यं तत्परं देहवृद्धयो

Mother's milk provides essential nourishment and is vital for the holistic development of the child.[23] Therefore, it is crucial for mothers to breastfeed their babies soon after birth.

Once both mother and baby are comfortable and clean, the mother should sit facing east and begin breastfeeding from her right breast within the first hour after delivery. This is significant because the first milk, known as colostrum, is rich in nutrients and vital for the baby's overall growth. It is important for the mother to establish a proper feeding routine from the first time itself as it will not only encourage adequate milk production for the mother but also train the baby on how to feed correctly, thus laying the foundation for successful breastfeeding in the future.

The mother should approach this moment with love and warmth, envisioning her milk as a potent elixir or *amrut* that bestows strength, power, longevity and divinity upon her baby. As recommended in the Sushrut Saristhana, she should recite the following mantra during this auspicious occasion of the baby's first feed:[24]

चत्वार: सागरास्तुभ्यं स्तनयो: क्षीरवाहिन:।
भवन्तु सुभगे नित्यं बालस्य बलवृद्धये।।
प्रयोऽमृतरसं पीत्वा कुमारस्ते शुभानने।
दीर्घमायु: अवाप्रोतु देवा: प्राश्यामृतं यथा।।

(Oh fortunate woman, let all the four oceans produce milk in your breast, resulting in the progress of your child. As the gods became immortal by consuming amrut, may your child also live a long life after drinking the elixir in the form of your milk.)

Even if the mother can't chant this, she should at least have these emotions while feeding her child. It is important here to note that many a times, perhaps out of ignorance, mothers feel that their milk is insufficient. However, she must be aware that the colostrum is thick and is produced in limited quantity, since the feed requirement of the baby is minimal. The mother, out of concern, might try to make up for it using alternate feeding methods such as top feed. However, this might get the baby used to the extra sweetness of the packaged infant milk and make it reject the natural feeding process. Furthermore, the mother should feed directly and not use any spoon or bottle as this is detrimental to breastfeeding and, as a result of this, the lactation of the mother will also get affected.

A Standing Ovation to Motherhood

As we experience the miraculous journey of childbirth, we are reminded of the profound beauty and resilience of life. From the divine moment of conception to the sacred moment of birth, the mother's unwavering love, care and dedication shape the foundation of a new existence. Through her sacrifices, prayers and unyielding determination, the mother not only ensures the physical well-being of her child but also fosters its mental, emotional and spiritual growth. Each contraction, each heartbeat and each breath during childbirth is a testament to her strength and courage. From the first cry that echoes the beginning of a new life to the nourishment of a mother's milk, every moment is imbued with the promise of growth, strength and divinity.

Dear mother, as you give birth to your little miracle, always remember this: 'Birth isn't just about welcoming a child—it's the rebirth of a mother, who is born all over again.'

Tracker Sheet for Preparing for Divine Delivery
(to be practised throughout pregnancy)

Physical Preparedness

Mental Preparedness

Emotional Preparedness

Spiritual Preparedness

Checklist for Hospital Bag

For Mother	
For Baby	

8

Care of New Moms and Newborns

'Embrace the beautiful journey from the womb to the world with profound tenderness and love.'

'Please, Maa, you know I don't like ghee on my chapati,' pleaded Rani as her mother-in-law fed her. It had been 15 days since Rani's delivery, and she was absolutely fed up with the postpartum diet she was being given. Even the list of do's and don'ts sounded like a punishment to her. As soon as her mother-in-law left the room, Rani quickly hid the chapati. Rani was proud of her career as a successful model and was very conscious about gaining weight since the time she had conceived.

Rani had absolutely no problems during her pregnancy, but post delivery was a completely different story. She had gone back to work in less than three weeks and had not been following any of the post-pregnancy, self-care advice suggested by either her mother or her mother-in-law and the other elders in her family. She presumed it to be too outdated and not in line with modern ways. In fact, she even tried various diet plans to quickly shed whatever little weight she had gained. And this only exterted a further toll on her body. She felt tired to such an extent that she could not even continue to feed her child beyond the first two months.

Initially, Rani did not feel the impact of her hasty decisions, but after a few months lapsed, she started feeling the pain and weakness growing in her body. She was soon diagnosed with arthritis and many other physical ailments resulting from a lack of self-care and improper breastfeeding. The immunity of the baby was also affected.

Instead of rushing to sets, Rani was soon found rushing to doctors, sometimes for herself and sometimes for her baby.

From Womb to Room: The First 40 Days

Remember, a woman is reborn during the delivery process. In fact, a mother is born first and then the child. The sudden transition from child-bearing to child-rearing for a new mother is absolutely tormenting. The first 40 days are considered to be the most important for the mother and the child as any mistakes made can have long-term repercussions for the life of both. As the mother grapples with physical and emotional issues at the same time, she is constantly judged and bombarded with conflicting advice from every direction. This is absolutely confusing, and she is unable to derive much wisdom from it. There are many practices associated with maternity care that have been followed since time immemorial. However, mothers have started questioning the scientific reasons behind them. Why do I need to confine myself? Why can't I take a head bath? Why should I bind my belly? Why should I cover my ears?

While they have these questions in their heads, the new moms are being pushed to follow age-old traditions which seem unnecessary and more like restrictions imposed upon them, than something to help them along the way. In her book *New Borns and New Moms,* Dr Farah Adam Mukadam has thrown light on the scientific relevance behind this wisdom of mother and child care that has been passed down through generations.[1] New mothers have the right to know the pros and cons behind each of these traditions and should be free to choose what is in their best interests.

Care of the New Mother

1. Forty days of rest: The most challenging aspect in the life of a new mother is the 40 days of rest, which actually seems like a lifelong prison sentence to her. By the end of the first couple of weeks, it seems to her as if she is being punished for becoming a mother.

   During pregnancy, the immunity of the body gets lowered to protect and nourish the development of the foetus, and the immunity of the mother gets lower post delivery. The process of giving birth to the baby, followed by the shrinking of the uterus to its original size and position, causes a lot of physical stress for the mother. It takes anywhere between three months to a year for a new mother to get back to her pre-conception immune levels. The body actually works overtime to repair and restore itself to its original form, and this recovery process can vary for different individuals. In some cases, the path to recovery is slow and steady, while in others, the body's immune system takes a drastic recovery course. Depending on the individual's body, the new mother can lie anywhere between the two continuums. It is thus advised that she should rest and minimize her contact with the outside world, as that might help her recovery process and prevent long-term health issues.

Furthermore, the new mother has to take care of her newborn as the child becomes her focus and deserves all her attention. So, when the mother is in this rest phase and not distracted by the outside world, it works in the best interest of both the mother and the child. However, this does not mean that she should subject herself to complete home imprisonment. She can definitely move out if she so desires or requires.

2. Belly binding: In Indian culture, it is a regular practice to bind the belly from the ribs to the hips by using an old cotton saree or belly binders that are commercially available. This is done with appropriate pressure that is tolerable for the new mother for a period of eight to ten hours a day for at least the first month. Care must be taken to not bind the belly while eating or sleeping. It is important for the mother to decide the level of pressure that suits her in order for this to be effective and not cause any adverse effects. This simple practice has lots of crucial benefits:

- It helps in reducing postpartum blood loss, as is evident by the higher haemoglobin levels.
- It helps to support the loose belly skin, thereby avoiding pressure being put on the stitches while walking or doing other activities. It thus helps reduce

pain in mothers who have had a C-section delivery.
- During pregnancy, the spine is under a lot of strain, as it curves excessively to balance the body. But now, due to belly binding, the abdominal pressure is increased, which helps to stabilize the strained spine.
- It also helps the relaxed ligaments realign to their pre-pregnancy state.
- The abdominal muscles handled the maximum stress during pregnancy while supporting the growing baby. The belly binder will help these muscles come together so that they can heal properly.
- Last but not least, it helps mothers achieve fast reduction of fat around the waist. The fleshy tissues get compressed, squeezed and distributed above and below the waistline, thereby aiding in a leaner muscle mass. Furthermore, as the belly binder holds the abdominal muscles under the right pressure, it prevents them from further expanding and becoming loose. However, tying the belly too tight is a big no, as belly binding is not for reclaiming the lost pre-pregnancy belly as a quick fix. This can, in fact, lead to uterus prolapse, a condition where the uterus sinks out of the open cervix and vagina. High pressure can even push the stomach up through the diaphragm, leading to life-long acid reflux.

3. Covering the ears: It is a common sight in most Indian households where the new mothers are compelled to place cotton in their ears and cover their heads with a scarf. They are also discouraged from going into a breezy, windy environments and are instructed to avoid cold air from air-conditioners, coolers or fans. It is important for new

mothers to know the scientific reasoning behind this.

Covering the head helps maintain the health of her ear-nose-throat region as any thermal shock (hot or cold) can lead to sinus infections. Respiratory tract infections in a new mother should be avoided under all circumstances as her immunity is already quite low and any further complication can worsen her health conditions.

Furthermore, the scarf that covers the head and ears also helps her to keep warm.[2] However, this does not mean that she should suffer in the heat and sweat. She can always remove the cover from her ears for her comfort.

4. Head bath: One thing the new mom craves is a good head bath so that she can feel fresh and clean after the strenuous labour. However, this is not advisable in our tradition immediately after delivery, since it might lead to headaches and dizziness.

In case of normal deliveries, a lot of pressure is already exerted onto the ear canal. Hence, it is wise to skip head baths for a couple of days. Even on later days, it is important to have a head bath with a cotton ball inserted gently into the ear opening, and further protect it by smearing some petroleum jelly around it to ward off any water or moisture entering into the ears. Care must be taken to bathe in warm water, dry the hair immediately with the help of a hair dryer, and also avoid air-conditioner or fan after coming out of a bath, as wet hair can lead to cold and cough due to lower immunity levels of the new mother. Excessive coughing can exert pressure on the stiches if the mother has had a C-section delivery and is also not good for the baby with whom you will always be in close contact. Always use a mask while nearing the

baby in case of any conditions of cold and cough.
5. Massage: Hormonal imbalance, the responsibility of being a new mother, and all the physical labour are instrumental in challenging the physical and mental health of the new mother.[3] Every new mother should get a daily massage from a trained masseuse for a minimum period of six weeks. Massages are a very important ritual in maternity care for the following reasons:
- Normal labour delivery is one of the most exhausting experiences that a woman has in her lifetime, with body pains and muscle aches being natural occurrences; a deep massage is a mandatory requirement to relieve and soothe her tired muscles and remove all the soreness.
- Pregnancy increases the level of body fluids by 50 per cent, which takes time to balance post delivery. Because of irregularity in body fluids, at times women experience swelling. Postpartum massage is a great way to slowly improve blood circulation and increase lymphatic drainage, which helps the body balance and drain the excess fluid. With balanced and regular blood circulation, the swelling will wear off and the body will return to its normal condition.
- During pregnancy, the placenta secretes the two most important pregnancy hormones—oestrogen and progesterone—into the blood stream. Oestrogen—the fat storing hormone—is responsible for preparing the mother's body for baby-bearing by giving it firm breasts, rounded hips, glowing skin and lustrous hair. Progesterone, on the other hand, is responsible for maintaining the pregnancy, supporting the baby in the womb and postponing lactation until delivery.

However, as the mother moves from baby-bearing to baby-rearing phase post delivery, the most important job is to strengthen the body of the mother and produce milk to build the body of the baby. Now, both these hormones are not required in great quantities. This is when the thyroid hormone—the fat-burning hormone—takes charge and the oestrogen production levels start decreasing. Further, as the progesterone levels start declining, the lactating hormone—prolactin—builds up. Thus, the baby-bearing hormones are steadily replaced by the baby-rearing hormones. Postpartum massage is helpful during this transitionary period as it encourages a balance of hormones. When they are adjusted and balanced, the mood is automatically uplifted, thereby lessening the feelings of stress and anxiety.

- A massage ritual helps the mother achieve a leaner body as it improves circulation and drainage of protein-rich fluids from the body, thereby reducing pregnancy-related swelling.
- Postpartum massage is effective in improving lactation as both back and breast massage relaxes the body, which increases lactation and helps feed the baby.[4]
- Last but not the least, a regular massage regime gives the new mothers the much-needed 'me time', as caring for a newborn gets difficult if the mother is sleepless and physically and mentally exhausted. An excellent postpartum massage by a professional massage therapist can do wonders to ease the pain, tiredness and sore muscles, help you with mental and physical relaxation, and improve sleep.

Care of New Moms and Newborns

Postpartum massage for new mothers is a very effective and therapeutic way for handling the physical and mental challenges posed by the pregnancy and after birth. Taking care of physical and mental health for new mothers should be the priority as a healthy and happy mother can take better care of the baby.

6. Skin Care: Since time immemorial, our grandmothers' favourite skin-care recipe has been paste made from gram flour (*besan*) with a pinch of turmeric powder (*haldi*) mixed with a little water. It is highly recommended that the new mother massage her skin with this beauty paste (*ubtan*) and then wash it off with a hot-water bath. This is because the ubtan massage increases blood flow to the skin, thereby rejuvenating it.

7. Sleep: Good sleep is very important for a faster recovery as well as ensuring an effective milk supply for breastfeeding. However, for the newborn, the night and the day are all mixed up. The first two months are hectic and tiring as the baby sleeps at the oddest hours of the day and is wide-awake at night. Thus, the best advice that I can give to new mothers is to sleep when the baby is sleeping and be the baby's perfect partner when it wants to play and have fun. This will ensure good rest, reduction in anxiety and irritation, and a better bond with the baby.

That said, sometimes it is not the baby but the phone in your hand that is the greatest culprit for exhaustion. The hormone melatonin is responsible for keeping us active during the day and helping us sleep at night. But the light emitted by the phone hampers melatonin secretion, thereby robbing us of our well-deserved sleep. Binge watching disturbs the body clock, which in turn secretes less of the satiety hormone leptin. Leptin is responsible for giving us satisfaction while eating and for reducing our appetite. Night-time exposure to screens reduces leptin levels, thereby increasing the appetite, which has a direct impact on the waistline.

8. Diet: It is important to note that a postpartum mother is recovering as well as preparing milk for her baby. A lot of confusing advice is bombarded on her. This may get in the way of her deciding what's correct for her and the baby and what's not. It is important for her to be judicious in her food selection as eating the wrong things after delivery could have serious long-term implications.

As a rule of thumb, the diet of the new mother should be light, fresh, nutritious, healthy and balanced. It should be rich in protein, fats, carbohydrates, vitamins and minerals. The new mother is often erroneously denied fresh produce. This poses an impediment to her and her baby's health as the essential iron, vitamins and other micronutrients available in fresh fruits and vegetables do not become readily available. The collagen produced by the body to heal the abdominal stiches is supported by vitamin C and zinc that is available in this fresh produce. Citrus fruits are abundant sources of vitamin C, which has an important role in repairing the body. One must avoid potatoes and cabbage in the first few weeks as they make breastfed babies gassy and uncomfortable.

It is important for the new mother to consume healthy fats like homemade ghee during pregnancy as it helps dissolve fat-soluble vitamins and aids in their absorption. It also slows the absorption of glucose from the food and protects from diabetes. So, eating boiled or raw food is not a good idea when it comes to weight loss for the new mother.

Legumes (not lentils or dals) like soyabeans, chickpeas, beans, etc., may be avoided in the postpartum period for at least two to three months as they are difficult to digest and can make the recovering mother feel gassy and uncomfortable. One thing to remember is that paneer is better than tofu during postpartum.

There are some special foods as per the individual's traditions, which are simply must-haves and should not be missed after delivery. Most of these foods are loaded with dry fruits and homemade ghee, which play a very crucial role in providing the required nourishment to the recovering and breastfeeding mother.

The following food types are recommended for effective breastfeeding:[5]

- Fenugreek (*methi*) Laddoos: These are undoubtedly the most favourite mid-meal snack. Methi seeds are excellent for increasing milk supply, while the jaggery in the laddoos is a rich source of iron, which is important to recover from the postpartum bleeding. Ghee supplies the short-chain fatty acids, thereby promoting metabolism and helping in the redistribution of body fat.
- Panjeri: It is a mix of dry fruits, coconut, dates and jaggery, lightly roasted in homemade ghee. This can be soaked in hot milk and eaten around dawn. A perfectly healthy replacement for breakfast cereals.

- Poppy Seeds (Khus Khus): A glass of khus khus milk is considered a wonder drink to be consumed during the day when you want to take your daytime nap with your baby. It is a rich source of:
  i. Iron, phosphorus and calcium, which are important for blood formation and bone restoration.
  ii. Zinc, which is necessary for healing.
  iii. Magnesium, copper and manganese, which are important for chemical balance in the postpartum brain.
  iv. High fibre content, which keeps constipation at bay.
  v. Oleic acid and omega-6 fatty acids, which help balance blood pressure and improving heart health.
  vi. Antioxidants, which are beneficial to the eyes and skin.
- Edible Gum (Gond): It is an excellent source of dietary fibre and helps in the promotion of postpartum metabolism, improves bowel movement, expedites weight loss and boosts milk production. It also reduces fasting glucose levels, thus being a boon for those recovering from gestational diabetes. It can be consumed in the form of laddoos or as a drink.
- Fox Nuts (Makhana): An excellent protein-rich snack that acts as a powerful milk-production booster, it can be consumed at any hour for a quick refill of energy.
- Power Seeds: A mixture of *ajwain*, *saunf*, *methi* and *kalonji* seeds is excellent for better digestion and lactation. They can be consumed as a post-meal digestive. Flaxseed is also an excellent source of Omega-3 fatty acids, which is great for the newborn's brain development. It can be consumed as a chutney

Care of New Moms and Newborns

during lunch time. Sesame seeds are excellent for lactation and can be consumed as laddoos, tahini, etc., as part of a mid-day meal.

- Decoctions: For the recovery and cleansing of the uterus post childbirth, ayurvedic decoctions (*ukala*) like *dashmularishta*, *devavyayardi kavath* and *balant kadha* are recommended to be taken for one to three months under the guidance of an Ayurvedic doctor. This helps to build immunity, reduce waistline, and cleanse the uterus, and also aids in lactation.

The body's initial need for replenishing nutrients post-birth is higher, which can increase appetite, so it is important for the mother to respond to the hunger cues by eating nutrient-dense food. However, within limits, it is important to incorporate her preferences in her diet as well, and she should not feel forced. Otherwise, the nutrient absorption and assimilation will not happen effectively. Once her body has recovered, the appetite will start reducing as the body adapts to the demands of breastfeeding. Then the mother can start with moderate portion control but should not suffer from hunger pangs.

9. Physical Workout and Weight Loss: It is quite amusing to find that the same people who used to appreciate you for your baby fat during pregnancy start ridiculing you the moment the baby is delivered. Many times, this body shaming is imposed by none other than the new mother herself. This is quite tormenting for the mother, to the extent that she forgets to enjoy her motherhood and in anxiety, takes some extreme steps that sabotage her health in the long term.

The moment the baby is delivered, there is a loss of

six to seven kilos of body weight (because the baby and the placenta are removed and blood escapes the mother's body). However, the excess fat that gets lined up in the belly that was created for the protection of the internal organs and the baby remains intact even after delivery. Thus, immediately after the delivery, the mother still looks six months pregnant. This is because the uterus is still very large and occupies a large space in the abdominal cavity. It takes around six weeks for the uterus to contract and go back to its original position and size in the pelvic cavity. Also, in the initial six weeks, there will be a loss of blood and debris called lochia from the uterus as vaginal discharge, which is quite uncomfortable and annoying. However, the good news is that it helps with your weight loss.

The visits to the gymnasium should be postponed to a minimum of six weeks and a maximum of three months post delivery. With low stamina post childbirth, even a 15-minute walk inside your house can be a good place to begin your workouts.

In fact, it is advisable for new mothers to do kegels every day to strengthen the pelvic floor muscles. To do kegels, tighten your pelvic floor muscles for three seconds and then relax them for three seconds. Repeat this 10 times to complete one set and as you feel your strength increase, you can increase the holding and relaxing time for a maximum of 10 seconds. You can also increase the repetitions in each set. In addition to tightening the pelvic muscle, kegel also prevents urine leakage while coughing or sneezing. Pelvic floor tilts help in strengthening the abdominal muscles. Lie flat on your back with your knees bent and tighten your abdominal muscles while pushing the pelvis up slightly. Hold for about 10 seconds.

The secret is that the more you breastfeed, the more the layers of fat are utilized. But impatient mothers miss this. They get paranoid that the weight they have gained will never go away because of the increased appetite, extended sitting while breastfeeding, and limited movement because of staying indoors. It is strongly recommended that the new mother does not start dieting because it will affect the nourishment of the breastfed babies as well. The mother should not cut down on the recommended diet and must definitely not be in a hurry to exercise as a recovering body needs both time and food to heal. The body will get lethargic and exhausted if one begins exercising too soon. The tired muscles need rest and massages to regain mass and strength. The hormonal levels went haywire during pregnancy and post delivery. Hence, a nutritious diet and adequate rest are important to let the entire body come back to its original conditions. Just give your body the love it deserves and don't feel guilty when eating the extra laddoo that you have been craving. The love you shower onto your body will be soon rewarded with the shedding of those extra kilos when the body feels that it does not need to store fat anymore.

Do remember that the best time to get started on a weight-loss journey is anytime between six weeks and three months, depending upon your gynaecologist's advice and also how your body feels. The mother should target achieving her preconception body conditions in terms of strength and weight within the first year of delivery, to take advantage of her postpartum metabolism and high-calorie utilization during breastfeeding. It has been found that those who are able to reach close to their preconception weight by the first birthday of their child are able to successfully shed off all the extra kilos added during pregnancy and post delivery very easily, as compared to those who start late in their weight-loss journey.

10. Mental Health Care: The fact that everything has suddenly changed in the mother's life, including the basics like food and sleep, is enough to make anyone feel out of control and depressed. Everything revolves around the baby and even the most basic requirements like going to the toilet is controlled by the baby. The body undergoes enormous physical stress during delivery and then the mother forgoes her much-deserved rest to look after the baby, drawing on the body's limited reserves. With this exhausted body and mind, taking care of the newborn seems to be a never-ending and tormenting task.

Sleep deprivation is a new norm for the new mom and it severely hampers the regeneration of brain cells and neural pathways. The prefrontal cortex, which is responsible for one's personality, complex thinking and decision-making, is greatly affected by lack of sleep, making the mother irritable and anxious, causing a lack of clarity in decision-making, as well as affecting short-term memory.

Moreover, the hormonal imbalance happening inside, with oestrogen and progesterone waning and prolactin and oxytocin building up, greatly impacts emotional stability. Further, all these postpartum woes create a stressful situation in the body that leads to an adrenaline rush, which is also accompanied by the rise of cortisol levels. Both of these hormones are harmful for the brain's regeneration, as it leads to accumulated brain cell death, which is the starting point of depression.

Postpartum depression seems increasingly prevalent and needs to be addressed properly. The best way to handle this is to create a strong support system at home by seeking help from your partner and mother (in-law), so that they can take turns to care for the baby and ensuring that you are able to rest. Also, don't make too many demands of yourself for the loss that is happening at work. The fear of missing out adds to your pre-existing anxieties. It's okay if your colleague gets a promotion or a raise and you missed it because of your maternity leave. Life is not a sprint but a marathon, and you will soon reach your goals if you learn to prioritize well.

Last but not the least, remember that this is not a permanent situation in your life and that it is soon going to change. So, don't let the hormonal cocktail dictate your life trajectory. Take charge of your life as you have always done. This, too, shall pass. But what will actually stay with you are the beautiful memories you create with your baby. Use this time to nurture a life-long bond with your baby through breastfeeding, massages and baths, and interacting with the baby by talking and singing to it. You can get rid of the baby blues by spending more time with the baby. The love that your baby showers upon you is actually a once-in-a-lifetime experience, so don't miss it.

Care of a Newborn

The growth and development of a newborn baby happens at a massive pace, so it is important that proper care be taken for the holistic well-being of the baby. The desirable baby weight at the time of birth is above 2.5 kg. Normally, the baby tends to lose some weight (approximately 10 per cent of its body weight) in the first few weeks. However, if by the end of six months, the baby's birth weight doubles, and by the end of first year, the baby's birth weight triples, then it is considered to be a healthy sign. First-time mothers actually face a challenging time as they are confused by the varying suggestions about baby care thrown at them every now and then. So it is important that every mother knows the basics of baby care really well.

Pee and Poop

In life, there is no other occasion when pee and poop are welcomed with so much excitement. These indicate that the baby's hydration, nourishment and overall health are in control. A newborn should pass stool in first 24 hours, and this milestone is eagerly awaited as it confirms the good health of the baby's digestive tracts. The initial stools—called meconium—are sticky in consistency and dark green or black in colour, as the baby excretes all that it has accumulated during the course of nine months. Within a week, this stool changes its colour to a regular yellow, which is again a moment of great joy.

The baby should urinate in the first 48 hours. Frequency of urination gives an indication of how well-fed the baby is. So, if the baby is urinating a minimum of six times a day and is exclusively on breast milk, then the probability that its stomach is full is quite high.

Bath and Massage

A baby does not need a bath for about three to four days as it does not get dirty. Plus, the protective covering on the body—called vernix—helps it protect the skin and regulate body temperature. You can get into a regular bathing routine after that. Every morning before bathing, it is important to massage the baby. Additionally, the mother can also massage the baby just before putting it to sleep at night, as this will ensure a peaceful, deep and long sleep.

Massage is a very important ritual for the baby and should be done either by the mother, a loving family member or an experienced masseuse. It can be accompanied by storytelling, singing or mantra chanting to engage and relax the baby. As the oil is applied, it gets absorbed by the baby's skin, thereby nourishing it. It helps strengthen the bones and the muscles, and adds softness and glow to the skin. It helps the baby gain weight due to increased blood triglyceride levels because of the oil application. Thus, through massages, the baby is fed through the skin. It ensures adequate physical growth, builds immunity and improves resistance to diseases. Moreover, it relaxes the baby and helps it drift into a peaceful, relaxed sleep. This is actually an indication that the massage is done properly and that the baby is enjoying it. If the baby is constantly and regularly crying during massage time, then please look into the matter seriously as something could be wrong. It is important that whoever is massaging should do it lovingly and with the right technique and strokes as any mistakes could lead to long-term injury.

A baby's skin is very sensitive, delicate and tender, so the mother should be very particular about the right kind of oil. The thumb rule to go by could be: if it is safe to eat, it could be safe to apply. Locally-produced *kachi ghani* oils like coconut, sesame, almond, sunflower, etc., are often used. It is better not to opt for packaged and perfumed baby oils as one cannot be sure of their quality. Also, it is important to note whether the baby is allergic towards any particular oil by applying it on a small part of the hand or stomach (of the baby) for the first time.

Sleep

Sleep is very important for the overall development of the baby. A newborn baby should sleep for 20–22 hours, waking up only when wet or hungry, the frequency of which reduces as the baby grows. A sleeping baby should not be disturbed by anyone under any circumstances.

Ayurveda recommends adherence to the following suggestion regarding sleep for babies:[6]

बोधयेत् सहसा सुप्तं नो न चैनं समुत्क्षिपेत्।

It is not good to suddenly awaken a sleeping child. The baby should not be lifted without waking it up beforehand.

The baby cannot differentiate between day and night in the first two months, which becomes the most challenging aspect for the mother. So it is important for her to consciously guide the baby's body clock to distinguish between day and night.

Morning Sun Exposure

Exposing the baby to the early morning sun will acquaint the baby's body clock with the understanding that it needs to stay up during the day and sleep at night. Moreover, morning sun is a source of vitamin D and its exposure also helps to get rid of mild jaundice, which most babies are born with. However, sun exposure should be done in the early morning hours as later during the day the rays become harsh and are not desirable.

Proper Night Regime

A proper night regime like a massage, change of clothes, feeding, lullabies, chanting of mantras, etc., gives the cues to the child's brain that it is night time and that it needs to sleep. Furthermore, by making the room darker and quieter, these cues get reinforced. This works positively and the child adapts to the night regime very soon.

Noisy Day Naps

Mothers should never let the baby sleep in pin-drop silence during the day. Rather, the baby should be made to have day naps in the busier areas of the house, like the living room, where the hustle and bustle is constant. This will help the baby to differentiate between short day naps and deep night sleep.

Whatever the baby hears before sleeping goes to its subconscious mind and stays there forever. So it is important that the baby is put to sleep by the mother very lovingly with the help of some soothing humming, soft singing or chanting of mantras, with gentle movements. Mothers can even give affirmations to the baby just seconds before the baby sleeps as, at that moment, the subconscious mind is most activated.

Once the baby falls asleep, transfer it to the bed with the head pointing east. Many mothers make the mistake of letting the baby sleep on their lap, which later becomes a problem as the baby refuses to sleep on the bed. Also, avoid using swings and rockers for putting the baby to sleep as this might form a habit and won't be feasible in the long run, especially while travelling.

Co-sleeping with the Baby

Co-sleeping refers to the practice of parents and infants sleeping close to each other in the same bed or within close proximity, such as in the same room. The bond between the mother and the baby gets strengthened by co-sleeping and lays a very strong foundation for the long term. It helps in creating a trusting, secure and meaningful relationship. However, there has been a never-ending debate on the pros and cons of the technique.

Co-sleeping, when practised safely, can have several potential advantages:

1. Bonding: Co-sleeping can promote a strong emotional bond between parents and infants, fostering feelings of closeness, security and attachment. According to child psychologists Mary Ainsworth and John Bowlby, babies who are held and remain close to their mothers are more secure, trusting, more adjusting and have well-rounded personalities.[7]
2. Convenience: Co-sleeping can make night-time breastfeeding more convenient, as the baby is within easy reach for feeding sessions, leading to better breastfeeding outcomes and increased milk production.
3. Promotes sleep: Some parents find that co-sleeping helps both parents and infants get better sleep as it can reduce night-time awakenings and help go back to sleep quicker.
4. Regulates breathing: Close proximity while sleeping can help regulate the infant's breathing and body temperature, providing a sense of security and comfort.

5. Encourages responsive parenting: Co-sleeping allows parents to respond more quickly to their infant's needs, such as soothing them when they wake up or providing comfort during times of distress.
6. Enhances attachment: The physical closeness and frequent touch that result from co-sleeping can enhance the parent–child attachment, which is beneficial for the child's emotional and social development.

It's important to note that the advantages of co-sleeping may vary depending on individual circumstances, parenting styles and safety practices. For example, when parents are heavy sleepers or the room environment is not conducive to sleep, then co-sleeping might be challenging for them. So, the decision finally rests on the parents.

Swaddling

It is the practice of wrapping an infant snugly in a blanket or cloth, creating a cozy and secure environment that is similar to the womb. This technique is often used to help soothe newborns and promote better sleep by providing a sense of comfort and warmth. Swaddling can also prevent the startle reflex in infants, leading to more restful sleep patterns. However, it's essential to swaddle safely, ensuring that the baby's hips have room to move and that the swaddle is not so tight that it can restrict breathing or cause overheating.

However, if the baby is not comfortable and struggles for freedom while it is swaddled, then respect the baby's wishes and avoid it. Please note that when the baby is coughing and sneezing, then it is best not to swaddle as the baby needs to be comfortable enough.

Use of Diapers

They are essential items used to absorb and contain urine and faeces, keeping babies and toddlers clean, dry and comfortable. They come in various sizes and types, including disposable and cloth diapers. For convenience, mothers have increased the use of disposable diapers. However, in case of newborn babies, the use of disposable diapers should be restricted to travel and for special occasions. It is not advisable to make babies wear disposable diapers round the clock or through the night as it keeps the genital region constantly moist and does not allow the delicate area to be exposed to air, increasing the risk of skin infections, inflammation and rashes. To mitigate these, it is important to apply diaper creams properly on the buttocks before making the babies wear diapers. Moreover, these are not friendly either to the pocket or the environment. Instead, for regular usage, it is advisable to use cotton cloth diapers which are soft to the baby's skin, reusable, affordable and environmentally friendly.

Some Important Care

As recommended by Ayurveda, these general guidelines should be followed with the baby under all circumstances.[8]

त्रासयेन्नाविधेयं च त्रस्तं गृह्नन्ति हि ग्रहाः।
वस्त्रपातात् परस्पर्शात् पालयेत् लंघनाच्च तम् ॥

The baby should stay away from any unnatural or loud noises, abnormal shapes and frightening sights or situations, all of which could potentially harm the baby. No stranger should be allowed to see or hold the baby when it is without clothes. Furthermore, the baby should not be swung into another person's arms or thrown up into the air. Such actions can lead to severe consequences.[9]

वर्षं स्ववसतेर्बाह्यां कुमारस्य न दर्शयेत्।
दीपमातपमग्निं च रुपमन्यच्च भासुरम् ॥

It should be noted that, especially in the first year, the child should be protected from excess heat, too much light, fire and fearful images. This does not mean that the baby should be kept in a dark room. There should be adequate light but it should not be so intense that it causes damage to the baby's eyes. It is also important to ensure that the baby does not look directly into a light source. It is extremely undesirable to place the baby's cradle directly under a fluorescent light or an electric lamp, or have the baby sleep near the television. The ability of a baby's eyes to respond to light by dilating and constricting its pupils only develops after the third month. Improper exposure before this can cause permanent damage.

The hearing centres of the brain get developed only a few months after the baby is born and speech also develops in conjuction. So, till these are properly developed, it is important to protect the baby from harsh exposure or injury, as any damage can lead to a lifelong disability in the baby.

Covering the baby's ears and head with a cap, especially after the morning bath, is recommended. According to ancient Ayurvedic practices:[10]

अहरह:श्वास्य श्रोत्रष्ट्रंगाटकं स्नेहाप्लुतेन प्लोतेन प्रच्छादयेत् ।

(A drop of lukewarm oil should be put in the baby's ears every day, and then covered with a cotton swab. Seek medical advice to confirm if this would suit the baby's needs.)

Breastfeeding: Continuing Garbha Sanskar Outside the Womb

While Garbha Sanskar is all about the principles a mother seeks to instil in her child while it is in her womb, one should know that it also continues after the birth of the child, well into the breastfeeding stage. The secretion of the mammary glands (breast milk) is a complete and wholesome food for the baby and is so powerful that it is considered to be amrut for the baby. Thus, since time immemorial, it has been believed and ensured that *'matureva pibet stanyam'* (the newborn) should have only the mother's breast milk. Breastfeeding is an extension of Garbha Sanskar outside the womb. During the pregnancy, the food, thoughts and emotions of the mother had a profound impact upon the womb. Similarly, while breastfeeding, whatever the mother is eating, thinking and feeling could be transferred to the baby through the milk.

This directly impacts the formation of the PQ, IQ, EQ and SQ of the baby. The first thousand days of a child's life, i.e., from conception (270 days) to two years of age, witness a very high growth phase and thus requires extra nutrition from the mother during pregnancy.[11]

Several scientific studies have recommended that it is best to feed mother's milk exclusively to a baby for a minimum of six months, and for best results, great health, and immunity, continued feeding till two years is highly recommended.

WHO and UNICEF recommends:

- Early initiation of breastfeeding within one hour of birth.
- Exclusive breastfeeding for the first six months of life.
- Introduction of nutritionally adequate and safe complementary (solid) foods at six months together with continued breastfeeding up to two years of age or beyond.

Thus, a mother should feed within the first hour of birth, exclusively feed the child for six months, and do continuous feeding for two years. This will ensure holistic growth of the child in all the areas—PQ, IQ, EQ and SQ.

The entire process of breastfeeding is highly divine and is one of the most satisfying experiences for the mother and baby. During the pregnancy, the mother can only imagine the way her child is, but loves it dearly; once it is born, she can hold her bundle of joy in her arms and her love has no bounds. She is filled with motherly love, and it showers upon the child in all spheres. One of the most tangible forms of expression of love is during breastfeeding. When done physically, while looking at the child, the mother can impart a whole world of kindness, love and power to the baby. It also helps her to deal with postpartum depression, relieves stress and, most importantly, helps her develop a bond with the baby that is imperishable and beyond time.

The Benefits of Breastfeeding for the Baby

There is no alternative to a mother's milk for a newborn. Breastfeeding has innumerable benefits that are irreplaceable. Some of the benefits are enumerated below:

1. Mother's milk is a complete food that provides all the essential nutrients in the right proportions that are easily digestible and are required for the baby to grow.
2. Breast milk is always fresh, pure and available whenever required at zero cost. It is at the perfect temperature and thus better and way more effective than any formula feed or any other alternative.
3. In addition to providing nutrients, breast milk has several special component such as growth factors, enzymes, hormones and anti-infective factors. It plays a crucial role in supporting and enhancing a baby's natural immune system. It contains Immunoglobulin A (IgA), lactoferrin, complement factors and lactoperoxidase, which protect the infant from various infections. The gut flora and the low pH of breast milk (pH 6.36–7.36) inhibit the growth of pathogens. The prebiotic bifidus factor in breast milk promotes natural gut flora. Antibodies and some viruses found in breast milk protect the gut mucosa. Exclusive breastfeeding protects against diarrhoea and upper respiratory tract infections. Breastfeeding also reduces the risk of allergic reactions in infants.

Thus, due to breastfeeding, antibodies pass from the mother to the baby through the milk, safeguarding the baby from future ailments, including infections, childhood obesity, type 1 and type 2 diabetes, and leukaemia, thereby increasing its PQ. Research has shown that breastfed babies are generally better nourished, healthier, and have stronger immune support throughout life. The incidence of diseases and mortality among breastfed infants is much lower than among non-breastfed infants.[12]

4. Research has proven that babies who were fed mother's milk for a longer duration have higher cognitive and brain development, leading to a better IQ than kids who were on formula feed.[13]
5. It promotes a stronger bond between the mother and the baby, gives the baby a sense of security, satisfies the emotional needs of the baby, and promotes EQ. In fact, the mother's love promotes the secretion of oxytocin, which in turn promotes lactation.
6. While feeding, if the mother chants mantras or reads scriptures, she sends healing energies to the baby, which helps in strengthening the SQ of the baby.

The Benefits of Breastfeeding for the Mother

It is not just the baby that benefits from breastfeeding. Today, it is surprisingly common for many new mothers to not wish to breastfeed their babies, and it can have a detrimental effect on the overall health and strength of the mother. Some of the breastfeeding benefits for mothers are enumerated below:

1. The entire journey of pregnancy can be very overwhelming for the mother. The process of the delivery is regarded as her second birth. Thus, this could also cause a lot of emotional and mental trauma for her. When the mother is breastfeeding, hormones like prolactin and oxytocin are released in her body that help her keep calm, feel loved, and also creates a defence against postpartum depression.
2. All the extra kilos that the mother puts on during the pregnancy can be easily burnt in the course of breastfeeding the child. Thus, it helps burn calories and facilitates weight loss after pregnancy.

3. Breastfeeding produces the hormone oxytocin, which helps in contraction and healing of the uterus post delivery.
4. The early reappearance of menstruation any time in the first five to six months after childbirth is detrimental to the health of the mother. Breastfeeding ensures that menstruation will generally not recommence as long as the child is being breastfed.
5. Breastfeeding mothers reduce their chances of breast cancer, ovarian cancer, obesity, type 2 diabetes, metabolic syndrome and cardiovascular diseases such as stroke and heart attacks.[14]
6. It also helps in family planning by usually delaying ovulation as the chances of conception while the mother is breastfeeding is low.
7. It builds up self-esteem and self-reliance of the mother, also helping her develop a stronger bond with her baby.

When Ruchi was in her thirty-fourth week, she gave birth to her baby girl, Kripa. Although Kripa's was a normal delivery and there were no developmental issues, her birth weight was considerably less.

This worried the doctors and Ruchi. However, the doctors said all would be well if she fed the baby enough breastmilk in a timely manner. The baby's body weight would increase, and things would be just fine. The only catch was that since the baby was preterm, it still did not know how to latch onto the breast properly. The doctors gave a prescribed weight-gain time chart for the next two months and told her that if the baby gained enough weight, she would be healthy.

Ruchi took up the challenge and decided to continue with her regime of Garbha Sanskar that she had been following. She stayed positive and blissful, fed herself healthy foods, rested whenever she could, continued to chant the mantras that she had been chanting throughout her pregnancy, and stayed connected to the baby through her positive talks. She would feed her baby for almost half an hour and then extract the leftover milk with a breast pump when the baby got tired. She would then feed her using a feeder spoon. Once happy with the feed, the baby would sleep, and by the time Ruchi sterilized everything and caught up with little rest, the baby would be hungry all over again! This went on for two weeks. But, to her delight, the baby was catching up with her target weight.

The doctors were amazed and asked her to continue whatever she was doing because it was yielding great results. Ruchi maintained her ritual and made sure not to use bottle feed because the baby would then have a tough time latching onto her once again. After a month, the baby was strong enough to latch onto the breast independently. In two months, Kripa had not only met but exceeded the target baby weight, being strong and perfectly in line with healthy development parameters, giving her the promise of a healthy life.

Garbha Sanskar is not just about what you feed to your child while it is still in your womb, it does go beyond and to the time when you really feed them, as you hold them tight in your arms!

Quality of Breast Milk

Like the baby was in the womb, it stays unified with the mother even after birth through her breast milk. The quality of the milk is affected by the mother's overall lifestyle, what she thinks, what she feels, and what she does and eats. As the child lives exclusively on breast milk for its complete nutrition, it is important that extreme care is taken by the mother for holistic well-being—physical, mental, emotional and spiritual. So a feeding mother should continue with all the holistic well-being principles as outlined in the previous chapters. This will ensure healthy and high-quality breast milk as shared by Acharya Carak in the following verse:[15]

स्तन्यसम्पन्नु प्रकृतिवर्णगन्धरसस्पर्शम्, उदकपात्रे च दुह्यमानमुदकं
व्येति प्रकृतिभूतत्वात् तत् पुष्टिकरमारोग्यकरं चेति ।

Breast milk of excellent quality should have the following features:

- Breast milk should have a natural colour, smell, taste and touch.
- Pure breast milk easily mixes with water.
- Breast milk provides nourishment and health to the child.

It should be noted that the overall quality of breast milk deteriorates with a negligent lifestyle.

Thus, for maintaining quality of breast milk and increasing its purity, it is important to add turmeric powder (haldi), asafoetida (*hing*), cumin (jeera) and fenugreek seeds (methi) in the food. Also, a mouth freshener can be made from sesame (*till*), carom seeds (*ajwain*) and fennel (*sauf*) to be consumed post meals to increase the purity of breast milk.

Commandments for Effective Breastfeeding

There are lot of myths and confusions regarding breastfeeding. However, it is a very natural process and should be done with extreme ease and relaxation. Some basic guidelines for effective breastfeeding are shared below:

1. Breastfeed your baby within an hour of delivery.
2. The first milk, which is translucent and yellow, is called colostrum and is the most important and highly beneficial nutrition for the newborn. It should not be discarded under any circumstances.
3. The amount of milk secreted increases gradually in the first few days after delivery, reaching the peak during the second month, and is maintained until about six months. An average Indian woman secretes about 750 ml of milk per day during the first six months and 600 ml of milk per day subsequently up to one year.[16]
4. The breasts must be cleaned before each feed, and for this, a vessel filled with boiled water should be kept covered ready for use. When the baby is hungry, the mother should wash her hands, then use a sterile cotton swab dipped in this water to wash her breasts, especially the nipples. A new sterile cotton swab should be used each time.
5. A quiet and calm place is best for breastfeeding. The mother should sit comfortably, ideally in a cross-legged position, on a soft seat. The baby should be held in such a way that the head is slightly above the level of its abdomen. Instead of the mother bending over, it is better to hold the child slightly higher on the arm, otherwise the weight of the breasts may cause breathing difficulties for the infant. The baby's head should not be entirely covered

with cloth as it could suffocate the child or cause difficulty in breathing. The child may have to breathe through its mouth, and the air, which then reaches the abdomen, may cause vomiting and colic.
6. The baby should latch on the areola and not just the nipple. This will not only ensure good feeding to the infant but also protect nipples from any damage.
7. There is no hard and fast rule about how long the infant is to be fed as it depends on various factors, such as age, hunger and the infant's ability to suckle. The baby will usually feed up to 15-20 minutes and stop suckling once it is satisfied. A weak or pre-term baby may feed up to 30-35 minutes. The mother will normally be able to determine the baby's requirements within a few days. It is important that the baby completes the feed from one side before switching on to the other side as then the baby receives all the essential nutrients because the composition of the milk varies at the beginning and towards the end of the feeding cycle; the milk coming later is richer in fat and should not be missed by the baby. In case the baby only takes feed from one side in the previous cycle, then alternate from the other in this cycle. This will balance milk production on both sides.
8. Caress behind the earlobes or pat on the cheek if the baby tends to fall asleep while feeding in initial days.
9. Ensure that there is no pressure on the baby's abdomen after feeding. This is best done by holding the baby on mother's shoulders with its back erect, close to the chest and gently stroking its back to facilitate burping.
10. Breast milk provides enough nutrition and immunity for the baby and it needs nothing other than a mother's milk,

not even water, until the first six months of its birth. In fact, feeding water reduces the breast milk and increases the risk of diarrhoea and is to be totally avoided.[17]

11. The baby should be allowed to feed whenever it's hungry. The initial interval between feeds (when the child is hungry) is usually about two to three hours, slowly increasing to three to four hours. If the baby is asleep at feeding times, it should not be woken just to feed. Similarly, it is not good to keep the child waiting if it feels hungry before the set feeding time.

12. The mother must feed the baby whenever and for whatever duration that is needed by the baby. The ideal demand for the feed is every one to three hours. She must 'feed on demand' and not based on a clock that is convenient for her.

13. The baby may vomit occasionally after a feed, but this is not usually a cause for concern. As long as it gains weight normally, sleeps quietly and is not irritable, one need not seek medical advice for occasional vomiting. Vomiting actually rids the baby's stomach of any excess accumulated phlegm. The incidence of vomiting usually reduces gradually, and ultimately stops when the child begins to turn onto its abdomen and crawl.

14. Care of your breasts should be done from the pregnancy stage itself. It's important to prevent the formation of lumps, and if any pain arises, ice application can provide relief. If your nipples are not erect, gently pull it out from the pregnancy stage itself.

15. In case the baby is consuming less milk than what is being produced, then it can cause a feeling of heaviness and a dull ache in the breasts. This excess milk should

be removed with some gentle pressure, else it could form clots that block the mammary ducts, leading to discomfort, or even fever. It could also cause decreased breast-milk production in some women. If required, a breast pump may be used to extricate the extra milk. It is important to be cautious as the repeated, indiscriminate use of a breast pump could lead to cracks in the nipples.

16. The nutritional well-being of a breastfed child relies entirely on the mother's milk. The quality of this milk is directly influenced by the mother's dietary choices, lifestyle and emotional state. Factors such as the mother's food intake, daily routines and communication style play a role in shaping the composition of breast milk, which in turn impacts the baby's nourishment. It is crucial for the mother to prioritize her own physical, mental and emotional health to ensure optimal breastfeeding outcomes for her child.

17. Many medicines (like antibiotics, painkillers and hormones) and addictive substances (caffeine, alcohol and psychotropic drugs) are secreted into breast milk and could prove harmful to breastfed infants.[18] Hence, caution should be exercised by lactating mothers and appropriate medical guidance should be taken for the above referred medicines or addictive substances.

18. Lastly, the mother should be totally committed towards breastfeeding and put in her best efforts. It might be less convenient but is infinitely more rewarding.

Guidelines for Working Mothers

The real challenge that the mothers face while breastfeeding is when they are either working or need to separate themselves from the baby frequently. The following tips may help them:

1. You should try to extend the maternity leave as much as possible for devoting maximum time to the baby. Otherwise, you should opt for a part-time job or work-from-home option so that breastfeeding does not get affected.
2. If the office is located near the house, then try to visit home during breaks and feed your child directly.
3. In extreme situations, express the milk with your hands or preferably by a breast pump in a clean container and refrigerate it. This milk should be used within six to seven hours of pumping out. Before offering to the baby, it is important to bring the milk to room temperature.
4. Mother's milk can be stored in a deep freeze for a year. However, care must be taken to bring the milk to room temperature by putting the bottle in a container of hot water and not by directly heating it
5. Always sterilize the pump equipment, bottles, nipples, etc., very carefully as not doing it might lead to infections.
6. It should be noted that direct feeding is always more beneficial then expressed feed as the quality of the milk deteoriates once it is expressed.
7. Always feed expressed milk from baby feeder spoons and never use bottle for feeding the baby as the sucking mechanism for bottle and breast nipples are totally different. If the baby gets used to bottle, it will refuse to suck from the breast, which can lead to decreasing milk supply.

How to Know if the Milk Supply Is Enough

The biggest challenge that any mother faces is in understanding whether her baby has had enough feed. Crying is not always a sign of hunger. The only language that a child uses to communicate any discomfort is crying. So, a mother needs to be intelligent enough to decode her child's crying.

The following guidelines can be used to know if the milk supply is enough or not:

1. A healthy newborn is expected to lose 7 to 10 per cent of the birth weight in the first four to five days of birth due to the loss of extra fluid that they are born with. Generally, it should regain that weight within the first two to three weeks after birth.
2. It should be noted that during their first month, if the newborn gains weight at a rate of about 30 g per day, it is a healthy sign of the baby being well fed. The general thumb rule for the healthy growth of a baby is if its weight increases by one to one-and-a-half kg at the end of the first month, doubles by the sixth month and triples on turning one.
3. A baby who consumes only breastmilk, not even additional water, and urinates a minimum of six times a day, is getting enough milk for its growth.
4. Crying is not always a sign of hunger. If your baby is active, happy, playful, sleeping well, gaining weight and urinating enough, then it is well fed.
5. It is an ignorant belief that if the mother has small and lean breasts, then she is not producing enough as the size of the breasts has no co-relation with lactation.
6. A leak from the other breast while feeding or when the baby has not taken feed from a long time is a sign of sufficient milk supply.

How to Increase Breast Milk Supply

According to Acharya Sushruta, many mothers experience a decrease in the quantity of their breast milk because of the following reasons:[19]

क्रोमशोकावात्सल्यादिभिश्च च स्त्रिया: स्तन्यनाशो भवति ।

(Experiencing emotions like anger, grief or a lack of maternal love and empathy, along with factors such as fasting, overexercising, excessive anxiety or worry can result in a decrease in breast milk supply.)

Many women today are working long hours, which is a constant source of physical and mental stress. Moreover, due to multiple commitments and time constraints, she is unable to meet the holistic guidelines prescribed in previous chapters. It leads to a decrease in the milk supply as breast milk is easily affected by minor changes in food habits or the mental state of the mother. This is one concern which is common with every lactating mother.

Guidelines to Increase Milk Supply

1. It is important to be full of love and have confidence in oneself while breastfeeding. A mother's positive emotions trigger the release of hormones like oxytocin, which supports lactation and boosts milk supply. Conversely, stress leads to cortisol production, which hinders lactation.
2. It is mandatory to feed within one hour of delivery or as soon as possible.
3. Chanting mantras while feeding can enhance the power, quality and quantity of breast milk.

4. Regular and frequent breastfeeding, including during night time, is crucial for effective milk production as the more often we breastfeed, the more our lactation increases.
5. It is important to ensure that the baby latches properly to the breast while feeding.
6. It is crucial to prioritize exclusive breastfeeding. If you need to leave the baby behind for some time, then it is important to make sure that you express and feed your milk. Under no circumstances should you miss your feed cycle as it can decrease the milk supply. However, direct breastfeeding is always recommended over expressed feeding because the quality of milk decreases once it is expressed.
7. Bottle feeding can contribute to breastfeeding challenges because it can confuse the baby between the mother's nipple and an artificial nipple. Since the sucking mechanisms for each are different, the baby may find it easier to suckle from a bottle nipple and eventually develop a preference for it, leading to potential breastfeeding difficulties or failure.
8. Breast-milk production adjusts according to the baby's needs. Adding formula milk to the feeding routine can reduce the baby's intake of your milk, causing a decrease in your milk supply over time and potentially leading to breastfeeding challenges.
9. Formula milk often has a sweeter and more palatable taste, which can lead babies to develop a preference for it. Therefore, it's ideal to avoid introducing formula milk unnecessarily to prevent your baby from acquiring a taste for it.

10. It is important to hug and physically bond with your baby as keeping the baby close to your chest triggers the secretion of oxytocin, a hormone that plays a crucial role in lactation.
11. Consistently give affirmations for breastfeeding and visualize your milk as divine and meeting all of your baby's needs.
12. Stay away from smoking, other addictions and certain medications that can impact the lactation process.
13. Sleeping in the prone position (on your stomach) can affect lactation as there is more pressure on your breasts, which can compress milk ducts and affect milk flow.
14. Maintain a balanced, nutritious diet and make healthy lifestyle choices.
15. Last but not the least, be a relaxed, blissful, happy and confident mother.

To sum it up, taking care of their physical, mental, emotional and spiritual wellbeing will help mothers with producing good quality and quantity of breast milk for their baby.

Foods for Increasing Quality and Quantity of Mother's Milk

According to NIN, during lactation, there is an increased demand for calories, proteins and micronutrients to maintain the health of the mother and ensure optimal breast milk production. In the first six months of lactation, an additional 600 calories and 13.6 g of protein are required daily. In the following six months, the additional requirements are 520 calories and 10.6 g of protein per day. While most of these nutritional needs can be met through a balanced diet, lactating women are advised to take daily supplements of iron and folic acid.[20] Some food items which help in improving quality and quantity of lactation are given below:

1. Ayurvedic preparation of asparagus or *satavari* powder with milk
2. Seeds and nuts with oil: fenugreek (*methi*), cumin (*jeera*), fennel (*saunf*), sesame (*till*), carom seeds (*ajwain*), coconut, almonds
3. Fresh fruits like unripe papaya, carrots, apricots, watermelon
4. Green vegetables like spinach (*palak*), fenugreek leaves (*methi*), mustard greens (*sarso*), basil (*tulsi*), bitter gourd (*karela*), drumstick (*sahjan*), asparagus (*satavari*)
5. Nutritious options like ragi, finger millet (*ragi* or *nachni*), oats (*jav*), barley (*jau*), tapioca pearls (*sabudana*), red lentils (*masoor dal*)
6. Dairy products like milk, paneer, ghee, tofu

Making the Process Divine

Breastfeeding is a sacred process and an excellent opportunity for bonding with your child. Sadly, many mothers miss this precious time by focussing on electronic devices and social media. It's crucial to utilize this time effectively by chanting mantras, sharing scriptures, affirmations or simply expressing love. The child is most receptive to the mother's voice during feeding, which helps in creating positive neural pathways in the child's brain.

Feeding is an extension of Garbha Sanskar, continuing the nurturing process even after birth. The brain undergoes significant development during pregnancy and the early years, making breastfeeding pivotal for fostering growth across various aspects like PQ, IQ, EQ and SQ. Though exhausting, breastfeeding is a unique opportunity for laying the foundation of immense love and connection with your child.

Devoting oneself to the child's care during pregnancy and the first year and prioritizing their needs set a strong foundation for their future. The cuddles and snuggles and the endless laughter over a simple peek-a-boo are what makes the life of a mother richer. The joy and love experienced during this time are priceless rewards, compensating for any sacrifices made. The love and adoration from your little one are unparalleled and irreplaceable, and as time passes, you'll cherish these moments more and more.

Divya Garbha Sanskar—A Salute to the Beautiful Beginning

Garbha Sanskar marks the powerful beginning of a journey that extends far beyond pregnancy. It's a reminder that as mothers, our responsibility only grows with time. Just as a farmer tends to every detail of his crop from seed to harvest, nurturing a life within us demands ongoing care, attention and love. The principles of Garbha Sanskar lay the foundation for a child's future, but our role as parents continues long after birth.

Our children are not just born; they are manifested from our deepest desires and intentions. With the right preparation and understanding, we can unlock their full potential and guide them towards a life of health, intelligence, creativity and resilience. As Maa Yashoda, Maa Sita and Maa Shakuntala exemplified in our scriptures, motherhood is a journey of strength, love and nurturing.

As we embark on this journey, remember that every challenge is an opportunity to nurture, every setback is a chance to grow. Like a diamond in the rough, our children need chiselling and nurturing to shine bright. Garbha Sanskar isn't just about pregnancy; it's about shaping a beautiful life and a meaningful parenting journey.

So, dear mother, embrace this divine responsibility with joy and determination. With fertility dwindling, values evolving, and many challenges posing a threat to our sustenance, it is important that each child that takes birth is a divine genius. It is not just about yourselves; it is the need of the hour to revitalize humanity. As we embrace the principles of Garbha Sanskar, we not only nurture individual lives but also contribute to the collective well-being of our nation, and humanity at large, with active participation collectively from the family, society, country and the world. Let us together focus on uplifting humanity by instilling in the womb all the powerful processes that will create a future that is capable of changing the shape of the world.

Just unlock the secrets shared here and give your 100 per cent to manifest your dream baby. Get ready to enjoy your baby who you have manifested; if you have manifested Lord Krishna, then enjoy his naughtiness like Maa Yashoda did, or take pride as Maa Kaushlya did if you have manifested Shri Ram. Enjoy all the love being showered upon you by your little bundle of joy. You deserve it all, dear mother.

> *'Mother is the first and foremost Guru taking the divine responsibility of sowing the first seeds of intelligence in her own Gurukul—The Divine Womb.'*

Tracker Sheet for Postnatal Self-Check
Preparation for Postnatal Maternity Care

Preparation for Neonatal Baby Care

Annexure 1

MONTH-BY-MONTH JOURNEY OF THE FOETUS WITH LIFESTYLE GUIDANCE

First Month: Foetal Growth

स सर्वगुणवान् गर्भत्वमापन्नः प्रथमे मासि संमूच्छितः
सर्वधातुकलुषीकृतः खेटभूतो भवत्यव्यक्तविग्रहः
सदसद्भूताङ्गावयवः ।।1।।

—चरक शारीरस्थान

तत्र प्रथमे मासि कललं जायते।

—सुश्रुत शारीरस्थान

During the first month, the embryo is shapeless and resembles a ball. It bursts like a bubble on the tenth day, takes solid shape after 15 days, and becomes a pea-sized flesh ball by the end of twentieth day. It weighs not more than a wheat seed. On the twenty-first day, it grows four times in size and the formation of heart, spinal cord and brain begins. The brain starts growing at a massive rate of 2.5 lakh neurons per minute, even before you realize that you are pregnant. By the end of the first month, the foetus is about half an inch in size.

Special Ayurvedic Diet

प्रथमे मासे शङ्किता चेद्गर्भमापन्ना क्षीरमनुपस्कृतं मात्रावच्छीतं
काले काले पिबेत, सात्म्यमेव च भोजनं सायं प्रातश्च भुञ्जीतः।

—चरक शारीरस्थान

During this initial pregnancy period, sufficient quantity of milk at room temperature (boiled and brought to room temperature) should be consumed both in the morning and evening. One must eat food that is wholesome and easily digestible.

(As the confirmation of pregnancy comes a little later, after a period is missed, it is advisable to follow this routine from the time the woman starts trying to conceive.)

Suggested Lifestyle due to Changes in the Mother's Body

In case it is a planned pregnancy and you are still awaiting the confirmation, then as a precautionary measure, go slow on your regular activities and don't take stress—physical, mental, emotional. Moreover, because of the sudden hormonal changes happening in the body, you might suffer from morning sickness, nausea, acidity, headaches, vomiting, etc. Thus, adapt your lifestyle accordingly.

Must-Do Activities

Listen to your body and start caring for it as if you are pregnant. Continue giving affirmations for conception, visualize as if you are pregnant, and do mantra chanting for getting confirmed results.

Second Month: Foetal Growth

द्वितीये मासि घन: संपद्यते पिण्ड: पेश्यर्बुदं वा।
तत्र घन: पुरुष:, पेशी स्त्री, अर्बुदं नपुंसकम ॥10॥

—चरक शारीरस्थान

द्वितीये शीतोष्मानिलैरभिप्रपच्यमानानां महाभूतानां संघातो घन संजायते,
यदि पिण्ड: पुमान, स्त्री चेत् पेशी, नपुंसकं चेदर्बुदमिति।

—सुश्रुत शारीरस्थान

In the second month, the embryo increases in density, and slowly becomes round, oval or like a teardrop. In the second month, the foetus starts showing cardiac activity, thus giving confirmation of the developing life. It is important to introduce changes in diet and lifestyle at this stage. In the second month, the head, limbs, heart and reproductive organs of the foetus start developing. The foetus starts to experience hiccups and bend its body. Most importantly the pituitary gland, which is the master gland that controls secretion of all the other glands, takes shape in the second month. The structure of the ear also begins to form now.

Special Ayurvedic Diet

द्वितीये मासे क्षीरमेव च मधुरौषधसिद्ध।

—चरक शारीरस्थान

In the second month of pregnancy, the pregnant lady should drink milk boiled with water and sweet-tasting herbs, such as shatavari, gokshur, bala and vidari to facilitate the massive growth of the body and brain.

Suggested Lifestyle due to Changes in the Mother's Body

The foetus is not yet strongly implanted, so it is important not do any physical exertion like bending forward, bowing down, standing for long time, etc. Moreover, due to the sudden physical and hormonal changes, expectant mothers may experience nausea, heartburn, restlessness, disinterest in food, mood swings, anxiety, etc. She should stay calm and refrain from doing any physical and mental activity that might cause stress to her body and mind. The mother should take a very healthy nutritious diet in small portions every two hours as an empty stomach aggravates nausea and vomiting.

The uterus is located in between the large intestine and the bladder and as it starts growing, it creates pressure on the bladder which results in the urge for frequent urination. Under no circumstances must the expecting mother suppress her urge for urination. As the foetus starts growing upwards, this problem gets mitigated from the third month.

Must-Do Activities

According to ancient rituals and beliefs, Punsavana Sanskar Ceremony keeps the child healthy for their entire life.

Since the expectant mother is anxious about the new experience, it is important that she is supported lovingly by her family members, especially her husband.

As the listening skills are developing, the mother should start doing Garbha Samvad (talking to the womb) as well as listen to Garbha Sanskar music, mantra chanting and powerful scriptures. The mother can further enhance the listening skills of the child in the womb by doing various activities like playing some musical games, identifying between various sounds and music, blindfolding and finding the direction of sound, playing

Chinese whisper, etc. Involving the father in these activities is a great idea as this will help him bond with the baby in the womb itself.

Since the foetus is delicate right now, it is important to chant the mantra given in Annexure 3 for its protection.

This is the best time to envision all the qualities that the parent wants in the child, as discussed in the previous chapter, and set affirmations and make a vision board for the same which the mother should meditate upon throughout the pregnancy for achieving the child of her dreams.

Third Month: Foetal Growth

तृतीये मासि सर्वेन्द्रियाणि सर्वाङ्गावयवाश्च यौगपद्येनाभि-
निर्वर्तन्ते ॥11॥

—चरक शारीरस्थान

तृतीये हस्तपादशिरसां पंचपिण्डका निर्वर्तन्ते अंगप्रत्यंग
विभागश्च सूक्ष्मो भवति।

—सुश्रुत शारीरस्थान

The tiny foetus develops its limbs and a head begins to take shape. The head, hands and legs and the five senses also develop at a microscopic level at this time. The expectant mother should get involved in activities that support development of the senses in the foetus. Umbilical cord is also developed in the third month, thus strengthening the bond between the mother and the foetus. The foetus starts experiencing all the emotions that are being experienced by the mother. Whatever the mother sees, hears, says and reads is experienced by the foetus in the same manner and intensity. The sense of tatste also starts to develop at this stage.

Special Ayurvedic Diet

तृतीये मासे क्षीरं मधुसर्पिर्भ्यामुपसंसृज्य

—चरक शारीरस्थान

In the third month, milk with ghee and honey should be taken every morning (one teaspoon of honey and two teaspoons of ghee in a cup of warm milk).

Suggested Lifestyle due to Changes in the Mother's Body

During this stage, the mother's body has adapted itself to the hormonal changes. So, by now, the vomiting and nausea starts getting better and are settled. Yet, it is advisable to eat gently cooked home food with less spices. The expecting mother should refrain from doing physical exertion at this stage. The couple should have a very loving relationship as this is being sensed and absorbed by the baby in the womb, but they should refrain from sexual acts throughout the first trimester.

Must-Do Activities

As the unborn child can sense all emotions, it is important for the expectant mother to always be in a state of complete bliss and have loving relations with all the people that matter to her and the baby. By regularly indulging in Garbha Samvad and expressing her love to the child, she must let it know how much it is wanted and welcomed. Affirmations and visualizations are a must for manifesting your dream child.

As the taste buds start developing, it is important for the expectant mother to include all the six variety (shadrasas)—sweet, sour, salty, spicy, bitter and astringent—so that the child in the womb starts developing acceptance towards all the rasas or tastes and adapts itself to all these tastes. Moreover, in order to develop the taste buds of the child, the mother can play a game wherein she experiences various tastes like the difference between the sweetness of sugar and jaggery, different flavors and delicacies, etc.

Fourth Month: Foetal Growth

चतुर्थे मासि स्थिरत्वं आपद्यते गर्भ:, तस्मात्तदा गर्भिणी
गुरुगात्रत्वं अधिकं आपद्यते विशेषेण।

—चरक शारीरस्थान

चतुर्थे सर्वाङ्गप्रत्यङ्गविभाग: प्रव्यक्तो भवति,
गर्भहृदयप्रव्यक्तीभावाच्चेतनाधातुरभिव्यक्तो भवति,
कस्मात्? तत्स्थानत्वात्।
तस्माद्गर्भश्चतुर्थे मास्यभिप्रायमिन्द्रियार्थेषु करोति,
द्विहृदयां च नारीं दौहृदिनीमाचक्षते।

—सुश्रुत शारीरस्थान

The foetus becomes stable, and as it grows in size, the expectant mother experiences a heavy feeling. The different body parts become better defined, the sense organ of vision gets developed, and the heart can now be experienced completely. Although heartbeats of the foetus can be felt from one-and-a-half months into pregnancy, the heart is fully developed by the fourth month.

In the fourth month, the pregnant woman is referred to as *dauhrudini*, i.e., one having two hearts, hers and that of her baby, beating inside her. The desires of the developing foetus, described as *dauhrud*, become evident at this stage. The baby is able to voice its wishes through its heart from this point, and it is important to fulfill these wishes. If not done, then it may have an adverse effect on the foetus. Furthermore, the sense of taste is fully developed by now and the baby in the womb starts sharing its desires for eating particular foods and flavours through its mother.

However, one should be cautious of not being overindulgent about these pregnancy cravings, in the garb of one's own desires.

Please note that if these desires are properly attended to, the child to-be-born will likely be healthy, happy and content, having a long life.

Special Ayurvedic Diet

चतुर्थे मासे क्षीरनवनीतमक्षमात्रमश्रीयात्।

—चरक शारीरस्थान

In the fourth month it is advised to have one tablespoon (12 g) of fresh homemade butter, to be consumed every morning with milk. Avoid stale butter as it might create heat in the chest.

Suggested Lifestyle due to Changes in the Mother's Body

Listen to the foetus, but do not get overindulgent in the garb of foetus's desire. Pregnancy cravings should not be taken lightly, but at the same time, family members should not stretch themselves too much to meet the demands that may cause adverse effects. It is suggested that the middle path be followed for the benefit of both the mother and the child. So, it is important to differentiate between the desires of foetus and creation of the mother's mind. When any desire comes suddenly to the mother without her thinking consciously about it or desiring it, then it is the actual desire of the baby.

The baby swallows the placenta water, which is not just

the water but has the taste of all the food that the mother is consuming. So, it is important that the mother should continue eating balanced sattvic food inclusive of all the six tastes and stay away from her food overindulgences.

You have now entered into the second trimester or the honeymoon phase of pregnancy and the foetus is much stable now. However, continue to be careful and refrain from doing anything that might physically or mentally exhaust you.

Must-Do Activities

To further develop the sense of vision, do a lot of creative visualization exercises. Engage yourself in creative activities such as drawing, painting, mixing palettes of different colours, which will strengthen the sense of vision. The mother should listen to the heart but should not get overwhelmed.

Fifth Month: Foetal Growth

पञ्चमे मासि गर्भस्य मांसशोणितोपचयो भवत्यधिकम्-न्येभ्यो मासेभ्य:, तस्मात्तदा गर्भिणी काश्र्वमापद्यते विशेषेण ॥21॥

—चरक शारीरस्थान

पचमे मन: प्रतिबुद्धतरं भवति।

—सुश्रुत शारीरस्थान

From the fifth month, the child's mind becomes sensitized to various feelings, events and surroundings. The brain becomes more active and alert. During this period the maximum development of muscle tissues and blood formation happens, thereby making the mother feeble. According to the Garbhopanishad, the vertebral column also gets properly developed in this month. Moreover, the mind of the foetus gets enlightened, and consciousness starts developing from this stage. The tactile glands become functional. So the sense of touch gets developed and the foetus starts responding to the touch of the mother. The baby has grown in size during this stage, and the mother can feel the movement of the foetus.

The stool and waste matter start to develop in the intestines.

Special Ayurvedic Diet

पञ्चमे मासे क्षीरसर्पि:

—चरक शारीरस्थान

From the fifth month, it is important to supplement the meals with seven to eight teaspoons of ghee daily to give an extra boost of energy. However, this ghee should be prepared by directly churning the milk into butter and not from curd.

Suggested Lifestyle due to Changes in the Mother's Body

In order to ensure the development of Sattvic Buddhi (pure mind), the mother should follow an extremely pure and divine lifestyle, adopt a sattvic or positive diet, and engage in activities that help create the desired values in the child.

Must-Do Activities

The expectant mother should focus on enlightening the mind of her unborn child by doing a lot of reading of good scriptures and powerful biographies, listening to divine music, chanting powerful mantras like 'Omkar', 'Gayatri Mantra', etc. She should refrain from negative emotions like anger, fear, grief, jealousy, and should not watch, read or listen to content that contains violence or horror. Instead, she should remain happy, contented and preferably in a state of bliss at all times.

Expecting mother should talk to the baby (Garbha Samvad) about all the values and qualities she wishes to inculcate in it.

From this point, the mother should do Garbha Samvad with her palm touching the womb as the baby is able to feel and connect with her touch. The father must also take this opportunity to bond with the baby by touching the womb lovingly with his palms and talking to the baby. In order to develop the sense of touch, the expecting mother can play games by blindfolding herself and recognizing various objects by merely touching them and feeling their texture—hard, soft, smooth, rough, cold, hot, etc.

Sixth Month: Foetal Growth

षष्ठे मासि गर्भस्य बलवर्णोपचयो भवत्यधिकम-न्येभ्यो
मासेभ्य:, तस्मात्तदा गर्भिणी बलवर्णहानिमापद्यते विशेषेण ।।22।।

—चरक शारीरस्थान

षष्ठे बुद्धि:

—सुश्रुत शारीरस्थान

According to Acharya Sushrut, the development of intellect or buddhi is seen in the sixth month of the foetus development. Acharya Carak focusses on the development of strength and complexion of the foetus because of which the mother loses her strength and complexion. He states that intelligence, strength and complexion develop during the sixth month. By this time, the internal development of the foetus is complete and focus is upon the development of the outer layer or the skin. In order to produce a strong, intelligent child, with a glowing complexion and healthy skin, the expectant mother must pay strict attention to her diet, health, lifestyle and behaviour throughout her pregnancy, especially during the sixth month. Adequate nutrition is, of course, extremely important for developing internal strength and focus should be put on the development of different parts of the brain.

Special Ayurvedic Diet

षष्ठे मासे क्षीरसर्पि: मधुरौषधसिद्धं।

—चरक शारीरस्थान

During the sixth month, the consumption of ghee infused with sweet herbs (like *shatavari* or *yashtimadhu*) is advised, ideally on an empty stomach, for the development of a powerful brain. Please consult with an Ayurvedic practitioner before starting any new herbal regimen.

Suggested Lifestyle due to Changes in the Mother's Body

In general, if the mother wishes her child to have glowing skin, she should regularly consume sattvic and liquid foods, such as ghee, milk, kheer, homemade butter, rice, buttermilk, tender coconut water and *panchamrut* with saffron and gold. These foods not only affect the child's skin positively but also provide nourishment for their development.

During this time, the mother should spend time on the kind of skills that she wishes her child to have, such as visual, verbal, musical, kinaesthetic, etc., and facilitate the development of different parts of the brain. She should consume almonds and walnuts (in limited quantity) for development of a strong brain.

The child in the womb has gained a lot of strength by now and its movements can be felt by the mother in the form of kicks, to which she should respond lovingly and encouragingly.

Must-Do Activities

As intelligence is formed in this month, the expecting mother should focus a lot on skill development. For the development of the brain, the mother should read rich and powerful texts, full of wisdom and knowledge. Some examples are the Bhagvad Gita and the Upanishads. She must try reading science journals and magazines and also get an understanding of the latest scientific inventions by watching Discovery and other educational television channels; and build logical skills by playing strategic games like chess and Sudoku, and solve puzzles, brainteasers, mathematical problems, etc. She should, in fact, allocate her time to skill development of the baby by indulging in activities that focus on the development of the Nine Intelligences as per her priority.

Seventh Month: Foetal Growth

सप्तमे मासि गर्भः सर्वैर्भावैराप्याय्यते,
तस्मात्तदा गर्भिणी सर्वाकारैः क्लान्ततमा भवति ।।23।।

—चरक शारीरस्थान

सप्तमे सर्वांगप्रत्यंगविभागः प्रव्यक्ततरः।

—सुश्रुत शारीरस्थान

The foetus is almost fully developed at this stage. All organs have essentially developed, lacking only in growth and maturity. Though the organs are still not fully grown, the child will be able to survive in the eventuality of a premature delivery. However, the baby will be underweight and have low immunity, thus needing extra care. Obviously, the ideal situation is for the baby to be born at full term (i.e., after nine months), when the development is complete.

The baby in the womb starts to use four senses—sight, hearing, taste and touch. The development of its lung capacity and temperature control is in progress.

Special Ayurvedic Diet

षष्ठे मासे क्षीरसर्पि: मधुरौषधसिद्धं, तदेव सप्तमे मासे ।

—चरक शारीरस्थान

During the seventh month as well, the expectant mother must continue with the consumption of ghee infused with sweet herbs, ideally on an empty stomach, for giving strength and power to the baby. For example, *Shatavari ghrut*, or *Yashtimadhu ghrut*. Please consult with an Ayurvedic practitioner before starting any new herbal regimen.

Suggested Lifestyle due to Changes in the Mother's Body

There is no substitute for the nourishment that the mother's womb provides, so it is important for the mother to have a very careful and balanced lifestyle in her third trimester to ensure a full-term delivery only.

The weight gain may give rise to physical discomforts like varicose veins, leg cramps or swelling, and also cause heartburn, indigestion, acidity and high blood pressure. Thus, it is recommended to reduce the intake of salt and avoid adding extra salt on food from top.

The expectant mother should now opt for whole-body massages, especially covering the back, pelvic region and thighs, with lukewarm oil, preferably sesame, for strengthening the body for normal delivery. However, it should be done very carefully by a trained masseuse and only while lying on the back or in a seated position.

As the brain is on its way to full development, the mother's focus should be more on creative activities as well as listening to various musical instruments or singing songs to the baby, thereby developing the visual and musical skills.

Must-Do Activities

Simantonayana Sanskar, wherein the expectant mother and the baby are pampered by close family, friends and relatives, is performed in this month. This makes the child feel adored and wanted.

From this point, the mother should sing a specific song at a specific time to the baby inside the womb and feel the baby gradually responding to the vibrations of the song. After birth, the same song can calm down the baby in case of crying bouts or when the baby is away from the mother for some time.

Engage in creative activities like painting, pottery, beading, sewing, decorating the house, etc.

Play musical games with the husband, like identifying sounds of various musical instruments like flute, violin, drums, etc., or identifying songs by different singers, etc.

Continue reading good scriptures and biographies of great men to instill these qualities in the unborn child.

Start giving affirmations and do visualizations for a happy, healthy, divine delivery, as well as for breastfeeding.

Eighth Month: Foetal Growth

अष्टमे मासि गर्भश्च मातृतो गर्भतश्च माता रसहारिणीभि:
संवाहिनीभिर्मुहुर्मुहुरोज: परस्परत आददाते गर्भस्या-सम्पूर्णत्वात् ।

—चरक शारीरस्थान

अष्टमे अस्थिरी भवति ओज:। तत्र जातक्षेत्र
जीवेत् निरोजस्त्वात् नैर्ऋंत भागत्वाच्च ।

—सुश्रुत शारीरस्थान

In this month, the Ojas or supreme energy is formed. It is unstable and flows alternately between mother and child. The mother-to-be appears extremely happy and enthusiastic when the energy flows to her, and tired and drained when the energy is transferred to the foetus. Because of this transfer of energy, delivery in the eighth month is not considered safe for either mother or child. For these reasons, any form of exertion, anxiety, stress, etc., is to be strictly avoided in the eighth month.

Special Ayurvedic Diet

अष्टमे तु मासे क्षीरयवागुं सर्पिष्मतीं काले काले पिबेत् ।

—चरक शारीरस्थान

From the eighth month, kheer made with milk, sugar and various types of grains, i.e., semolina, rice or wheat, should be eaten daily. It is important to add two spoons of pure, homemade ghee to it as this not only helps in giving strength and weight to the baby but also kickstarts the lactation process in the expecting mother.

Suggested Lifestyle due to Changes in the Mother's Body

The expecting mother should not undertake any form of physical, mental or emotional exertion as a premature delivery in this month is not desired. She should avoid travel altogether. She should be totally relaxed and rested and must always be under medical guidance. She must be alert to the bodily changes such as swelling in feet, increased blood pressure, etc.

Must-Do Activities

The expecting mother should be physically, mentally and emotionally in a state of relaxation and bliss. Start taking appropriate care of your breasts and do affirmations and visualizations for a safe and healthy delivery as well as lactation.

Ninth Month: Foetal Growth

तस्मिन्नेकदिवसातिक्रान्तेऽपि नवमं मासमुपादाय
प्रस-वकालमित्याहुरादशमान्मासात्।
एतावान् प्रसवकाल:, वैकारिकमत:
परं कुक्षावस्थानं गर्भस्य ॥25॥

—चरक शारीरस्थान

नवमदशमैकादशद्वादशानामन्यतमस्मिञ्जायते,
अतोऽन्यथा विकारी भवति ॥30॥

—सुश्रुत शारीरस्थान

The Ojas gets stable in the ninth month and thus the ideal time of delivery is between the thirty-seventh and the fortieth week; delivery beyond this time (post-term delivery) is not very desirable.

Special Ayurvedic Diet

यदिदं कर्म प्रथमं मासं समुपादायोपदिष्टमानवमान् मासात्तेन गर्भिण्या गर्भसमये गर्भधारिणीकुक्षिकटीपार्श्वपृष्ठं मृदु भवति, बातश्चानुलोम: सम्पद्यते।

—चरक शारीरस्थान

From the beginning of the ninth month, in order to achieve a comfortable delivery, it is very important for the expectant mother to get a perineal or perineum massage, under expert guidance, for widening the birth canal to prevent tearing during childbirth with a vaginal delivery.

Suggested Lifestyle due to Changes in the Mother's Body

Due to the increased weight of her body, the expecting mother faces issues in her day-to-day activities like walking, sitting, sleeping, etc., and gets exhausted very fast. Also, due to expansion of the uterine walls, the bladder gets squeezed, and there is an urge to urinate, because of which she is unable to have a sound sleep. Furthermore, with the due date round the corner, the expectant mother gets anxious and nervous. But the mother should remember that this is just a temporary phase and accept these developments with a lot of excitement and happiness.

Must-Do Activities

The expecting mother should be at rest—physically as well as mentally—and start visualizing a divine and healthy delivery. Mild massage of waist, thighs and legs with warm oil will provide strength and relaxation, and prepare the expecting mother for the delivery process.

Give affirmations, do visualizations, and chant mantras for a safe and happy delivery.

Keep your hospital bag for delivery ready for avoiding last-minute anxiety while hospitalization. It is advisable to always have an experienced woman with the expecting mother for any complication that might arise. Just sit back, relax, visualize, and wait for the child of your dreams to come in your arms really soon.

***Note:** All the dairy products, including milk, homemade butter and ghee, mentioned above must be made from A2 milk sourced from indigenous cows only.

ॐ

Annexure 2

AFFIRMATIONS

Affirmations on Physical Quotient (PQ)

- My baby is developing well in my womb.
- All the body parts and organs of my baby are fully developed and properly working.
- My baby's birth weight is 3.5 kg.
- My baby is tall/My baby has dimples/My baby has grey eyes/My baby has sharp features/My baby has a round face (affirmations around physical looks).
- My baby's heart is developing well/My baby's sense organs are fully developed/My baby's brain cells are developing fast (affirmations for achieving monthly milestones).
- My baby is very active physically/I love my baby's kicks/My baby loves to dance in my tummy/My baby is fantastic at sports.
- My baby is quick at mind—body coordination/My baby's body responds fast at her brain signals.

Affirmations on Intellectual Quotient (IQ)

- My baby is doing great with logic and numbers.
- My baby has good command over language/My baby is learning a new language/My baby can express himself well with words.

- My baby responds well to my talks.
- I love my baby's sense of humour/My baby can mimic so well/I love my baby's acting.
- My baby has a very good sense of music/My baby is learning [musical instrument name] very well/I love when my baby starts dancing on music in my tummy.
- My baby is very creative/My baby's beautiful fingers can create artistic things.

Affirmations on Emotional Quotient (EQ)

- My baby can connect with people well.
- My baby can forgive easily/My baby can seek forgiveness/My baby doesn't hold grudges/My baby has gratitude.
- My baby is an ocean of love/My baby can understand the feelings and emotions of all/My baby believes in win-win.
- My baby has extreme clarity of mind/My baby has good decision-making power/My baby's thoughts are clear and steady/My baby can understand her emotions well.
- My baby can accept ups and downs of life/My baby can differentiate between good and bad.
- My baby is kind towards all living things in nature/My baby loves playing with animals/My baby loves planting trees.

Affirmations on Spiritual Quotient (SQ)

- My baby is a very powerful and divine soul.
- My baby has come to my womb to fulfil his life purpose/My baby is born to release all his karmas/My baby is born to finally merge with the Almighty/My baby is born to do great deeds.
- My baby is always in a state of *sat-chit-anand*/My baby is always happy and peaceful.

- My baby has a lot of faith and devotion towards God/My baby is God's most special child.

Affirmations for the Mother

- I am calm and composed.
- My delivery is a moment of celebration.
- I am enjoying every moment of my pregnancy.
- I am lactating very well.
- My weight gain is around 12 kg.

ॐ

Annexure 3

PREGNANCY MANTRAS

Various Pregnancy Mantras to Be Chanted by Expecting Mothers

Bhaktamar Pregnancy Cluster

Shri Bhaktamar Stotra is the most famous stotra in the Jain community. It has 48 verses written in Sanskrit by Acharya Manatunga in the seventh century ce.

There are four shlokas in the pregnancy cluster of Bhaktamar Stotra. Shloka 20 helps in conception, Shloka 9 is focussed on attainment of a divine holistic child of your dreams, Shloka 34 helps in the protection of the womb, and Shloka 26 is focussed on divine delivery. The expectant mother should chant the shlokas, either 9 or 27 times, followed by chanting of Mantra Jaap and Riddhi Jaap in multiples of 108.

Bhaktamar Shloka 20–Conception

ज्ञानं यथा त्वयि विभाति कृतावकाशं
नैवं तथा हरि-हरादिषु नायकेषु।
तेज: स्फुरन्मणिषु याति यथा महत्त्वं
नैवं तु काच-शकले किरणाकुलेऽपि ॥20॥

Annexure 3

Mantra Jaap

ॐ श्रां श्रीं श्रं श्र: शत्रु भय-निवारणाय ठ: ठ: नम: स्वाहा ।
ॐ नमो भगवते पुत्रार्थ सौख्यं कुरु कुरु स्वाहा हीं नम: ॥

Ridhhi Jaap

ॐ ह्रीं अर्हं णमो चारणाणं झौं झौं नम: स्वाहा ।

Bhaktamar Shloka 9–Wishful Child

आस्तां तव स्तवन-मस्त-समस्त-दोषं,
त्वत्सङ्कथाऽपि जगतां दुरितानि हंति ।
दूरे सहस्र-किरण: कुरूते प्रभैव,
पद्मा-करेषु जलजानि विकास-भाञ्जि ॥9॥

Mantra Jaap

ॐ ह्रीं श्रीं क्रीं इवीं र: र: हं ह: नम: स्वाहा ॥
ॐ नमो भगवते जय यक्षाय हीं हूँ नम: स्वाहा ॥

Riddhi Jaap

ॐ ह्रीं अर्हं णमो अरिहंताणं णमो संभिण्ण-सोदाराणं झौं झौं नम: स्वाहा । ॐ ह्रीं ह्रीं हूँ ह: फट् स्वाहा । ॐ ऋद्धये नम: ।

Bhaktamar Shloka 34—Protection of Womb

शुम्भत्प्रभा वलय-भूरि विभा विभोस्ते
लोक-त्रये द्युतिमतां द्युति-माक्षिपन्ती।
प्रोद्यद्-दिवाकर-निरन्तर-भूरि-संख्या
दीप्त्या जयत्यपि निशा-मपि सोम-सौम्याम् ॥34॥

Mantra Jaap

ॐ नमो ह्रीं श्रीं क्लीं ऐं हौं पद्मावती देव्यै नमो नम: स्वाहा ।
ॐ प च य म हाँ हीं नम:।

Riddhi Jaap

ॐ ह्रीं अहं णमो खेल्लो सहि पत्ताणं झौं झीं नम: स्वाहा ।

Bhaktamar Shloka 26—Divine Delivery

तुभ्यं नमस्त्रि-भुवनार्ति-हराय नाथ!
तुभ्यं नम: क्षिति-तलामल-भूषणाय।
तुभ्यं नमस्त्रि-जगत: परमेश्वराय,
तुभ्यं नमो जिन! भवोदधि-शोषणाय ॥26॥

Mantra Jaap

ॐ नमो ॐ ह्रीं श्रीं क्लीं हूँ हूँ
परजन शान्ति व्यवहारे जयं कुरु कुरु स्वाहा।

Riddhi Jaap

ॐ ह्रीं अहं णमो दित्त-तवाणं झौं झीं नम: स्वाहा ।

Santan Gopal Mantra

Santan Gopal Mantra is the eleventh shloka from the Santan Gopal Stotra aimed at achievement of a desired child with good health and a sharp mind. If the expectant mother can listen or chant the entire Santan Gopal Stotra, this can be highly beneficial. The Santan Gopal Mantra which should be chanted in multiples of 108 to get the desired results.

ॐ देवकीसुत गोविन्द वासुदेव जगत्पते देहि मे तनयं कृष्ण त्वामहं शरणं गत:।

(I come to surrender to you, give me a son, O Krishna, the Son of Devaki, Lord of the Universe.)

Durga Devi Raksha Kavach Beej Mantra

Durga Kavach is a very powerful stotra aimed at the overall protection of an individual. When chanted by an expectant mother, it helps in the protection of the foetus. In case the expectant mother is unable to chant the entire stotra, she can still get the desired benefits by chanting the Durga Devi Raksha Kavach Beej Mantra in multiples of 108.

ॐ दुर्गे दुर्गे रक्षिणी ठ:ठ: स्वाहा ॥

Krishna Gayatri Mantra

This mantra is called Krishna Gayatri and can be safely chanted during pregnancy. Lord Krishna, as you know, was the only surviving child of Vasudev and Devaki. Lord Krishna is, thus, the survivor and also the only God to have such extensive experiences and teachings even during his infancy. For best results, chant in multiples of 108.

देवकीनन्दनाय विद्महे वासुदेवाय धीमहि, तन्नो कृष्ण: प्रचोदयात्॥

Gayatri Mantra

The Gayatri Mantra is considered to be among the most revered and powerful mantras in Hinduism. By chanting this mantra, the expectant mother is able to foster spiritual development and knowledge in both herself and the baby in the womb. It helps to cleanse the mind, body and soul, and should be chanted in multiples of 108.

ॐ भूर्भुव: स्व: तत्सवितुर्वरेण्यं भर्गो देवस्य धीमहि
धियो यो न: प्रचोदयात्॥

(We meditate on that most adored Supreme Lord, the creator, whose effulgence [divine light] illumines all realms [physical, mental and spiritual]. May this divine light illumine our intellect.)

In addition to these, chanting or listening to other stotras like Hanuman Chalisa, Madhurashtkam, Ram Raksha Stotra, and Durga Saptsati is very beneficial.

Garbha Rakhsha Stotram

This stotram has been written by Sage Saunaka to ensure the safe delivery of the child in the womb. There are nine shlokas chanted for the nine months of pregnancy.

First Month

एहैही भगवान ब्रह्म, प्रजा कर्ता, प्रजा पाथे,
प्राग्रुहशीनिवा बलिम चा इमाम, आपथयम रक्षा गर्भनीम ॥

(O Lord Brahma, the creator of the world, graciously accept the sacred obeisance of this pregnant woman. Accepting all the hardships, she has started on this family path.)

Second Month

अश्विनी देवेसौ, प्रग्रनीथम बलिम द्विमं,
सपथ्यं गर्भनीम चा इमाम, चा रक्षथम पूजा यनया ॥

(O Ashwini Dev, please accept the holy obeisance and worship of this pregnant woman and protect her who is fighting all odds and risks to complete her family.)

Third Month

रुद्राश्च एकादश प्रोक्था, प्रग्रुह्न्थु बालिम द्विमम्,
युष्माकम प्रीथाये वृथम, नित्यं रक्षथु गर्भनीम ॥

(O Eleven Holy Rudras! Please accept our prayers and offerings, which are in harmony with your will. Please protect this pregnant woman who is going through all the hardships and risks to complete her family. Keep your kindness and blessings on her.)

Fourth Month

आदित्य द्वादसा प्रोक्था, प्रग्रहनीथवं बालिम द्विमम्,
युष्मगम थेजसम वृध्या, नित्यं रक्षा गर्भनीम ॥

(O Twelfth Holy Sun God, you fill our lives with a bright glow like yours. I bow before you. Accept my prayer and save this pregnant lady from all kinds of danger, who is on her way to complete the family.)

Fifth Month

विनायक गणध्याक्ष, शिव पुत्र महा बाला,
प्रग्रह्रीश्व बलिम चा इमाम, सपथ्यं रक्षा गर्भनीम ॥

(O Vinayaka, O Ganesha, O Son of Lord Shiva, you are mighty. Please accept our obeisance and save this pregnant woman from suffering and danger. Help her on her way to the completion of her family.)

Sixth Month

स्कंद षणमुखा देवेसा, पुथरा प्रीति विवर्धन,
प्रग्रहनीश्व बालिम चा इमाम, सपथ्यं रक्षा गर्भनीम ॥

(O Skanda, O Lord of Six heads, O Chief Lord of the Devas, Lord Who Increases Our Love for Sons. Please accept this holy sacrifice and protect this pregnant lady who is on her way to complete her family risking all the dangers.)

Seventh Month

प्रभास: प्रभावश्याम: प्रत्याउशो मारुथोएनालाह
द्रुवोधुरा धरशैव, वासवोष्टौ प्राकीरथिथा
प्रग्रह्री थवं बलिम चा इमाम, नित्यं रक्षा गर्भनीम ॥

(O Ashtavasu Dev Clan, which includes Dhar, Dhruva, Soma, Ah, Anil, Anal, Pratyusha, Prabhash, I bow down to all. O Lord, receive this holy sacrifice. May you protect this woman who is on her way to complete the family, bearing hardships and risks.)

Eighth Month

पिथुरदेवी, पिधुश्रेष्ठे, बहू पुत्री, महा बाले,
भूत श्रेष्ठ निशा वासेय, निर्व्रथा, सौनाकाप्रिये,
प्रग्रह्रीश्च बलिम चा इमाम, सपथ्यं रक्षा गर्भनीम ॥

(O Goddess of my forefathers, who is in the form of daughters of all women, O Goddess who is extremely powerful, O Goddess who is more powerful than all beings, O Goddess who protects us in the night, O Goddess who is without faults, O Goddess who is worshiped by Saunaka. Please accept this priceless sacrifice and keep this lady safe from all dangers while on the way to the family.)

Ninth Month

रक्षा रक्षा महादेव, बक्था अनुग्रह कारक,
पाक्षी वाहन गोविंदा, सपथ्यं रक्षा गर्भनीम ॥

(O Lord, who is the best, who protects his followers and is happy to bless, O Govinda, riding on the bird, please protect the pregnant woman who overcomes the dangers and risks to complete her family, who are on the path.)

Instructions on How to Chant during Pregnancy

Daily sit in front of photo of the Goddess with any small offering and recite as follows:

- During the second month, read the first two shlokas 108 times daily.
- During the third month, read the first three shlokas 108 times daily.
- During the fourth month, read the first four shlokas 108 times daily.
- During the fifth month, read the first five shlokas 108 times daily.
- During the sixth month, read the first six shlokas 108 times daily.
- During the seventh month, read the first seven shlokas 108 times daily.
- During the eighth month, read the first eight shlokas 108 times daily.
- During the ninth month, read all the nine shlokas 108 times daily.

In case one is unable to chant the mantras, then even listening with trust, devotion and surrender will help to achieve desired results.

Furthermore, it should be noted that all mantras from all religions and faiths are extremely powerful and, if chanted or listened to with reverence, can definitely help in raising our consciousness and bless us with the desired results.

Endnotes

Chapter 1: The Beginnings

1. 'The Sixteen Sanskars in Hinduism', *RitiRiwaz*, http://tinyurl.com/nzw2nfpn. Accessed on 22 February 2024.
2. GBD 2021 Fertility and Forecasting Collaborators, 'Global Fertility in 204 Countries and Territories, 1950–2021, with Forecasts to 2100: A Comprehensive Demographic Analysis for the Global Burden of Disease Study 2021', *The Lancet*, Vol. 403, No. 10440, 20 March 2024, pp. 2057–99, http://tinyurl.com/cetb9tm7. Accessed on 14 May 2024.
3. Jha, Durgesh Nandan, 'India Staring at a Shortfall in Births by 2050, Warn Experts', *The Times of India*, 21 March 2024, http://tinyurl.com/ymc5uvzn. Accessed on 14 May 2024.
4. 'Median Age of India 1950-2025 & Future Projections', *database.earth*, 11 July 2024, ttps://tinyurl.com/v8ksast3. Accessed on 15 January 2025.
5. Jogal, Devangi, and Nilesh Jogal, *Garbha Sanskar*, Yuti Publication, Ahmedabad, 2021, p. 47.
6. Vidyanath, R., *Illustrated Caraka Samhita Vols 1, 2*, Chaukhambha Prakashak, Varanasi, 2023, p. 545.
7. Joseph, R., 'Fetal Brain Behavior and Cognitive Development', *Developmental Review*, Vol. 20, No. 1, March 2000, pp. 81–98.
8. Partanen, E., et al., 'Learning-Induced Neural Plasticity of Speech Processing before Birth', *Proceedings of the National Academy of Sciences*, Vol. 110, No. 37, 26 August 2013, pp. 15145–50, http://tinyurl.com/2bpme5vp. Accessed on 1 March 2024.
9. 'Language Attainment May Begin in the Womb', *123helpme*, https://tinyurl.com/558nvz68. Accessed on 1 March 2024.
10. Partanen, E., et al, 'Learning-Induced Neural Plasticity of Speech Processing before Birth', *Proceedings of the National Academy of Sciences*, Vol. 110, No. 37, August 2013, https://tinyurl.com/2faa592n. pp. 15145–50. Accessed on 23 May 2024.

11. Austin, Diana, '"Neighbours" Theme Learned in the Womb', *The Independent*, 16 January 1994, http://tinyurl.com/ye26m92c. Accessed on 1 March 2024.
12. 'What Can My Baby See and Hear inside the Womb?', *Happiest Baby*, http://tinyurl.com/bdc325pe. Accessed on 16 February 2024.
13. 'Weeks 15 & 16', *Lozier Institute*, tinyurl.com/46hp564c. Accessed 23 May 2024.
14. Fleming, Amy., 'How a Child's Food Preferences Begin in the Womb', *The Guardian*, 8 April 2014, http://tinyurl.com/3nbz65c4. Accessed on 16 February 2024.
15. Ustun, B., et al., 'Flavor Sensing in Utero and Emerging Discriminative Behaviors in the Human Fetus', *Psychological Science*, Vol. 33, No. 10, 2022, pp. 1651–63.
16. Fleming, Amy, 'How a Child's Food Preferences Begin in the Womb', *The Guardian*, 8 April 2014, tinyurl.com/3nbz65c4. Accessed on 16 February 2024.
17. Varendi, H., R.H. Porter and J. Winberg, 'Does the Newborn Baby Find the Nipple by Smell?', *The Lancet*, Vol. 344, No. 8928, pp. 989–90.
18. Klaus, Marshall, and Phyllis Klaus, *Your Amazing Newborn*, Perseus Books, 2000.
19. Ackerman, Sandra, 'The Development and Shaping of the Brain', *Discovering the Brain*, National Academies Press, Washington, DC, 1992.
20. Ibid.

Chapter 2: Creating Intelligence in the Womb

1. Tambe, Balaji, *Ayurvedic Garbha Sanskar: The Art and Science of Pregnancy*, Balaji Tambe Foundation, Pune, 24 July 2011. p. 20.
2. Schechter, Harold, *Fiend: The Shocking True Story of America's Youngest Serial Killer*, Gallery Books, 2000.
3. Sharma, P.V., *Susruta Samhita Part-2*, Chaukhambha Visvabharati, Varanasi, 2022. pp. 145–6.
4. Ibid. 146.
5. Gardner, Howard, *Frames of Mind and Multiple Intelligences: The Theory in Practice*, Basic Books, 2011.
6. Ibid.
7. Sharma, P.V., *Susruta Samhita Part-2*, Chaukhambha Visvabharati, Varanasi, 2022. p. 149

Chapter 3: Maintaining Physical Well-Being

1. 'Dietary Guidelines for Indians', *National Institute of Nutrition*, 2024.
2. Vidyanath, R., *Illustrated Caraka Samhita Vol. 2*, Chukhambha Prakashak, Varanasi, 2023. p. 686.
3. 'Dietary Guidelines for Indians', *National Institute of Nutrition*, 2024.
4. Tambe, Balaji, *Ayurvedic Garbha Sanskar: The Art and Science of Pregnancy*, Balaji Tambe Foundation, Pune, 24 July 2011. pp. 72–80.
5. 'Dietary Guidelines for Indians', *National Institute of Nutrition*, 2024.
6. Ibid.
7. Ibid.
8. 'WHO Calls on Countries to Reduce Sugars Intake among Adults and Children', *World Health Organization*, 4 March 2015, https://tinyurl.com/2dsat5jn. Accessed on 15 January 2025.
9. 'Dietary Guidelines for Indians', *National Institute of Nutrition*, 2024.
10. 'Sodium Reduction', *World Health Organization*, 14 September 2023, https://tinyurl.com/2b99ckax. Accessed on 15 January 2025.
11. 'Dietary Guidelines for Indians', *National Institute of Nutrition*, 2024.
12. 'Processed Foods and Health', *Harvard T.H. Chan School of Public Health*, August 2019, http://tinyurl.com/ymf664pp. Accessed on 14 May 2024.
13. 'Dietary Guidelines for Indians', *National Institute of Nutrition*, 2024.
14. Ibid.
15. Tambe, Balaji, *Ayurvedic Garbha Sanskar: The Art and Science of Pregnancy*, Balaji Tambe Foundation, Pune, 24 July 2011. p. 86.
16. Birsner, Meredith, and Cynthia Gyamfi-Bannerman, 'Physical Activity and Exercise during Pregnancy and the Postpartum Period', *The American College of Obstetricians and Gynecologists*, December 2015, https://tinyurl.com/4tzyryew. Accessed on 16 May 2024.
17. 'Dietary Guidelines for Indians', *National Institute of Nutrition*, 2024.
18. Emoto, Masuru, *The Healing Power of Water*, Hay House, 2007.
19. Yardi, M.R., *The Yoga of Patanjali*, Bhandarkar Oriental Research Institute, Pune, 1979.
20. Ma Xiao, et al, 'The Effect of Diaphragmatic Breathing on Attention, Negative Affect and Stress in Healthy Adults', *Frontiers in Psychology*, Vol. 8, No. 874, 6 June 2017, https://tinyurl.com/399bu3sd. Accessed on 1 March 2024.
21. 'Pregnancy and Smoking', *Better Health Channel*, 2022, https://tinyurl.com/jwem6956. Accessed on 1 March 2024.
22. 'Drinking Alcohol While Pregnant', *NHS*, 2 December 2020, https://tinyurl.com/ypsr9z5n. Accessed on 1 March 2024.

23. 'How Electronic Gadgets Have Outcomes on Pregnancy', *Plunes*, 8 November 2023, https://tinyurl.com/4urvey2j. Accessed on 1 March 2024.
24. R. Vidyanath, *Illustrated Caraka Samhita Vol. 2*, Chaukhambha Prakashak, Varanasi, 2023, p. 729.
25. Ibid. 65.
26. Ibid.
27. Tambe, Balaji, *Ayurvedic Garbha Sanskar: The Art and Science of Pregnancy*, Balaji Tambe Foundation, Pune, 24 July 2011.

Chapter 4: Developing Mental Well-Being

1. Tambe, Balaji, *Ayurvedic Garbh Sanskar: The Art and Science of Pregnancy*, Balaji Tambe Foundation, Pune, 24 July 2011. pp. 19–20.
2. Hay, Louise, *You Can Heal Your Life*, Hay House Publishers, India, 2009.
3. Philamon, Jan, 'Brain Waves and Hypnosis', *M1 Psychology*, https://tinyurl.com/3x9f6bz4. Accessed on 13 May 2024.
4. Rios, Armando, 'The Power of Repetition: How It Shapes and Creates New Habits in Humans', *Medium*, 16 August 2023. Accessed on 16 May 2024.
5. *The Bhagavadgita or the Song Divine*, Gita Press, Gorakhpur, 2008.

Chapter 5: Ensuring Emotional Well-Being

1. 'Prenatal Maternal Stress', *Douglas Mental Health University Institute*, 2013, https://tinyurl.com/86ptnunk. Accessed on 23 May 2024.
2. Zeindler, Christine, 'Prenatal Maternal Stress', *The Douglas Institute*, 21 January 2013, https://tinyurl.com/2pwe372t. Accessed on 13 March 24.
3. Ibid. p. 132.
4. Vidyanath, R., *Illustrated Caraka Samhita Vols 2*, Chaukhambha Prakashak, Varanasi, 2023. p. 611.
5. 'Music for Babies', *BluenetHospitals*, https://tinyurl.com/4akarp2m. Accessed on 13 May 2024.
6. 'How Music Affects Your Baby's Brain: Mini Parenting Master Class', *UNICEF*, https://tinyurl.com/4wvf4yzm. Accessed on 13 March 2024.
7. 'Play Mozart, Not Adele, to Baby in Womb: Study', *The Times of India*, 14 June 2018, tinyurl.com/48vknmhb. Accessed on 23 May 2024.
8. 'Garbh Sanskar: Why Your Unborn Baby MUST Listen to Music', *iMumz*, https://tinyurl.com/4s84kevy. Accessed on 13 March 2024.
9. 'Sing to the Bump: Because Music Makes a Difference in the Womb',

The Times of India, 15 June 2018, https://tinyurl.com/3mctjjv2. Accessed on 13 March 2024.
10. 'Garbh Sanskar: Why Your Unborn Baby MUST Listen to Music', *iMumz*, https://tinyurl.com/4s84kevy. Accessed on 13 March 2024.

Chapter 6: Imbibing Spiritual Well-Being

1. Tambe, Balaji, *Ayurvedic Garbh Sanskar: The Art and Science of Pregnancy*, Balaji Tambe Foundation, Pune, 24 July 2011, pp. 103-4.
2. Sharamon, Shalila, and Bodo Baginski, *The Chakra Handbook*, Motilal Banarsidass Publishers, Delhi, 2006.
3. 'The Transformational Power of Mantra', *Himalayan Yoga Institute*, http://tinyurl.com/bdfbmcds. Accessed on 10 April 2024.
4. 'Mantras are Frequencies That Can Heal, Kill and Transcend', *BooksFact*, 28 January 2015, https://tinyurl.com/5h2yy5ta. Accessed on 10 April 2024.
5. Pundir, Anubha, and Akshya Chauhan, 'Positive Effects of "AUM" Chanting on Mental Health Well-Being', *Traditional Medicine*, Vol. 4, No. 2, 19 May 2023, http://tinyurl.com/mrvjr42j. Accessed on 13 May 2024.
6. Ibid.

Chapter 7: A Miracle Is Born

1. Jogal, Devangi, and Nilesh Jogal, *Garbha Sanskar*, Yuti Publication, Ahmedabad, 2021, p. 120.
2. Ritchie, Hannah, and Edouard Mathieu, 'How Many People Die and How Many Are Born Each Year?' *Our World in Data*, 5 January 2023, tinyurl.com/5x9mksdu. Accessed on 23 May 2024.
3. 'The World Counts', *The World Counts*, 2022, https://tinyurl.com/ykx9xe2u. Accessed on 11 March 2024.
4. Desai, Ninad M., and Alexander Tsukerman, 'Vaginal Delivery', *PubMed*, StatPearls Publishing, 24 July 2023, http://tinyurl.com/yf33b847. Accessed on 13 May 2024.
5. Tambe, Balaji, *Ayurvedic Garbha Sanskar: The Art And Science Of Pregnancy*, Balaji Tambe Foundation, Pune, 24 July 2011, p. 135.
6. 'Oxytocin: What It Is, Function & Effects', *Cleveland Clinic*, 27 March 2022, tinyurl.com/mtpdrnxp. Accessed on 13 May 2024.
7. Prajapati, Suresh Alka, *Garbh Sanskar*, Dreamz Institute, Surat, September 2022, p. 92.

8. Prajapati, Suresh Alka, *Garbh Sanskar*, Dreamz Institute, Surat, September 2022, p. 92.
9. Vidyanath, R., *Illustrated Caraka Samhita Vols 2*, Chaukhambha Prakashak, Varanasi, 2023, p. 686.
10. Tambe, Balaji, *Ayurvedic Garbha Sanskar: The Art and Science of Pregnancy*, Balaji Tambe Foundation, Pune, 24 July 2011, p. 130.
11. Jogal, Devangi, and Nilesh Jogal, *Garbh Sanskar*, Yuti Publication, Ahmedabad, 2021, p. 125.
12. Tambe, Balaji, *Ayurvedic Garbha Sanskar: The Art and Science of Pregnancy*, Balaji Tambe Foundation, Pune, 24 July 2011, p. 167.
13. Sharma, P.V., *Susruta Samhita Part-2*, Chaukhambha Visvabharati, Varanasi, 2022, p. 225.
14. Vidyanath, R., *Illustrated Caraka Samhita Vols 2*, Chaukhambha Prakashak, Varanasi, 2023. p. 748.
15. Ibid. 750.
16. Sharma, P.V., *Susruta Samhita Part-2*, Chaukhambha Visvabharati, Varanasi, 2022.
17. Tambe, Balaji, *Ayurvedic Garbh Sanskar: The Art and Science of Pregnancy*, Balaji Tambe Foundation, Pune, 24 July 2011, p. 167.
18. Sharma, P.V., *Susruta Samhita* Part-2, Chaukhambha Visvabharati, Varanasi, 2022, p. 227.
19. Jogal, Devangi, and Nilesh Jogal, *Garbha Sanskar*, Yuti Publication, Ahmedabad, 2021, p. 139.
20. Mukadam, Farah Adam, *New Borns and New Moms*, Pan Macmillan, India, 2020.
21. 'Kangaroo Mother Care: A Practical Guide', *World Health Organization*, 2003, https://tinyurl.com/ywppy8fs. Accessed on 23 May 2024.
22. 'Kangaroo Mother Care: A Practical Guide', *World Health Organization*, 2003, https://tinyurl.com/dmu9enbe. Accessed on 11 March 2024.
23. Jogal, Devangi, and Nilesh Jogal, *Garbha Sanskar*, Yuti Publication, Ahmedabad, 2021, p. 139.
24. Sharma, P.V., *Susruta Samhita* Part-2, Chaukhambha Visvabharati, Varanasi, 2022, p. 231.

Chapter 8: Care of New Moms and Newborns

1. Mukadam, Farah Adam, *New Borns and New Moms*, Pan Macmillan, India, 2020.
2. Pandey, Kirti, 'Postpartum Care Traditions in India: Science behind Why New Mothers Are Asked to Wear Scarves Covering Their Ears', *TimesNow*, 28 April 2022, https://tinyurl.com/2p9ywwb7. Accessed on

11 March 2024.
3. 'Benefits of Postpartum Massage', *WebMD*, 19 April 2023, https://tinyurl.com/ybwunwju. Accessed on 11 March 2024.
4. Patel, Umesh, 'Effect of Back Massage on Lactation among Postnatal Mothers', *International Journal of Medical Research and Review*, Vol. 1, No. 1, 31 March 2013, https://tinyurl.com/yzw43n3x. Accessed on 11 March 2024.
5. Mukadam, Farah Adam, *New Borns and New Moms*, Pan Macmillan India, 2020.
6. Tambe, Balaji, *Ayurvedic Garbh Sanskar: The Art and Science of Pregnancy*, Balaji Tambe Foundation, Pune, 24 July 2011, p. 179.
7 Mukadam, Farah Adam, *New Borns and New Moms*, Pan Macmillan, India, 2020.
8. Mukadam, Farah Adam, *New Borns and New Moms*, Pan Macmillan, India, 2020.
9. Ibid.
10. Tambe, Balaji, *Ayurvedic Garbh Sanskar: The Art and Science of Pregnancy*, Balaji Tambe Foundation, Pune, 24 July 2011, p. 179.
11. Ibid. 180.
12. 'Dietary Guidelines for Indians', *National Institute of Nutrition*, 2024.
13 Ibid.
14. Ibid.
15. Ibid.
16. Ibid.
17. Ibid.
18. Ibid.
19. Prajapati, Suresh Alka, *Garbh Sanskar*, Dreamz Institute, Surat, September 2022.
20. 'Dietary Guidelines for Indians', *National Institute of Nutrition*, 2024.

Dreamstar Baby—Manifest Your Divine Genius

Embark on a transformative journey with DreamStar Baby—an innovative pregnancy app blending ancient Garbha Sanskar wisdom with modern science for a holistic motherhood experience.

Key Features of the Path-Breaking App

- Introducing a pregnancy app using the amalgamation of ancient wisdom with modern science through an array of impactful and structured activities and experiences to manifest the divine baby of your dreams.
- Experience the transformative impact of Sonal's Intelligence Model for Holistic Development© through nine thought-provoking daily activities tailored to focus upon each of the nine intelligences.
- Immerse yourself in a wide range of enriching daily activities, including engaging audios, informative videos, insightful experiments, stimulating brain-booster exercises, introspective self-reflection and more, to holistically develop physical, intellectual, emotional, and spiritual quotients (PQ, IQ, EQ, SQ).

- Discover a treasure trove of practical tools such as engaging prenatal exercises, uplifting motivational boosts, soothing mindfulness practices, harmonious music and mantras, serene meditation sessions, and more, all infused with the science of positive affirmations for a holistic motherhood experience.
- Stay informed with general milestone updates on foetal development, ensuring a confident and informed motherhood journey.
- Connect with a vibrant community of like-minded mothers for support, growth and solidarity.
- A perfect companion for all aspiring mothers throughout their pregnancy journey irrespective of caste, creed or religion, at zero subscription fee.

Scan the QR Code below for daily enriching activities to manifest your divine genius through the **DreamStar Baby** App.

Acknowledgements

I express my deep gratitude to my Guru, Dr Avdhoot Baba Shivanand, whose guidance blessed me with motherhood. This book is a compilation of his teachings that I followed during my pregnancy, and now, with his blessings, this divine knowledge is accessible to all.

My gratitude goes to Acharya Amit Hisariya-ji who keeps guiding us about righteous living with his divine knowledge and helping us to raise our consciousness.

I am grateful to my parents, Shri Santosh and Lalita Jain, for instilling in me deep-rooted values, and to my in-laws, Shri Manoj and Manisha Jayaswal, for providing me with the wings to venture into the world of spirituality.

My heartfelt thanks to my husband, Shri Abhishek Jayaswal, for his unwavering and unconditional support that continuously motivates me to push my boundaries and broaden my horizons.

I am profoundly grateful to Dr Vijay Darda and the late Smt. Jyotsna Darda, whom I lovingly call Bade Papa and Badi Mummy, for their invaluable mentorship and guidance. I am thankful to my guide Dr Manju Jain who encouraged me to pursue research in Garbha Sanskar, which has now become my life's mission.

I am thankful to all the expectant mothers who trusted me and followed my guidance during their pregnancy, providing practical insights that have shaped this book.

I'm very grateful to my family and friends, in particular my soul sister Ms Richa Bora, for the unconditional love and guidance in moments of desperation, so that I could become a source of inspiration.

Special appreciation goes to Ms Namita Bajaj Sonthalia for her meticulous creative editing and enhancing the quality and impact of the content, and also to Dr Partha Guha Roy and Dr Ranjana Tibrewal for taking out time from their immensely busy schedules to review the medical content of the book.

I am grateful to Rupa Publications for their constant support, professionalism and commitment to bringing this book to fruition.

I thank my bundles of joy—Ishaan and Shambhavi—for shaping me into who I am today. They were the reason for my penance, and little did I know then that I would be chosen to guide thousands of others to help them achieve their dream baby.

Most importantly, my deepest gratitude to the Almighty for blessing me with such a beautiful life. Every day, every breath and every blessing inspire me to serve You and all of Your creation. Please continue to bless me.

Made in the USA
Monee, IL
03 May 2026

49438413R00187